Doing Fieldwork

W9-DFZ-321

Doing Fieldwork

Ethnographic Methods for Research in Developing Countries and Beyond

Wayne Fife

DOING FIELDWORK
© Wayne Fife, 2005.

All rights reserved. No part of this book may be used or reproduced in any manner whatsoever without written permission except in the case of brief quotations embodied in critical articles or reviews.

First published in 2005 by
PALGRAVE MACMILLAN™
175 Fifth Avenue, New York, N.Y. 10010 and
Houndmills, Basingstoke, Hampshire, England RG21 6XS
Companies and representatives throughout the world.

PALGRAVE MACMILLAN is the global academic imprint of the Palgrave Macmillan division of St. Martin's Press, LLC and of Palgrave Macmillan Ltd. Macmillan® is a registered trademark in the United States, United Kingdom and other countries. Palgrave is a registered trademark in the European Union and other countries.

ISBN 1–4039–6908–6
ISBN 1–4039–6909–4

Library of Congress Cataloging-in-Publication Data

Fife, Wayne.
    Doing fieldwork : ethnographic methods for research in developing countries and beyond / by Wayne Fife.
        p. cm.
    Includes bibliographical references and index.
    ISBN 1–4039–6908–6 (alk. paper)
    ISBN 1–4039–6909–4 (pbk. : alk. paper)
      1. Ethnology—Field work. 2. Ethnology—Developing countries—Field work. 3. Ethnology—Developing countries—Research. 4. Ethnology—Developing countries—Methodology. I. Title.

GN346.F537 2005
305.8′0072′3—dc22   2005048686

A catalogue record for this book is available from the British Library.

Design by Newgen Imaging Systems (P) Ltd., Chennai, India.

First edition: September 2005

10 9 8 7 6 5 4 3 2 1

Printed in the United States of America.

In Memoriam

This book is dedicated to the memory of my niece, Alana Fife (1981–2003). Lanny wanted to be a teacher and died in an accident while working as a volunteer in the country of Indonesia with orphans and street children on basic literacy and other life issues. She had strong convictions and she acted on them. Her courage challenges us to find our own convictions and apply them to our everyday lives.

Contents

List of Tables

Acknowledgments

There are many people to thank for helping to make this book possible. First, the Social Sciences and Humanities Foundation of Canada has, through their generous support over the last two decades, made the cumulative research experience on which this book is based possible. Without this institution and the people who have served it so well, Canadian scholarship would be a ghost of its present form.

During my research in Papua New Guinea in the late 1980s, upon which this book draws so heavily, a number of individuals deserve to be remembered. Peter Humphries, Steven Laupau, Joe Maza, and Paul Kavan all provided help when it was needed. Unexpected and much appreciated friendship was offered to me during my research period by Danny Wakikura, John Ellison, Matthew Sil, Terry Killoran, Jack and Margaret Fenton, Sheldon Weeks, Michael Crossley, and Graham Vulliamy. At home at McMaster University, Matthew Cooper, Richard Preston, and especially my Ph.D. advisor David Counts gave me the support and encouragement that I required to become a professional anthropologist. My fellow graduate students Karen Szala-Meneok, David Black, Tom Maschio, Sam Migliore, and Cath Olberholtzer gave unselfish friendship in some difficult times. In the earlier years of my studies, Chris Meiklejohn of the University of Winnipeg and Susan Hornshaw of the University of Western Ontario gave me the kind of mentoring that I try to pass on to my own students.

More recently, I have become indebted to a number of companions of the intellect. During two years at the University of Massachusetts at Amherst, I was privileged to know and share ideas with Oriol Pi-Sunyer (a scholar and a gentleman), Susan diGiacomo, Jackie Urla, John Cole, Stuart Kirsch, Deborah Gewertz, and Frederick Errington. During four years of teaching at St. Thomas University, Paul Morrissy, Suzanne Prior, and Colm Kelly gave me refuge, and Vice President Rick Myers gave me support when I wasn't sure that I even had a job. In my present post at the Memorial University of Newfoundland, Rex Clark, Robin Whitaker, Mark Tate, Tom Nemec, and Elliott Leyton have all, in their various ways, helped make this not just an institution but a lively home for me. Gerry Sider also deserves a special mention for his encouragement not just to myself but also to so many others who have bumped into his anthropological orbit.

I owe a special thanks to Michael Crossley and Graham Vulliamy, who gave me copyright permission to make use of parts of my book chapter "The Importance of Fieldwork: Anthropology and Education in Papua New Guinea," which was originally published in their book *Qualitative Educational Research in Developing Countries* (Garland Publishing, Inc., 1997).

At Palgrave Macmillan, I want to thank editor Farideh Koohi-Kamali for believing in the project and Lynn Vande Stouwe for her ongoing editorial support—without presses willing to take risks and the people who nurture them there are no books.

Above all, Sharon Roseman has been there for me as a partner and a fellow anthropologist for over fifteen years. She has not only influenced everything I have ever written, but also made it possible for me to live in the world rather than to merely inhabit space. For that, there can be no adequate thanks to give.

Believe me, I'm quite capable of making my own mistakes—none of these people had anything to do with any errors or omissions in my book.

1

Introduction to Ethnographic Research Methods

Open up any introductory textbook in sociocultural anthropology and you will find a section explaining the importance of the concept of holism. The author will typically go on to explain that anthropologists are generally more interested in gaining an understanding of how human lives "make sense" within the contexts in which they live than we are in arriving at universal generalizations or "laws" regarding human behavior. This is particularly true of ethnographic researchers, who traditionally make extensive use of the participant-observation method in their work. Two key terms for an ethnographer are context and pattern. The goal of ethnographic research is to formulate a *pattern* of analysis that makes reasonable sense out of human actions within the given *context* of a specific time and place. This task of holism may seem simple enough when a student is reading about it in an introductory textbook, but when the same person turns into a researcher s/he is inevitably confronted with the following two questions: (1) how much context do I have to cover, and (2) how will I recognize a pattern when I see it? These are other ways of asking how a researcher who follows a qualitative, ethnographic strategy can ever know when a "holistic" understanding has been satisfactorily achieved.

Unfortunately, there are no straightforward answers to these questions. The answers can never be fully determined for the simple reason that ethnographic research occurs simultaneously as an art form and as a scientific endeavor. As a social or human science, empirical evidence must be gathered so that the readers of the ethnographic product (e.g., book, article, thesis, report) can weigh the evidence and therefore judge the researcher's analysis of the patterns of human behavior that s/he delineates in the work. Ethnography is also an art form because ethnographic literature requires the writer to make an aesthetic judgment about when the context that has been presented is "whole enough," or when the examples that illustrate a particular pattern of behavior are complete enough to give the reader a proper understanding of the words and actions that led to the analysis. As a method, or more accurately a changing set of methods for gathering information, ethnography is a kind of science; as a written literature that does not have a programatic style of writing (as might be said of more strictly scientific approaches to research, such as most forms of psychology), it can also be seen as an art form or as a part of the humanities (i.e., as a literature). Writing (from note-taking to book production) is normally not separated from the other "methods" of information gathering in qualitative research; both are seen as forming an insepa-rable ethnographic whole (e.g., Emerson, Fretz, Shaw 1995; Kutsche 1998). Because of the aesthetic dimension of ethnography, it is not possible to provide simple answers to the research questions noted above, ones that could be consid-ered valid in all times and for all places. This is, therefore, a book for researchers who want to conduct their studies with the understanding that context cannot be left out of our work simply in order to create the illusion of authoritative infalli-bility or universal scientific completeness. There are common methodological tools that will help any researcher learn how do deal with working with disadvan-taged populations (and you will learn about them in this book), but that does not mean that we have to pretend that there are no differences between doing our research in Papua New Guinea, New Zealand, the Ivory Coast, Canada, or India (for good examples that demonstrate similarities and differences related to quali-tative research approaches in regard to education in quite different developing countries, see Crossley and Vulliamy 1997). An open-ended approach, such as the one advocated in this book, will allow scholars the necessary flexibility to cope with the particularities of the contextual differences that they encounter while conducting their own fieldwork. I see research methods as being rather like tools within a tool kit. Well informed scholars should be able to reach into their kits and extract the method or technique of research that will best help them deal with the situation they currently face—enabling them to get the most complete informa-tion possible within that specific research context. This book provides readers with just such a tool kit so that they can go on to modify it through their own individ-ual experiences.

The Craft of Ethnography

Formulated in another fashion, we might think of ethnography as a kind of craft and the new researcher as an apprentice who wishes to learn that craft. My goal is to ensure that any scholar (whether a graduate student or professional researcher) who follows the advice contained in this book will learn how to conceptualize a project, collect the information for it, analyze and write the project up in such a way as to create a professional quality article, thesis, or book. Not everything can be covered in this book. For example, it is useless to attempt to discuss how to go about obtaining research permits, as every country has its own specific require-ments for them. The focus here, then, is upon the parameters of research that we can expect to find while working with disadvantaged groups of people in virtually any developing or industrialized country.

As a craft, research methods can best be learned through experience. Therefore, the most effective way to teach other scholars ethnographic research methods is to provide them with examples of the decisions that a researcher has actually made in response to a particular research project. I propose therefore to use extensive examples from my own doctoral and postdoctoral research, carried out during a one-year period in 1986–1987 in the country of Papua New Guinea and during three months of 1994 in the missionary archives of the School of Oriental and African Studies at the University of London. My Papua New Guinea fieldwork focused on the issue of formal primary school education and its relationship to expectations for economic development in that country. Whereas the 1994 archival work was part of an attempt to gain a deeper understanding about the British missionaries who went to Papua New Guinea in the last 1800s and began this formal educational system. Overall, this key example will be supplemented now and again by research experiences I have gained in other field-work contexts, such as a study of old age homes in Southern Ontario or the long-term fieldwork project that I am currently engaged in that involves a con-sideration of the effects of tourism on the Northern Peninsula area on the island of Newfoundland, Canada. I draw on these examples in order to teach the reader how to go about conducting an ethnographic study of disadvantaged people. Ethnographic methods can only be properly taught through specific encounters with real methodological problems in a living research situation. I firmly believe that scholars who wish to conduct a field study of educational practices, medical beliefs, or community development (to name only a few potential projects) in countries such as Kenya, Australia, China, or Fiji will be able to adapt the experi-ence-based methods of this book for their own work in a more useful manner than they would if I presented the material as a set of decontextualized "rules" for qualitative research. Using my own trials and tribulations to illustrate specific research techniques will enable other scholars to think about their own unique situations in a more concrete manner, as well as reassure the scholar that things will not always proceed smoothly, information will not always be "gathered" in a timely fashion, and that constant, imaginative innovation informed by a knowledge of the methods that have worked elsewhere will always remain the touchstone of a good ethnographic study.

In this book, then, I discuss many of the decisions that I made during a year-long field research project concerning education and social change in the province of West New Britain, Papua New Guinea. Along the way, I explain how I arrived at what proved to be workable answers to the two questions listed on the first page of the book. The reader is provided with specific examples of how I collected evidence about individual actions and words, shared forms of cultural expression, and the structures of social formations in such a way as to make it possible to produce a consistent, empirically valid argument regarding education and social change in West New Britain.[1] Owing to the constraints of this type of book, only a very small portion of the actual overall argument can be reproduced here. Therefore, I have chosen to focus upon one particular aspect of my research proj-ect. This concerns the impact that the implementation of a state-run educational system has had on issues of social inequality within Papua New Guinea. Throughout the book we return often to the question of social inequality as an illustration of the kind of analysis that can be formulated within each method-ological level of the total research project. In addition, I utilize material that I gathered during my archival work at the School of African and Oriental Studies in

1994 in chapter 2 as part of the consideration of the relative merits of using primary versus secondary historical sources in contemporary projects.

Macro and Micro Levels of Research

The book is divided into three main sections, with each of the first two sections corresponding to the methods that are most useful for carrying out research at either the macro or micro level of analysis. It is easiest, for example, for most researchers to begin their initial work (long before they enter the field situation) at the macro level. To take the specific example of educational research, it is no longer adequate to treat individual classrooms or even whole schools as if they formed independent and fully bounded cultural or social units. Education must be seen within its larger social, cultural, and historical context if it is to provide us with useful knowledge about the kinds of relationships that exist between schooling and other social formations inside of a developing (or any) country. It should be obvious that formal education, for example, is closely related to the developing economic institutions of a society and greatly impacts larger trends such as regional patterns of employment/unemployment or the contemporary or potential creation of knowledge-based industries. Perhaps less immediately obvious is the fact that education is intimately tied to religious institutions in most developing countries (and some subregions of industrialized countries) and that trying to arrive at an adequate understanding of education without also learning something about the specific historical relationship between education and religion in these countries will likely lead to seriously underestimating the impact of the moral dimension of education on the citizens of a contemporary nation-state. Schooling is not just about secular concerns such as learning how to read and write, but also about creating the "ideal" citizen—an ideal that has been strongly influenced by moral values that are themselves often at least partially grounded in "missionary" (e.g., Christian, Buddhist, or Islamic) influenced notions of human conduct. In the Papua New Guinea of the twentieth century, for example, various forms of Christian mission institutions were heavily involved in every level of education, from the elementary schools to the Teacher Training Colleges that turned out the future educators of that country. During the period of my primary field research in the late 1980s, the national school system was officially "secular" and had collapsed all of the previously distinct Protestant and Catholic school systems inside of the formerly much smaller government system in order to create a single federally controlled school system (with the exception of the Seventh Day Adventists, who insisted on maintaining a fully separate board). In reality, as the reader will see later in this book, even the most "secular" school was greatly affected by the built-in Christian morality that had become a standard feature of most Papua New Guineans' education prior to the independence of their country in 1975.

All this is to suggest that we cannot really understand what a particular school or even a local school system is about unless we are also able to interpret something of the relational role it plays inside of a larger educational system and the society as a whole—including its articulation with preexisting forms of education.[2]

I would suggest this kind of a contextual lesson is equally valid if we want to understand the place of old age homes in the United States, worker-peasant food production in Spain, or a cigar factory in Cuba. This is the reason behind our concern with macro levels of information gathering and analysis. It is important to note that the boundary between macro and micro levels of research is a relative rather than an absolute distinction. It is obvious, for example, that the world-market system (the buying and selling of commodities on a global level), structures of nation-state formation and re-formation, national educational or medical systems, and so forth would be considered by virtually every researcher as involving macro level research and analysis. Conversely, actual conversations between students and pupils, the interactions between tourists at a heritage site, or the minutiae of a resident's council meeting in a home for the aged would normally be seen as part of the micro level of an educational, tourism, or aging study. But what happens when the two levels meet and merge? To take the educational example, a researcher intensively studying the interactions present in one or two classrooms may consider the school as a whole to make up the most salient macro feature of his/her project; while a scholar studying two or three schools might consider a provincial or statewide school system to be the critical macro feature of his or her study. To a certain extent, what is considered to be "macro" and what is considered to be "micro" levels of information gathering and analysis within a specific study depends upon where the researcher decides to create a primary focus for the project. In my own education study, for example, the essential focus fell upon three different primary schools (grades 1–6) in the province of West New Britain, two of which served urban students and one of which catered to rural students. This meant that anything immediately related to the operation of these three schools (from classroom interactions to parent–teacher associations) were considered by myself to form the micro level of analysis, while anything that fundamentally influenced and was influenced by these schools (from the provincial and national forms of school system organization to national employment structures or the history of the educational system in Papua New Guinea) were considered to be part of the macro level of concern. That in the final analysis the concepts of macro and micro levels of research turn out to be heuristic devices is not only *not* a problem but rather something that must be acknowledged in order to eventually bring these two "levels" of research and analysis back together to form a whole ethnographic study—the goal of any good qualitative project.

In terms of the specific example of research I offer here, the kinds of research methods that belong within each "level" of analysis become much clearer as we proceed through the sections of the book. Again, concrete examples are more useful than abstract rules for illustrating how the researcher can make use of these kinds of conceptual categories for organizing a specific project. I, however, pause for a moment here in order to give readers a brief overview of what they can expect to find within each of the three major sections of this book and the chapters that make up each section of the book.

There are three main parts and ten chapters in this book (including this introductory chapter). Part A is concerned with examples of methods for macro level research, part B with examples of methods for micro level research, and finally part C deals with how researchers bring the disparate elements together in order to create a single work. Part A begins with chapters 2 and 3, each of which is about preliminary research that can be accomplished before the researcher enters the field.

It is a truism in ethnographic studies today that one needs to begin with at least a brief historical overview of the background that informs the contemporary research project. Chapter 2 of this book explains the use of both secondary and primary forms of historical research and why it is necessary to develop a proper contextual understanding of education (for example) within countries that have been undergoing intense amounts of social and cultural change over the last century (the time period when the modern educational systems have largely been created within these nations). I explain why secondary sources are often sufficient for a scholar engaged in a research project involving contemporary education in developing countries, and also explicate the advantages of utilizing primary sources whenever possible. These historical considerations are just as valid for the researcher doing fieldwork about the role of "women's work" among the urban working-poor of Egypt, a comparison of ecotourism in British Columbia versus Alaska, or the very uneven impacts of so-called natural disasters among different social groups in Bangladesh.

Many scholars do not make sufficient use of current sources before they enter the field. Chapter 3 makes a case for a thorough review of the contemporary specialized (e.g., educational) and nonspecialized literature (e.g., literature relating to the overall political economy of the country). Knowledge about both the past and present context of a country is required if the scholar is going to arrive at the fieldwork site with enough information to allow for flexibility in the inevitable case of plans going awry. Upon arriving in Papua New Guinea (PNG), for example, I was informed by an important educational researcher at the University of Papua New Guinea that my research plan was not feasible because a British sociologist was at that very moment conducting similar research in the province of West New Britain. Because of a relatively thorough grounding in the history of Papua New Guinea education, coupled with a knowledge of certain emerging trends in the country, I was able to sit down and type out a new research plan within two days— one that met with the approval of both local researchers and government officials (who had control over whether or not I would be issued the necessary permits to conduct research in that country). Such situations are very common in fieldwork and the researcher needs to be prepared to deal with them. The researcher should be willing to change his or her plans upon arrival in a new country (or even a new area of the country in the case of internal researchers); however, it should also be kept in mind that "open minded is not empty headed" and that a scholar has a responsibility to know as much as possible about the research situation before entering the field in order to undertake the actual project.

A thorough grounding in the literature of the past and present situation in regard to a specific topic such as education will also allow the researcher to develop a general theoretical orientation or approach that will guide methodological decision-making in the field. Theory can be thought of as both a guide for the collection of information and as forming an explanatory boundary within which one will eventually place much of the information that has been gathered. There are no "facts" outside of a theoretical orientation; no "information" without a problem or an issue that requires informing. More will be said about this issue at the end of chapter 3, but it is sufficient to note here that it is quite impossible to enter the field without any preconceived notions regarding education or any other social institution or cultural formation. It is, therefore, much better if a researcher's preconceptions are built upon patterns of understanding that have been created through a careful reading of the available historical and contemporary literature concerning the provision of formal education (or medicine, or social services, etc.) in a particular country than it is to enter the field blissfully unaware of one's own ethnocentric biases. The cultural *bricolage* of one's own life experiences are not sufficient preparation for fieldwork. Again, open minded is not empty headed.

Chapter 4, which involves using newspaper and government documents for research, begins the section of the book involving primary fieldwork. Many fieldworkers neglect newspapers (and, we could add, other mass media sources such as radio programs, print magazines, and web sites) because of the medium's well-earned reputation as an inaccurate source of knowledge. I suggest ways that local newspapers within developing countries such as Papua New Guinea can be used to gather certain kinds of information that is important for understanding education and that is available nowhere else in the country, while simultaneously warning the reader about the kinds of evidence for which newspapers cannot be relied upon. Again, this instruction is equally applicable to a project focused on soccer clubs in northern England, the social impact of feature films in Thailand, or politicians and public life in Argentina.

Government documents are often only available in relatively up-to-date forms within the country and therefore the field researcher will have to allow for the time needed to gather these sources together from what is often a wide variety of venues. Although a separate chapter (chapter 6) will be devoted to the art of the interview, chapter 4 also includes a discussion of the relevance of interviewing government workers (including local academics) during an initial period of field research. These interviews can often save the researcher considerable time and trouble later in the project.

Part B (Methods for Micro Research) begins with chapter 5, which concerns the basic field methods of participant-observation that an ethnographer will need to master in order to collect accurate information regarding behavior within (and in relation to) educational or other settings. The chapter opens with an explanation of the standard method of participant-observation and then goes on to suggest how various forms of observation may be carried out. Researchers are taught in this chapter how to work from more general to more specific information gathering. In the case of schooling, for example, I suggest that the researcher should begin by learning the best ways to take notes based upon their unfocused observations of various forms of behavior both inside and outside of the classroom setting. Using material gathered in the preliminary observations, I then show readers how to turn that knowledge into more focused forms of observational note-taking—ones that allow for evidence gathering according to specific themes that have been identified as important in the earlier research period. The tricky issue of reliability in qualitative research will also be discussed in this chapter. How do we know when our observations are accurate? I draw upon my own experiences and offer specific examples of how I went about cross-checking my information and developing tools for testing my own initial observational impressions. These reliability techniques require nothing more than a pen or pencil, paper, and time and they could be applied equally well to the observation of young girls in play settings in a suburban playground or to the study of campers in Yellowstone National Park, to name only a few noneducational settings.

Chapter 6 is about the art and science of interviewing. In it, I explain the differences between structured, semi-structured, and unstructured interview formats and discuss why qualitative researchers tend to make extensive use of both semi-structured and unstructured interviews but seldom use the fully structured interview technique (which forces answers into preconceived conceptual boxes). This chapter also includes a discussion of the advantages and disadvantages of single person versus group interviewing and why both will likely be necessary in your work. Children in the primary schools of West New Britain, for instance, responded best within group interviews, while government officials and schoolteachers generally preferred to be interviewed within one-to-one situations.

In chapter 7 I explain the potential uses of various forms of self-reporting. For example, during my research in West New Britain I arranged for school children to write essays for me based upon the theme of "my future work" within the context of their normal English language classes. Using this material, I was able to compare the expectations of grade five and six students in three different schools regarding their ideal futures. This material could then be related to other evidence that had been collected during teacher interviews or classroom observations. Such methods could just as easily be productively used in a study of corporate executives in New York, or when trying to understand the lives of Christian monks in France. In this chapter, readers will be able to see how a researcher can use self-reporting material to supplement the more direct researcher-gathered material to give an extra subjective dimension to information gathering.

In part C of the book we turn toward learning how to put the information gathered together in our studies to form a single ethnographic whole. In chapter 8, I discuss how to move from a preliminary conceptual analysis of particular data to a secondary analysis in which the researcher is able to discern larger social, cultural, and behavioral patterns. Specific examples are used to illustrate why individual differences exist within any pattern and how scholars can know when they have reliably identified a larger pattern of significant behavior despite these singularities. Analysis is the heart of ethnographic writing and I explain in this chapter why the process of analysis is both an art form and a science in and of itself.

Chapter 9 is a consideration of how analysis can turn into the creation of new theory and/or be used to consider the worthiness of older theory. How do we "test" existing theory in relation to our own study? Can new theory be created out of a specific project alone, or is it always related to previous theories, ideas, and assumptions? I answer these questions and show readers how they can develop both new theory and test older theoretical formulations through the use of the information that they have gathered in the course of their own research projects.

Finally, chapter 10 deals with issues of ethnographic writing (for both academic and practical audiences). Academic writing has its own conventions and some suggestions given should make your book, thesis, or other form of scholarly writing easier to complete. At the same time, even a project that was not initially conceived of by the researcher as a form of "applied research" often has practical significance. I would contend that any good research involving issues of education in developing countries, for example, has implications for educational practice in that country. My own experience with offering "practical" advice based upon an "academic" research project is utilized to show that there is no true dividing line between academic and applied research, and that as scholars we do not have to give up our more theoretical concerns in order to satisfy local expectations for us to conduct "relevant" research on formal educational matters in a developing country. Similar conclusions about the mutual relevance of academic versus applied orientations can be drawn for working with small business owners in the rural communities of Nova Scotia, or diamond miners in South Africa.

I have written this book in such a way that any researcher with a pen, a pad of paper, a tape recorder with a dozen tapes (and even the use of a tape recorder is optional), and the necessary money to put him or her self in the field for a year or so can do the research. The advantage to this approach is: (1) it makes it possible for nonacademic researchers (including school teachers in a developing country, social workers in India, or a sports activist in Great Britain) who may not have access to substantial financial resources to carry out a basic study, (2) it allows graduate students (or academics for that matter) who were not able to secure a grant to undertake a quality research project in the face of that restriction, and (3) it emphasizes basic skills over technical tricks and therefore allows fieldworkers to expand their research from this solid foundation if subsequent opportunities arise for them to do so. Therefore, researchers who wish to make use of this book do not need access to field computers, fancy photographic or video or audio equipment. All of the methods taught here can easily be adapted for use with more sophisticated equipment (e.g., for use in computer programs that utilize qualitative sorting and analysis applications such as NUDIST or ETHNOGRAPH), but it is *not* necessary to have this kind of infrastructure to carry out a sophisticated study. That is part of the beauty of an ethnographic approach to a study or a project—it is a very cost-effective method of doing research in a rich or a poor country. It produces a tremendous amount of information for very little cost and allows the researcher to present that information in a manner that is understandable to nonspecialists concerned with education, sports, tourism, or other special areas of interest in that country.

Research Ethics and a Critical Stance

It should be obvious to the reader by now that I expect a researcher to take a critical stance in relation to the study of education or any other social or cultural topic that they might wish to pursue. It is important, therefore, to consider how such a stance can be achieved while keeping within generally accepted ethical guidelines for our work. An example of a stumbling block that I faced in my own fieldwork in Papua New Guinea should help to put this issue into perspective. Soon after arriving in the province of West New Britain and during the very first period of my interview process with provincial government officials I noticed that the bureaucrats most directly responsible for education were very reluctant to cooperate with my project, even though higher government officials had instructed them to do so. Not wanting to force myself upon these individuals, I finally asked one male official who played a key role in the provincial educational system why he didn't seem to like the idea of my doing research on primary schools in his province. He took a deep breath and let loose with a stream of angry words, the gist of which was that they, the people directly responsible for educa-tion in the province, were sick and tired of outsiders coming in and "telling us that everything we are doing is wrong." He likened the situation to one of neocolonial-ism, in which researchers from much richer countries came into Papua New Guinea and told local practitioners that they were "backward" in their educational methods without realizing that the local context made many of the educational practices of wealthier countries impractical. He sat back, looked downward at this desk, and said that he knew that the Provincial Minister of Education had person-ally approved my project and that he would therefore not be able to block it, "but that doesn't mean that I have to like it." Looking somewhat abashed, he then waited for me to speak. I told him that he was quite right and that anthropologists firmly believed in the importance of context in understanding education in a specific place, and that it would in fact be quite colonial of me if I came into his province and started saying that I knew better than anybody else what the goals of education should be and how to "fix" anything that might seem to be wrong with the system. After a lengthy discussion, we arrived at an accord of a sort, although he still seemed to hold considerable reservations about both my work and myself as a researcher. In fact, it was only some months later when I stopped to admire a house with a beautifully landscaped yard and garden in a part of town that I did not normally visit that we reached a real understanding. A man came out of the house to see what I was doing. It turned out to be the same government official and when I expressed my very real delight in his garden we launched into a long discussion about horticultural practices in West New Britain. This discussion eventually became a consideration of education as a metaphor for gardening. From that time onward, this key bureaucrat and I had a very good working relationship and he seemed to accept that I was not out to criticize him personally because of any "failures" that the educational system might hold in and of itself due to the financial and structural limitations of life in the province of West New Britain.

The important point about the story above is that this encounter made it nec-essary for me to rethink my critical approach to educational research in Papua New Guinea. At one level, he had been right about me. I did (and do) pride myself on my "leftist" leanings and had planned on a critical evaluation of education in his province. Furthermore, I had unthinkingly adopted a critical stance that had largely been informed by theorists who had conducted their studies in wealthy countries and who did not have any experience in developing countries. Pondering my problem, I remembered about some of the material that I had gathered from the various federal government offices while I was in the capital city of Port Morseby prior to commencing my provincial research (see chapter 4 on this issue). Reading through some of it, I was able to discover that both the federal and provincial governments had very specific goals for education in Papua New Guinea. They wanted, for example, to ensure that the benefits of education reached as many people in the country as possible, that both males and females received equal chances at education, and that schooling helped to create independent thinkers who could act as entrepreneurs capable of moving the country forward economically, socially, and culturally (e.g., Department of Education 1985). In other words, government officials and educators in Papua New Guinea wanted education to achieve a number of very specific goals in their country. Realizing that led me to understand that I could maintain a "critical stance" toward education in PNG *without* unnecessarily relying upon "external" expectations for education. I could, for example, critically examine schooling practices that might lead to boys being favored over girls in the classroom (or vice versa), or negatively evaluate pedagogical methods that seemed to lead to dependent and docile identity formation, in the light of Papa New Guineans' own goals for gender equality in education or their desires for the development of independent entrepreneurial citizens. By adopting *internal* goals and relating my critical research to these goals I was able to obviate the ethical dilemma of taking a seemingly colonialist stance on the directions that Papua New Guinea education ought to take in the future. A similar approach can be taken to research virtually anywhere. The scholar could work with the members of a craft guild, for example, in identifying desirable goals for potters or metal workers of a specific region and then do a critical study of whether contemporary practices are encouraging or blocking the realization of these goals. Such an approach does not obviate the use of other, more external, critical stances—but it does suggest that the researcher has the obligation to reconcile these stances with more localized concerns in order to avoid becoming the ugly colonialist.

All research takes place within an ethical framework. In Canada, where I am employed as a professor, national standards exist for the ethical conduct of research and each university has a duly constituted committee that vets every research project for ethical considerations. Most researchers also belong to professional associations (such as the Canadian Anthropology Society or the American Anthropological Association). Most of these associations also publish their own guidelines for ethical research. Every researcher must become familiar with the ethical guidelines of their own country and/or professional association(s) before they undertake field research *and* seriously consider the ethical context that exists in the place in which they conduct their project. I cannot possibly cover all of the relevant issues in this short section, but I would like to briefly consider a few of the more important topics here before we continue on into the next chapter.

To begin with, all ethical guidelines require the researcher to come to terms with the issue of informed consent. Such consent involves informing individuals who participate in a study in such a way that they can reasonably be considered to have a conscious understanding of the goals, methods, and implications of the research project in which they are participating. Such consent is often culturally specific. For example, it might involve a formal presentation to the leaders of a band council in the case of a First Nations society in Canada, or to various levels of government responsible for education in a developing country, in order to gain official acceptance for the study. In addition, each individual involved in the project (whether adult or child) should be aware of the basic reason for the study and how it is being carried out. In some fields, such as psychology or sociology, informed consent often involves research participants signing a sheet of paper indicating that they understand the basic rationale for the study and who is responsible for its ethical conduct. In fields such as anthropology, in which we attempt to conduct research in a culturally appropriate manner in various locations around the world, we normally use oral consent as it is generally recognized that a request for written consent will often be viewed with hostility (e.g., due to different comfort levels with literacy as well as to local political situations in which people may have good reason to worry about signing anything that they feel might be held against them by an authoritarian government). In each case, to obtain (written or oral) consent, the researcher should have a short statement ready that includes information about who is conducting the study, why it is being carried out, and what the researcher (and others) might reasonably hope to gain from the project.

Part of the statement usually contains an offer of anonymity to those participating in the study if they so desire. In anthropology, for example, it is commonplace to disguise the name of the place (or places) in which the study occurs and names of all of the study participants. This is done to in order to fulfill one of the main ethical tenets of research: to ensure, insofar as it is humanly possible to do so, that no participants of the study will ever be harmed by their participation or by the publication of the results of the study. This is not always easy to do, and it may involve taking great care during the publishing stage of the work. In addition, not all groups of people, or individuals, wish to remain anonymous in a study and researchers have to take that into account in their work. In my own case, for example, both local researchers and educators told me that following the common anthropological convention of disguising the schools involved in my study would render the research useless to both them and to future scholars in Papua New Guinea. I therefore modified the standard writing practice and named the actual schools involved in my written work, while simultaneously taking great care to disguise individual teachers and pupils who were behind specific words or behaviors as they were presented in the study. Even ethical considerations sometimes have to be negotiated.

Other key ethical considerations involve the storage of research notes and the dissemination of study results. Care must be taken to store research notes in a secure place (often using a small trunk and a lock) both in the field and after fieldwork is completed in order to ensure the protection and privacy of those involved in the study. In my case, simple procedures were enough to ensure the safety of my notes. In a country in which the police, the military, or the government have a reputation of interfering with the safety of local populations, the researcher may have to go to substantial lengths to ensure the well-being of the study participants, including (but not limited to) keeping all notes in a form of personal code—one that does not reveal the true names of the participants themselves.

As researchers, we often have a responsibility to make sure that our results are made available in some fashion to the people with whom we conducted our study. In my case, for example (see chapter 10), this involved both short presentations to interested parties before leaving the country and also a much larger report that I sent back to the country some months after my departure.

Much more can be said about ethical considerations, but these are the key topics that the researcher will have to consider as a part of any educational study. Above all, use your own sense of justice when conducting research. Does the research have potentially significant findings that make it important for me to find a way to conduct the study? Am I doing anything that might impact on the dignity of the people with whom I am working? Will I have to withhold this or that information in my publications to make sure that there are no repercussions for those involved in the study? How can I best fulfill my obligation to share my research results with relevant groups or individuals? As in so many other areas of research, a little imagination and lot of empathy may be necessary to obtain the best results.

Part A

Methods for Macro-Level Research

2

Using Historical Sources for Ethnographic Research

H istory has become a major part of virtually every ethnographic research project. For example, in order to develop an understanding of how a contemporary educational system came to take its present form, it is necessary to begin with a history of that system and its relationship to other important social institutions within the country. Similarly, if I wanted to understand why a particular area was receiving special funding today for the development of tourism, I believe it is also necessary to learn about the history of economic change in that area and how tourism fits into that overall social and economic history.

In an ideal world, researchers would be able to follow an initial study of secondary (i.e., published) historical sources with research into primary (archival) historical sources before beginning the actual fieldwork stage of a project. In the case of educational research in Papua New Guinea, for example, primary historical work would require spending time in research archives contained in both Australia and Papua New Guinea itself (and possibly Great Britain as well). For most of us, whether first-time researchers (and therefore likely graduate or perhaps even undergraduate students) or professional researchers (and therefore likely professors or employees of government or nongovernment agencies) the time constraints imposed by financial and professional limitations generally render an extensive use of primary sources in the initial research project impossible. I therefore begin this chapter by concentrating on the use of secondary historical sources and suggest that a careful consideration of these materials can create an adequate, if not ideal, platform upon which to generate an understanding of the most important historical trends affecting the special area of research interest.

Secondary Sources for Historical Research

In my own initial Ph.D. study, I was forced to rely extensively upon secondary sources, saving primary historical research for a later period of postdoctoral work. Luckily, Papua New Guinea had a relatively rich secondary literature on the history of education available to me prior to field research.[1] Obviously, there will be considerable differences in relation to the amount of secondary historical material available to researchers depending upon the project topic, the site at which the author is doing the preparatory work, and the developing or industrialized country that contains the project site. Going to graduate school in Canada, for example, did not make it easy to find material concerning the topic of education in Papua New Guinea within local libraries. It might require some "digging" to ferret out the resources that are available in your home country (a task that should be somewhat easier for those who also live in the country in which they are doing their research, unless of course they live in a more remote part of that country). Even though I was located at a large university in Canada (McMaster University in Hamilton, Ontario) with a good general library, I was still forced to travel to another even larger Canadian city (Toronto, Ontario) in order to make use of its specialized education libraries (attached to various educational institutions there). Many countries have interlibrary loan systems, but this may not prove to be sufficient if scholars do not yet know what sources they need to ask to borrow (a common enough situation at the beginning of a project). Anyone having difficulty obtaining at least six to twelve good secondary historical publications about the topic they are interested in should consider whether they can afford the time and expense of a trip to an urban center with a larger library system. Alternatively, if that is not feasible, I would suggest that you build three or four weeks into your field research that will initially be devoted to using the research country's university library system in order to gather basic information about the history of your topic in that country. This is a feasible option for most researchers, even those working in developing countries, as it is normally necessary to fly into either the national capital or one of the major city of a developing country in order to gain eventual access to one's (possibly) more remote field research site. Local academics are ordinarily extremely helpful, especially to neophyte researchers, and can generally be counted upon to point out the classic historical and contemporary works available in their libraries and bookstores. Don't be shy about asking for their help—they want you to understand what you are doing so that you can properly contribute to the knowledge base of their country.

To use my own study as an example, the secondary literature on the history of education in Papua New Guinea alerted me to the notion that there had been three main phases of educational policy in that country (corresponding roughly to three political phases): (1) 1873–1945: an era of almost total missionary control over rudimentary education for the purpose of Christian "salvation," (2) 1945–1960: a period of rapidly expanding the primary school system for the purposes of a "basic education" for the masses, during which time the colonial government and missionaries began to work in a closer partnership, and (3) 1960 until the present: a phase in which first the colonial government of Australia and then the independent government of Papua New Guinea (post-1975) took over primary responsibility for the total educational system (see Fife 1995b, 1996). It was during this last period that large amounts of money were invested in the rapid expansion of the secondary and tertiary levels of education in order to prepare an educated "elite" for independence in 1975. An important impact of this overall trend was the creation of an educational system that fueled regional, urban/rural, and class inequalities within the country (e.g., see the papers in Bray and Smith 1985). It was because I had taken the time to familiarize myself with some of the secondary historical material before the beginning of my on-site work that I was able to realize that signs of these emerging forms of social inequalities could be expected to appear when I conducted my micro-level field research within the primary school system of West New Britain. Later in the book, it becomes evident that this was exactly what occurred.

Researchers will normally only have a short period of time available (because of the exigencies of graduate school or professional duties) to read secondary historical material before beginning field research and they should therefore concentrate during the beginning stage of their work on the broadest outlines available that help to explain the development of their topic of interest (e.g., small business enterprises in Brazil, or cash cropping within communist China). After the field-work has been completed, they can then return to either secondary or primary sources in order to look more closely at material that speaks directly to the development of the most important themes discovered during the on-site research. To give an example from my own work, my initial readings were what alerted me to the importance of missionary influences in Papua New Guinea's primary school system. This eventually led me to notice a number of behavioral interactions between teachers and pupils that seemed aimed more at the creation of a moral order within the schools and classrooms of West New Britain than they were tied to any specific or official educational goals in the secular school system. Follow-up reading (after the completion of the on-site fieldwork) on the history of education (using both additional secondary sources, as well as primary sources) allowed me not only to confirm my micro-level fieldwork evidence concerning the creation of a moral order, but also to link specific historical practices to contemporary practices even though teachers and other educators themselves no longer recognized these linkages as existing within the newer government-run "secular" school system (e.g., Fife 1994). This make it possible for me to conclude that much of the "hidden" morality embedded within teachers' attitudes toward students' behaviors (which could be seen in classroom interactions as well as heard in teacher interviews) had their origins in missionary influences. Without at least some knowledge of historical missionary endeavors within education I would never have been able to recognize these cultural patterns when they appeared within the interactions between teachers and pupils in the classrooms of West New Britain during the actual in-site fieldwork part of the project.

It should be evident that a scholar must read the secondary historical literature on their topic (e.g., education) for a given country with an eye toward delineating the major ways that specific themes will appear within that topic (e.g., educational history). For example, have gender relations always been problematic in Papua New Guinean education (e.g., is there an ongoing historical imbalance between males and females in the higher levels of educational attainment, or in terms of specific subjects such as mathematics) or have they been relatively equitable? Has education historically fueled the growth of class differences, rural/urban differences, or differences between ethnic subgroups? Researchers may approach reading the secondary historical literature having already been pre-sensitized to certain issues (such as gender inequality) or they may simply begin reading the literature confident that specific themes will soon emerge that are worth noticing for future reference. In either case, they are reading to gain a basic understanding of the context that will prove to be necessary in order to "place" or "give meaning" to the more specific words and behaviors they will come across during the in-site phase of the project. In my own case, I was already interested in general themes of social inequality and wanted to pursue them in some form within my field research. I therefore read the initial secondary historical literature, both the literature concerned directly with education (as above) and that which outlined the wider history of the political economy of the area that later became the country of Papua New Guinea,[2] with the intent of delineating various themes of social inequality and how they might relate to the emerging educational system.

How can themes be "pulled" from the secondary historical literature that will prove to be of use to researchers planning to do fieldwork on a specific topic such as education in a developing country? Some examples from my own work should illustrate the kinds of themes that a reader might glean from secondary historical literature and explain how they may be of use in the overall project. Due to space constraints, I limit myself here largely to those themes that most directly relate to the topic of emerging social inequalities—though the reader should understand that a parallel process can be followed for his or her particular interests (e.g., an interest in the relationship between gender and education, the economics of education, religion and education, changing organizational design and policy in education, and of course noneducational issues as well).

What we are really after here is what Anthony Giddens has referred to as the "structuration" of institutions: "The structural properties of social systems exist only in so far as forms of social conduct are reproduced chronically across time and space. The structuration of institutions can be understood in terms of how it comes about that social activities become 'stretched' across wide spans of time-space" (Giddens 1986: xxi). Structuration refers to the active and ongoing historical process by which the traces of social change are left behind in the form of institutional *structure*. Even this is misleading, as "structure" itself is constantly undergoing new change. Most change, however, occurs in a regular direction and therefore gives the viewer the illusion that not much *is* changing—at least in terms of the broader outlines of institutional forms. It is the illusion of stability, or structure, and how it is *used* by practitioners (educational, economic, political, artistic, and so forth) that we find of interest for our projects.

Strangely enough, I began my search for historical influences on Papua New Guinean education with a brief reading of some of the archaeological (i.e., prehistoric) literature. It seemed important for me to know that human occupation went back in this part of the world at least 40,000–50,000 years (Kiste 1984; Howe 1984) and that several large waves of populations swept out from Southeast Asia at different periods of time, bringing new lifeways and languages with them and influencing the mixture of cultures that previously existed in the area. One such wave, for example, can be seen in the archaeological evidence for approximately 5,000–6,000 years ago, when large numbers of migrants arrived in outrigger canoes, bringing with them technology appropriate for root crop horticulture and the domestication of pigs—the dominant form of subsistence production up until the present period of time in Papua New Guinea (Howe 1984).

Some readers might be thinking: "Yes, but what does this have to do with education?" My answer would be that an educational researcher might wish to know, for example, about the waves of migrants who form the foundations for the contemporary division of Papua New Guineans into Austronesian speakers versus non-Austronesian speakers—which in turn forms the platform for the tremendous language diversity (more than 800 separate languages) that exist in the contemporary country. The educational challenge that must be faced in a country with so many different indigenous languages (along with the European influenced "contact" languages of English, Tok Pisin, and Motu) and the various forms of social inequalities that are fueled by these language patterns is, I would argue, informed by knowing about how this situation came to pass in the first place.

Just as importantly, there is still a great deal of misinformation concerning the history of social change in developing countries (and of so-called backward regions in industrialized countries). Influenced by various forms of modernization theory, many researchers, educators, politicians, and others both inside and outside of Papua New Guinea still believe that processes of social change are something that only really began with the arrival of Europeans to the shores of the region that eventually became the nation of Papua New Guinea. This notion regarding the existence of an "unchanging tradition" prior to the arrival of Europeans, embedded as it is in the ethnocentric assumption that "primitive peoples" live within "simple and unchanging" social and cultural formations, has to be directly challenged by the researcher if s/he is going to give proper weight to the role of both indigenous and foreign influences affecting the contemporary education (or other) institutions of a country such as PNG (or Kenya, or Bolivia, or Thailand, or Tonga). Similar statements could be made about the situation of working on First Nations reserves in Canada, in the Appalachian region of the United States, or in other similar areas that have a history of cultural clashes between more powerful and less powerful populations. A brief knowledge of the archaeological record, for example, allowed me to point out that many small villages in Papua New Guinea were not "isolated" in pre-European times, despite many peoples' assumptions in this regard, as extensive trade networks existed in several different regions as early as 6,000–7,000 years ago and likely before this as well (Lacey 1983: 8–9; for a good regional example, see Harding 1967). In effect, the continuous history/prehistory of this part of the Pacific Islands points to an extremely long period of ongoing adaptation to new peoples and technological changes. This information allows us to view the effects of the arrival of Europeans as simply one more in a long series of social changes in which the inhabitants of Papua New Guinea have adapted to, transformed, and selectively rejected outside influences in their areas. This form of understanding lets us see Papua New Guineans (pupils, parents, educators, bureaucrats, and others) as social agents actively engaging in the ongoing creation of their educational system rather than as passive receptors of "outside" or "western" forms of education. Similar *caveats* are necessary in all of our project areas.

Something along the same lines can be said about why we need to study the secondary historical sources regarding both formal education and the social formations within which it is embedded. Local agency can be seen in various historical encounters, as can some of the effects of emerging structural formations. Only a few examples from my Papua New Guinea study will be given here. Again, the focus is upon large-scale historical themes and their relation to emerging forms of social inequality.

Despite early and very limited excursions by Portuguese, Spanish, and Dutch "explorers" into the New Guinea[3] area as early as the 1500s and 1600s (Howe 1984; Kiste 1984; Blythe 1978), there were very few significant effects from the European intrusions into this region prior to the 1870s—the period when the first missionaries (such as those who came from the London Missionary Society) began their work. In 1884, under pressure from traders, missionaries, and would-be planters, and under the political threat of the German annexation of the New Guinea territory (the area that makes up the north-eastern quarter of the main island), Great Britain in turn annexed the south-eastern area generally known as Papua. Thus began a long colonial history of administration, a history that saw Australia assume control of Papua in 1906 and of the New Guinea territory in 1914, which it maintained (with only a brief interruption by partial Japanese occupation of the island from 1942–1945 during World War II) until full independence was achieved in 1975 (e.g., Delbos 1985; Easton 1985; Fife 1995b).

Since missionaries began the educational system (or more properly, educational systems) in Papua New Guinea and colonial administrations created the policies under which education operated, it is clearly important for an educational researcher in that country to understand something about the history of those two social institutions in relation to education. A similar statement could be made if I had been interested in studying the creation of mass media (such as radio and newspapers), social services, or changing kinship patterns in the rural versus urban areas of Papua New Guinea.

Education was understood as a key to colonization in New Guinea from the very first period of European influence. Dr. Christian Barth, for example, wrote in a German magazine in 1911 in relation to the German colony that "For a country to show a healthy progress in its development it is necessary to lift its population to a higher level, to train it. In other words, all colonization, if understood correctly, is nothing but a certain kind of education" (Barth, available in Smith 1987: 30). Europeans associated directly with the colonial enterprise, such as government officials and colonial planters (agricultural plantation owners and overseers) often defined education as much more than just schooling. A paper published by the New Guinea Planters Association in 1928 suggested, for example, that "The only real education available to the native at present is provided in the homes of colonists, in the workshops, on the ships, in the Christian missions, and most particularly on the plantations and trading concerns of the planting community" (available in Smith 1987: 122).

For missionaries, morality could only be achieved through numeracy and literacy (especially true for the Protestant missionaries) and it is worth noting that the first school appeared in 1873, only two years after the London Missionary Society

(LMS) became the initial mission agency to set up shop in southern New Guinea (Hecht 1981; Weeks and Guthrie 1984). They were soon followed by the Methodists in the Duke of York Islands in 1875; Catholics in the Gazelle Peninsula (East New Britain) in 1882; Lutherans in Finschhaffen in 1890; and by the Anglicans in Milne Bay in 1892 (Weeks and Guthrie 1984; Delbos 1985). All of these missions (and the many others that followed them in the 1900s) ran schools with one basic goal—the creation of a new people who would display a Christian character—a people that would operate more "comfortably" inside of a colonized New Guinea, with its newly European forms of government, religion, and economy (Thomas 1976; Hecht 1981; Fife 1995b).

Although missionary educators, planters, and the members of the colonial government did not agree about many things, there was a widespread feeling that one of the main purposes of mission education was to "civilize the primitive, backward, amoral and lazy" indigenous villager. For example, a resident magistrate declared in 1908 when he discovered that planters were having a difficult time recruiting workers for their plantations in the Kerema area: "Nowhere in Papua, I venture to say, will you find a more lazy, indolent set of male natives than in these villages. With them laziness is carried to a fine art and their chief and only occupation is dancing" (quoted in Lacey 1983: 36).

With no understanding of local cultural formations, the various mission groups set themselves the task of instilling discipline into the resisting bodies of the villagers (e.g., Fife 2001). The L.M.S., for example, did this through the creation of fenced-in mission stations alongside of but not within larger clusters of villages or hamlets (Langmore 1989). The goal was to convince parents to turn their children over to the missionaries for "education." These small stations were to be models or "beacons for civilized Christian life" among the heathen savages, as most missionaries characterized the adult indigenous islanders. Children who grew up on these stations (a very small minority of the children in the country as a whole) gained basic numeracy and literacy skills, learned to follow the European standards for personal hygiene, and often took on the Protestant (or Catholic, as the case may be) work ethic. They were highly sought after as employees by the other Europeans living in New Guinea. Thus began an enduring set of social inequalities, one that continues to have reverberations for the contemporary period in Papua New Guinea. Villagers who grew up near mission stations had vastly greater opportunities than the majority of villagers within that country in terms of familiarizing themselves with the educational, economic, and social ways of Europeans (and because of that to work on plantations, in mines, and eventually as clerks in government and commercial enterprises). This meant that when Papua New Guinea became an independent country in 1975, a minority of the people (and a minority of the collective cultural groups) living there had many decades of experience in learning, understanding, and manipulating the various European-derived organizational forms (e.g., economic and political) that came to characterize "opportunity" in the new Papua New Guinea (for an example of how this affected models of masculinity and hence opportunities for employment, see Fife 1995a). This situation also helped lead to huge differences in collective educational attainment among local populations (e.g., coastal versus highland peoples) and therefore also affected their relative abilities to access the new government or other cash economy jobs (such as becoming a school teacher, a construction worker, or an office worker) or to access such related opportunities as obtaining bank loans in order to begin local coffee plantations for the export market (for a fascinating take on how these complex issues of "modernity" worked out among the Karavar people, see Errington and Gewertz 1995). These were also the beginnings of substantial class differences, although "class" formation in Papua New Guinea involves such complex factors as living in urban versus rural environments and is not a straightforward artifact of those who own the means of production versus those who work for them (as it would be expected if we followed more classic forms of Marxist theory).

Without a solid understanding of some of the major historical patterns of the area that became Papua New Guinea it would be extremely difficult for a researcher to arrive at an adequate understanding of such contemporary issues as social inequality within that country and the role that education (or social services, or financial services, etc.) plays in these processes. Patterns such as social inequality are not timeless, universal entities; they are historical patterns that change forms over both time and space. There are many other aspects of these forms of inequality in Papua New Guinea and its relationship to historic educational patterns, such as the great historical differences that have existed in various parts of the country in terms of the amount of resources families and kinship groups are willing to put into the education of their young females. However, the above examples will serve to show why the ethnographic researcher needs to begin his or her work by reading secondary historical sources *before* entering the research field. The same would hold true if the scholar's interest was in banking policy formation, the impact of radio on trade and travel, or any of the other numerous potential topics to pursue in a developing or industrialized country.

Primary Sources for Historical Research

As stated above, the use of secondary historical sources is perfectly adequate for many contemporary ethnographic research projects. I wish to take a moment, however, to point out the advantages of adding the use of primary archival sources to your work (if not immediately, then perhaps in subsequent research periods). As a first consideration, let's return to the example that was given above regarding the L.M.S.'s use of mission stations to discipline and hence to "civilize" (or more properly, Europeanize) their educational charges. If I wished to write about this process more specifically for purposes of publication, the use of primary archival material would allow me to substantiate the patterns I first found in secondary sources and also suggest more of the texture of life that was involved at these stations. Primary archival sources, for example, led me to this description by the Reverend John Holmes about what life was like at his Urika station in the

New Guinea of 1918:

> At 8 am. the siren calls all hands to work every day of the week, Saturday excepted, and when all have assembled in the large workshop I call the register. [He then gives a five minute address and service] . . . After the service each group of workers [which includes the students] is consulted about its work each day. The leader of each group has to be able to account for the work of the previous day and if there has been any slackness it has to be accounted for before all hands. Teacher, lay workers and headboys all have to toe the line, no quarter is given to anyone, it is driven home to them over and over again that we are fellow-workers together with God in this work. (Holmes 1918: 2)

In a related fashion, the Reverend Caleb Beharall makes a forceful statement about the "industrial" model of total education that was followed to at least some extent at most L.M.S. stations and the effects they wished it to have upon villagers:

> The ideal we have before us is the training of character, mind and body of the child. The new conditions of affairs [i.e., the influence of an industrial style mission] have compelled us to give the last a prominent place. Our methods are physical drill and manual labour. The results are very satisfactory. The young people are becoming cleaner in their habits, stronger in body, more industrious and are beginning to learn the value of time. (Beharall 1917: 1)

Primary archival material also allows us to notice the similarity between the physical discipline of work on these stations and the content of mission education in the classrooms. For example, the reverend Archibald Hunt wrote about the content of the first written school examination given at Murray Island by the Reverend MacFarlane:

> The paper in Geography covered:—(1) Definition of Terms; (2) General Geography of the World; (3) Europe. In the first division the questions were correctly answered in nearly every case. In (2) the answers were very good, but one question proved too much for them all—viz., the names of the five oceans. They all remembered "Indian," and some could manage "Pacific," but the rest they could not pronounce, much less write. . . . In (3) the answers were exceptionally good—the names of all the countries in Europe, the location of such places as Berne, Christiania, Athens, &c., and the capitals of such countries as Ireland, Germany, Turkey, Italy, &c., being among the questions. (Hunt 1888: 392)

What direct sources such as these show us is that just as the physical aspects of education involved teaching village children how to "locate" their bodies within regimes of a Christian moral discipline, the content of education also involved locating their minds within the political geography of a European-centered world.

It was in the archives that I first became aware that military style "drill" was considered to be a normal part of education on many mission stations. I eventually discovered that this existed largely because of the introduction of the Boys Brigade (similar to the Boy Scouts) movement on many mission stations around the year 1900 (Springhall, Fraser, and Hoare 1983). Drill was actually "graded" and often examined in combination with regular academic disciplines during school finals. Examinations of every type were commonplace at the stations and were usually very rigorous. As Reverend John Holmes (one of the greatest proponents of the Boys Brigade) notes in 1918, he and his wife were:

> Conducting a monthly examination of everyone who attends school and everyone includes everyone on the station apart from babies who cannot yet lisp letters. . . . [Native] Teachers and scholars are on their mettle. The former know if they are slack in their work and in the maintenance of discipline they will have to account for the slackness before their pupils. (Holmes 1918:1)

Notice how the above themes parallel material found by myself at a much later period in contemporary Papua New Guinea (presented below). The following is taken directly from my fieldnotes (chapter 5 deals with how to take such research notes) and are based upon observations conducted at a primary school in the provincial capital (Kimbe) of West New Britain.

> Assembly is outside today and students form into squares, each square subdivided into several classrooms. They stand at attention, gathered around the flagpole. Start off with some hand clapping, in unison, then they sing the national anthem. . . . After the announcements they do marching in place; hands clapping, then hands behind the back, in response to shouted orders from the assistant headmaster. While still marching in place, he calls out the names of individual classes, which then proceed to peel off in single files and march toward their classrooms. As each reaches its classroom building, they wait outside the door, still marching, until the teacher comes over to give them orders. I follow the class that I am observing today, and the teacher drills them in front of the door before she allows them to go inside, making them turn around a number of times in place; standing at ease, at attention, at ease, at attention, and so forth.

It was not until I came across passages in the archives of London, England that described pseudo-military styles of assembly, the importance of drill, and the influence of the Boys Brigade that some of my contemporary fieldnote descriptions began to make sense to me as a larger pattern that speaks about disciplining the body as a moral agent (see Fife 2001). When I asked teachers themselves about why assembly and many other moments of physical aggregation (such as preparing to go outside for recess) had such a "military" style, they uniformly said that that they didn't really know why. Most teachers simply stated to me "this is the way we do it," or "it is good for the students to do things this way." Not a single educator that I spoke with connected these forms of physical discipline to the missionary history of education in Papua New Guinea and no one mentioned the Boys' Brigade as a possible source of influence on contemporary pedagogical practices. Without my primary archival knowledge of history, I would never have been able to make these kinds of connections in my subsequent publications.

In a similar fashion, other aspects of the content of education continues to parallel concerns that first show up in the missionary archives of the relatively distant past. Contemporary educators in Papua New Guinea, for example, remain committed to frequent "testing," just as the Reverend Holmes and his colleagues did at the beginning of the twentieth century. Strict grade six, grade eight, and grade ten examinations determine which students are eligible to continue with their formal education beyond each of those grades and who will be "left behind." Similarly, the content of education continues to show a tremendous concern for social "placement," as we also saw in the quote from the Reverend Hunt in 1888. Compare that quote with the following classroom exchange that I recorded in 1986:

> "Okay, who can tell us what we're doing this week in community life?" Michael answers, "Local Government." The teacher continues: "Right, do we have one here?" Several respond at once: "Yes." "What is it called?" she asks. Several boys and girls shout, "NAKANAI GOVERNMENT COUNCIL!" "How many more are there around this area?" Sheila responds, "Eight." "Right," the teacher says, and gets the children to name each one . . . "All right, who can give the local government councilor's name?" After Matthew gives her name, she asks, "If he [it is actually a woman] has a problem that he cannot handle who will they bring the problem to?" Several children answer, "Parliament." "No," she responds, "You don't jump from here to your house, you must climb the ladder properly." The students then name the office holder in the provincial government and then the one in the national government to whom problems would be taken.

It should be obvious by now that there are many parallel themes that show up in both the history of missionary education and in the contemporary educational practices of Papua New Guinea, despite the fact that modern educators generally do not make these connections themselves (though modern research academics, including those working inside of Papua New Guinea, certainly do). It is true that a number of these themes should become visible through the researcher's knowledge of secondary historical sources, but it is also true that much of the texture of these patterns and how they come to be played out in both the past and (in comparison) present situations would remain invisible without primary source research. Such research need not involve half a dozen archives located in the four corners of the world (as might well be required for the professional historian). We are concerned here with fleshing out our knowledge of contemporary practices, rather than for example, researching and writing formal histories of education in developing countries. In my case, a three-month visit to a single archive in 1994 (located in the School of Oriental and African Studies at the University of London, in England) has provided me with invaluable primary source material about the L.M.S. and other mission groups who pioneered educational practices in Papua New Guinea. The extent to which a researcher should be concerned with archival work depends upon his or her use of the historical material. Writing educational history for its own sake clearly requires a much more extensive exploitation of primary archival material than the more limited reading that can help make sense of contemporary educational practices (the approach I am advocating here).

This approach to historically grounding one's ethnographic project has similar advantages in most research situations. To illustrate this point, I give one other short example here of a quite different study that I conducted in 1981. Over two decades ago, I was engaged in a project (my M.A. thesis) in which I was trying to understand how rural people who entered a home for the aged in the Canadian province of Ontario went about trying to maintain an image of themselves as independent adults. Although most residents that I spoke with during my project took great care to praise the institution in which they lived as a real "family-like home," occasionally, very bitter remarks would emerge that indicated that at least some individuals felt denigrated at least some of the time to be living in such an environment. Some of these statements made only partial sense to me, as when one older man told me a long story that included the statement that when he died, "they are going to take my body up in a plane and toss me out of it—just to get rid of me. That's how it's around here. Nobody cares if I die or what happens then." Or when a well-respected female resident remarked: "They try to get us to do things—but I just hide away. I'm retired and if I wanted to work I wouldn't be here. I know some people [i.e., some members of the outside communities] think funny things about us—but we don't have to work you know! We've done our part." Given the emotional depth of statements such as this, I was sure that they meant more than just the surface words could tell us. On the other hand, it was not until I began to investigate the history of the home and found out that it had been built in the early 1960s on the same site as a much earlier "workhouse" (that itself went back to the 1930s) that I gained a greater understanding of these kinds of statements. The workhouse had been created largely for indigent farm laborers such as tobacco and fruit pickers who, for one reason or another, could no longer find work in this part of southern Ontario (e.g., owing to individual health problems, or local economic depressions). Some of the workhouse inhabitants were actually transferred into the then newer home for the aged so that the older institution could be torn down. Partly because of this transfer, in the 1960s and 1970s the home for the aged was often viewed by surrounding rural dwellers [including some of those who now resided in the home] as something of a "home for the indigent." The man above who complained that after his death they would "throw him out of an airplane" was in fact one of the last remaining individuals who had been transferred from the old home for the indigent. In this light, his feelings of neglect and lack of connection to others—both in the home itself and within the surrounding community—becomes much more understandable. The older woman who spoke above, conversely, was from one of the more prosperous families in the region and, in hindsight, I realize that she wanted to give me the message that this was in fact a home for the aged and not a "workhouse" through her (and other residents') emphatic statements about the *voluntary* nature of resident participation in "work" situations around the home. Without the historical dimension to add to the contemporary ethnographic research, I would have missed the analytical richness of these seemingly idiosyncratic statements.

There is one last advantage that I would like to briefly discuss in favor of adding at least some primary source research to your project. Secondary source material has a tendency to "summarize" large-scale trends or to "gloss over" important individual differences that can be found in the actions of real historical actors. As researchers, we wish to create patterns of analysis out of our own readings of primary actions and voices, rather than simply adopt those of other scholars. Only the primary source material will give you access to the competing voices that existed during a specific historical moment. One small example should suffice here. I mentioned earlier in this chapter that the various European groups present in the region of what eventually became the country of Papua New Guinea sometimes differed quite strongly in their opinions about what was good for the country and good for the people of the region (e.g., Fife 1995b). I have published an article (Fife 1998), for example, about the nearly disastrous clash between Captain Morseby of H.M.S. Basilisk as a representative of British authority in the New Guinea islands and the Reverend Murray as the first missionary in charge for the L.M.S. of the New Guinea mission in the early 1870s. A heated disagreement, documented to at least some extent in the primary source material located in the archives, broke out over who was ultimately responsible for the deaths of four "Polynesian teachers" who had been left ill-supplied by the Reverend Murray on the brand new mission field of Bampton Island (just south of the main island of New Guinea). Though generally a supporter of missionaries, Captain Moresby seemed to feel that the Reverend Murray was negligent in this case. Let me give you some of the flavor of the exchange that occurred by quoting from only a very few of the series of letters that were exchanged between Captain Morseby, the Reverend Murray, and others. Captain Moresby stated, for example,

> From Bampton Island now comes the report that the native [Polynesian] Teachers landed there some months ago, and never since visited by any agent for the Parent Society have been cruelly murdered on account of refusing to make the natives any return for fish supplied. . . . The question is *could* the Teachers make any return? I have never yet seen that they were supplied with any trade [goods with which] to purchase food which is absolutely necessary before the yam season commences. . . . after making all due allowances, the want of a proper vessal [*sic*] to visit the stations + an insufficient supply of food, Medicines and support cannot be excused. . . . Were the Pearl Shellers [traders working in the same area] to act thus to the natives in their employ they would deservedly be subject to action at law. (Moresby 1873: 4–6; underlined emphasis in original, as in all quotes below)

One of Murray's many replies was as follows:

> In regard to Bampton Island, I beg to say *emphatically*, in reply to your question, "could the teachers make any return" for the fish—that the error at Bampton Island was not in the teachers having too little property but in their having too much. If they left half of what they had, as I wished them to do, on Cornwallis [Dauan Island] I believe they would have been exposed to less danger. They were bent on taking all they had with them + when we reached the Island the prospects were so assuring that I did not further object to their taking all on shore. (Murray 1973: 5–6)

As I show in the journal article that I wrote about the case, the Reverend Murray is very much overstating his position. The Polynesian teachers[4] (two men and two women) very likely did not have sufficient supplies to see them through their time on the island and Murray left them there after spending only a few hours on shore, unable to communicate with what were then an unknown people because no one in the mission party could speak their language. Reverend Murray was eventually forced to defend himself to the Directors of the L.M.S., after correspondence made it clear that they did not accept his initial "excuses" for the Bampton disaster. Perhaps in desperation, he eventually suggested that the deaths might have been a kind of divine retribution for things that he had "found out" about the Polynesian teachers:

> Some thing has come to light, which you and the Directors at least should know, which furnishes a sad explanation of the melancholy affair on its God-ward side. . . . It came to light . . . that Cho was a wicked man. Shortly before he left Lifu [the mission station from which all four teachers came] . . . he attempted to draw into sin the wife of Mataio [the other male teacher]!—and another married woman, . . . Mataio must have known about the affair and wickedly concealed it, and there can scarcely be any doubt that Cho's wife must have known also. Thus the whole party seem to have combined to impose upon man and deceive man, *but* "God is not mocked"—their sin has found them out. (Murray 1873 Report: 2–3)

There is indirect evidence that the Directors were not at all impressed by this theological argument and Murray softened it to some extent (though never fully withdrew it) in future correspondences. By 1875 he was replaced as the head of the mission by the Reverend MacFarlane, although no direct blame was ever formally attributed to him by the Directors of the Society (or at least, none that survives in documentary sources).

The point here is that this incident, and many others like it, changed the course of educational history in Papua New Guinea. The Polynesian teachers provided the vast majority of the Christian evangelists that were used by the L.M.S. in the first few decades of the mission to New Guinea. These teachers were actually able to wrestle better wages out of MacFarlane and the directors back in London because of the Bampton incident. Several things might have happened if Captain Moresby had chosen to make an official accusation against the Reverend Murray and the L.M.S. in relation to their treatment of the Polynesian teachers. The resulting scandal would have likely destroyed or at least severely impacted the donations that the L.M.S. depended upon as an independent mission society (the standard design for mission societies in Europe at that time) and therefore forced them to withdraw from New Guinea altogether. Or, the British government might have forced the L.M.S. (and therefore all other subsequent missionary societies in New Guinea) to severely curtail their use of "native teachers" for the pioneering and very dangerous work of establishing new mission stations. What happened instead was, if anything, Polynesian and other native teachers solidified and even improved their position as important members of the New Guinea mission. Famous among European missionaries for their "Old Testament" style of Christianity, with its emphasis on rule making and strict bodily (i.e., moral) discipline, they went on to set the tone for education in Papua New Guinea. This is a tone that could have been quite different if the historical balance had tipped even slightly in other directions because of specific historical incidents such as the Bampton Island massacre.

People make history. Without some access to primary sources it becomes much more difficult to appreciate this fact and much more tempting to create very broad portraits of particular historical periods that fit neatly into contemporary concerns but ignore the complexities of the past and their effects (or potential effects) on the present.

The ideal, of course, is to eventually combine the knowledge available from both secondary and primary historical sources to arrive at an adequate context for the analysis of a specific ethnographic topic in a country such as Papua New Guinea, Sierra Leone, Argentina, or Egypt. Before this can be done, however, contemporary sources of information must also be consulted, as is evident in chapter 3.

3

Contemporary Scholarly Sources and a Theoretical Orientation

We use historical sources as researchers in order to provide ourselves with the necessary depth to allow for us to develop an understanding of the context that embed our projects. In a similar manner, we also turn to a study of the contemporary scholarly sources in order to give ourselves the necessary breadth that will make it possible for us to accomplish the same goal. When the two research methods are combined, it enables us to arrive at a basic theoretical orientation, one that is specific to the individual scholar but which ties his or her work into the broader trends in the scholar's field of study.

In this chapter, I continue to use my own project experiences to show potential researchers how to make use of contemporary sources that illuminate the political economy of a specific country and combine it with the general theoretical literature on a specific topic to form a unique theoretical orientation for his or her own research.

Political Economy as an Overview of a Contemporary Situation

The fieldworker need not consider him or herself to be a "Marxist" scholar in order to benefit from a reading of political economy perspectives (and s/he should also understand that while it is true in anthropology that most researchers taking a political economy perspective tend to be influenced by one form or another of Marxist thought, not all political economy perspectives are Marxist). In order to simplify here, let us consider any set of writings that is concerned with the relationship between broader economic structures (such as who owns the means of production and how the labour in that production process is organized) and the forms of political organization and expression that coincide with these economic structures (such as the creation and maintenance of social classes, or the ways various agencies of the state, such as the educational system or the legal system, are organized) to be what we mean by the term *political economy*.

In this regard, specific questions should immediately leap to mind for a person doing educational research. What is the relationship between education and employment opportunities in the country? Are divisions of social class being created through the formal educational system of a developing or industrialized country (or maintained, or disrupted)? What economic ramifications does the current process of education have for the future citizens of an area, or region, or country? For example, are most students being trained in the liberal arts while the nation is badly in need of engineers, medical personnel, and agriculturalists? Or, has a reliance on technical training severely limited the general (i.e., liberal arts) education of the population and therefore citizens' abilities to participate in "democratic" political processes in their own country as well as in international forums in informed and critical ways?

In order to show how political economy writing can inform one's research, I give the example of my own use of material that focuses specifically upon the potential relationship that existed in Papua New Guinea between education and employment in the cash economy at the time of my research in the late 1980s. First, let me note that the scholar who is trying to learn about the basic political economy of the current period is in a sense really pursuing a reading of the economic and social processes that have emerged during the last twenty-five years within that country. In other words, we are building a contemporary framework of understanding to stand on the shoulders of our previously constructed historical framework.

Let me begin by informing the reader a little about the overall situation of Papua New Guinea from approximately 1960 until my primary field research period of 1986–1987. For example, it is important to know that at the time of this research less than 20 percent of the national population lived in urban settings and even fewer of them had direct access to a job in the cash economy. Most continued the trends long since established in their largely small-scale village societies: they grew root crops, engaged in pig husbandry, and lived within localized political formations. In these political situations, kinship units (e.g., lineages or clans) usually controlled access to the means of production—such as the land that was available for growing foodstuffs. At the same time, local forms of leadership (big men, chiefs, elders, or other small-scale and usually informal or semiformal methods of leadership) dominated. Most Papua New Guineans were able to grow enough food to feed themselves and their families in the normal course of events (though natural disasters and localized disease epidemics, or rain, or horticultural problems could and did create local food disasters) and any competent adult had at least some say in how things were organized and expressed in his/her relatively small-scale society.

In the 1960s, two main avenues were developing for the indigenous populations to participate in the cash economy: (1) involvement in the independent agricultural production of export commodities such as copra, coffee, and cocoa, and (2) working for expatriate (i.e., primarily Australians, British, or New Zealanders) interests on plantations or in the emerging resource extraction enterprises. Both of these economic sectors were expanding relatively rapidly under a push from the colonial government for "a form of development" that was ultimately aimed at making PNG less dependent upon financial aid from Australia to run its European style infrastructure, as Ian Downs explained in his book about "The Australian Trusteeship" of PNG (Downs 1980).

Kenneth Good (1986) and Bryant Allen (1983) have described the economic changes of the 1960s and early 1970s that were part of this overall drive for independence (which came finally in 1975). The colonial government of Australia wanted to encourage the production of commodities for export. Led by the traditional four Cs (copper, coffee, cocoa, and coconuts), production soon expanded in the 1970s to also include timber cutting, oil palm growing, and large-scale gold mining. Agriculture (including horticulture) continued to form the backbone of both the subsistence and cash economy, but beginning in the 1960s and increasingly thereafter it also began to provide the basis for widespread social inequality based upon differential opportunities to participate in the cash economy through commodity production (such as coffee growing in specific areas of the highlands, or oil palm production in places such as the province of West New Britain—where I did my own research). These were the economic beginnings of regional inequalities (though of course the missionaries and other colonial agents had begun this larger social process in the late 1800s).

As the political economy literature shows us, equality of participation did not necessarily exist even in the regions in which there was a better overall chance of participating in the cash economy. Kenneth Good (1986: 26) believes, for example, that

> By the 1960s, the class nature of the government aid programmes was increasingly evident. Assistance for coffee production in the highlands concentrated on relatively large-scale production by a few villagers, and it aims to produce, as one proponent of the policy later put it, "a small class of purposeful elite farmers capable of responding to opportunities opened up to them."

Allen (1983: 222) referred to these as a "rich peasant class" and noted that at least some of them had begun to press for such capitalist-friendly social practices as individual ownership of what had heretofore been collectively owned land, no minimum wages for rural workers, and government policies that favoured the production of agricultural commodities over subsistence-based horticulture.

In 1964 the first elections were held for the legislature. No real "national" issues emerged as key topics of debate among the inexperienced electorate, but what did become clear was that large numbers of both urban and rural peoples wanted representatives who would be able to persuade "the government" to provide their areas with "development" in the form of roadways, medical aid posts, schools (both primary and secondary), air strips, and above all employment in the cash economy (Griffin, Nelson, and Firth 1979: 133). This would prove to be an enduring set of concerns, one that emerges every election from that time forward. Equivalent situations are of course common to many developing countries and to the poorer regions of wealthier countries as well (e.g., on First Nation reserves in Canada).

All of this had tremendous implications for education in PNG. During most of the 1960s there were good opportunities for those who qualified (i.e., those with secondary educations) in public school teaching or in the increasingly localizing public service (Smith 1987: 231–232; Pomponio and Lancy 1986: 41). It was understood, for example, that the civil service would have to be handed over to Papua New Guineans if true Independence was to be achieved. This meant that the first few generations of formal school finishers, especially those with a higher level of secondary education, had tremendous opportunities for employment with both private employers (banks and other commercial enterprises) and in the emerging government administration.

This situation did not last long. By the middle of the 1970s, the expanding cash economy could not keep up with the number of higher school leavers who wanted wage employment. "Even an aggressive nationalization program designed to replace expatriate with their Papua New Guinea counterparts failed to accommodate all of the newly schooled manpower. In the private sector, plantations and mines continued to employ unschooled younger men from their villages on short-term contracts" (Pomponio and Lancy 1986: 42). Many employers wanted to ensure the continued existence of a largely uneducated pool of potential manual laborers and not create a large educated population that might question the contracts they were asked to sign, the wages they were offered, or the orders of their mostly expatriate bosses. This left an overall situation in the 1980s of a greatly expanded educational system that operated at all three levels (primary, secondary, and tertiary), pumping out growing numbers of school graduates who thought that their education entitled them to a job in the cash economy but who increasingly faced the prospect of either returning to their home villages to engage in subsistence horticulture or of becoming one of the growing number of unemployed youth haunting the fringes of urban centres in the country (for an excellent general critique of the notion of "development" as the route to modernity, see Escobar 1995). This was the economic/political/educational situation that I walked into in 1986 to conduct my fieldwork on primary schools in West New Britain and their relationship to larger social and cultural processes of change in that province.

A quick reading of books and articles concerned with the general political economy of a developing or industrialized nation should bring the scholar up-to-date on the overall trends in the country and give him or her ideas about the role that education, medicine, small businesses, or local political structures may be playing within those larger processes. Again, the scholar who has a home base in a smaller centre within a developing or industrial country, or within a country that has few ties with the developing country s/he is interested in (as was true in my own case), may have some difficulty in obtaining numerous sources regarding the social, economic, and political situation of a specific country. However, this is less true now than it was fifteen or twenty years ago. For those with access to the internet, for example, basic statistical and other information for many developing countries can be accessed (e.g., employment rates, information on the dominate economic sectors, overall numbers registered in various levels of schooling, etc.). This alone should give you a basic sense of the current situation, though the usual *caveats* regarding internet information applies here (i.e., there is a lot of misinformation on the net, so although it can be a good source of quick information a good scholar should double-check that information with an independent source, such as published government documents, before using it as "evidence" in their research). The existence of huge "bookstores" on-line, such as Amazon.com, also makes it much more likely that a scholar can gain access to a much needed source provided he or she has the funds to purchase it (remember to include books in your research budget if you are applying for a grant). The larger university presses, such as the University of California Press or Cambridge University Press, generally have similar on-line services now. In addition, many university and even large public library catalogues are now on-line as well. Combining the above situation with interlibrary loans and trips to larger centers should provide researchers with all they need in terms of a basic knowledge about what has been going on during the last few decades in a specific country. Read these sources well. I would suggest that reading a single good source thoroughly is superior to skimming through half a dozen sources and obtaining bits and pieces of decontextualized information. A little information, poorly understood, can be worse than no information at all— as it will often lead to assumptions that might take months of on-site research to correct. Quality therefore is better than quantity in this regard. There will be time for additional reading once the fieldwork portion of the project is completed, during which period the researcher can read about selected (historic and contemporary) subjects in more depth as this is needed for the specific project.

Research and Theory: Setting the Stage

Scholars should be conversant with the major theoretical trends in their topic before they begin their fieldwork. This will be necessary if he or she is going to create a personal theoretical orientation that will guide the on-site study and eventually result in collecting the kind of evidence that will allow for a proper ethnographic argument to be constructed after the work is completed.

I limit myself here to the example of the kinds of theory that I considered prior to my own 1986–1987 project so that the reader can properly judge how this guided my later research choices.

By the mid-1980s, theoretical writing about educational processes could be divided into two main categories: (1) those concerned primarily with macro level processes, and (2) those concerned primarily with micro level processes. As the reader might imagine, there is considerable overlap in some specific educational theories regarding these two "levels" of analysis, but scholars will find that most theoretical orientations focus primarily upon one or the other of these two "sides of the same coin." This division may not work for theoretical literature about every topic—but I suggest that it would be a useful device for most bodies of theory. At any rate, a good case can be made for using this division as an organizing tool in order to make sense of the large number of extant theories concerning education. Due to space constraints, I reduce the number of theories used here in comparison to the actual number that I originally considered before beginning my fieldwork. The purpose is not to give an exhaustive survey of pre-1990 theories of education, but rather to show the scholar how to read these types of theories in order to make use of them for their own theoretical constructions. Also, by using only the same sources that were actually available to me before my research began I eliminate the easy corrections that hindsight might afford me at this point in time. The material offered here is the same material that I studied prior to my original research period.

At the time of my preparation, I made a conscious decision to limit myself largely to theoretical orientations that derived from either the anthropology of education or the sociology of education, due to my interest in relating education to larger social and cultural issues. Other researchers might have added the psychology of education if they were interested primarily in individual motivations or reactions, the philosophy of education if they were primarily concerned about policy formation, and so forth. Similarly, any large topical areas such as health care, tourism, or peasant production, will need to be considered wisely in order to limit the number of theoretical orientations that a specific researcher will take into account. Make your decision based on your prior reading of the history and political economy of your topic in the specific context of the region in which you will conduct your fieldwork.

Macro Approaches to the Study of Education

We begin by viewing macro approaches to understanding education. One of the earliest such approaches is associated with the functional perspective of Emile Durkheim and his school of thought (e.g., Durkheim 1961, 1977). Functionalists or neo-functionalists often assume that school practices can be explained in terms of their adaptive value for society as a whole (Feinberg and Soltis 1985: 69). The institution of education, despite being described by Durkheim as an "organism," is normally given no real life of its own outside of the much more important "social organism" (i.e., society as a whole) (Durkheim 1977: 6). Education here is seen as reproducing society rather than as changing society (Thompson 1982: 163). This makes sense for Durkheim, as the key issue in his theory of society is the way in which overall social order is achieved and maintained (Blackledge and Hunt 1985: 64). However, this kind of approach leaves education as little more than an efficient tool for inculcating the young into whatever social reality already exists at the moment.

Not all functionalists assigned education such a static role. Talcott Parsons, for example, added new dimensions such as an emphasis on the construction of "culture and personality" to Durkheim's basic social position. Parsons, however, still considered education's primary function to be that of creating people who "wanted" to play the kinds of social roles they would "have to play" in order for a general social integration to be maintained. He suggested that this was done primarily through a teacher-led competition, in which students were encouraged to "achieve" in a manner that was in-line with teachers' attitudes, which in turn were finely tuned to the values of society as a whole (Parsons 1951: 240).

All this suggests that functionalists generally view education as playing a conservative role in society. Durkheim, for one, thought that this was a good thing.

"Just as the priest is the interpreter of God, he [the teacher] is the interpreter of the great moral ideas of his time and country" (Durkheim 1961: 155). The teacher becomes, in this kind of a scheme, primarily an agent for social discipline—the creator of a kind of moral authority that will eventually be taken up and internalized by the student (144). Functionalism could be viewed then as a specific kind of "structural" analysis, one in which cultural practices such as education and morality are ultimately socially determined (Thompson 1982).

A different kind of structural approach has emerged out of orientations for understanding education that have centered around the key idea of the social reproduction of inequality, which in turn has its basis in the work of both Max Weber and Karl Marx. "This view . . . [holds] that both cultural and political socialization reflect the influence of the structure of society in terms of class relations and differential power over the definition and distribution of knowledge" (Trent, Braddock, and Henderson 1985: 307). This perspective adds class considerations (i.e., it assumes social differentiation rather than social homogenization within a society) to the structural equation. Like functionalists, its practitioners see teachers as "reproducing" society; unlike functionalists, they believe that this kind of reproduction is inherently undesirable as it reproduces or exacerbates already existing social divisions and makes it largely impossible for students who come from the lower social strata to change their lot in life.

Max Weber, for example, tied the emerging forms of modern education to the overall increase in the bureaucratization of life in these societies (e.g., Weber 1948: 240). Examinations and educational certifications were being used, he said, to "qualify" a new European elite to run modern society. This was very different from the old elite, which was based upon noble birth. This process "rationalized" class divisions and made them appear as though they were based upon a meritocracy rather than an aristocracy. Once this new elite was in place, education then became the means to restrict access to the upper classes. "When we hear from all sides the demand for an introduction of regular curricula and special examinations, the reason behind it is, of course, not a suddenly awakened 'thirst for education,' but the desire for restricting the supply for those [status] positions and their monopolization by the owners of educational certificates" (Weber 1948: 241). For Weber, then, education could be used both as an agent of social change and as a force for social conservation, depending upon the historical conditions of the moment. Frank Parkin points out that much of Weber's theorizing about education concerned the process of "social closure." By social closure he means the process by which various groups attempt to improve their lot by restricting access to rewards and privileges to a limited circle (Parkin 1982: 100). In other words, Weber has been concerned, as were the functionalists, with the social reproduction of society—differing from them in that he largely viewed this process as something that created and maintained social divisions rather than as something that was "good" for everyone.

While Weber has influenced the "reproduction" school of critical thought, it is the work of Karl Marx that has most heavily been drawn upon by contemporary theorists in this regard. This is somewhat ironic, as Marx himself makes no major statements about the place of education in the social scheme of things. What he does do is provide a framework for educational research that makes the economy as important as the classroom for understanding the role of education in a given society. Researchers influenced by Marx tell us that education cannot really be understood outside of the politics of the social reproduction of class-based society (which is assumed to ultimately be based upon economic divisions within that society). Michael Young, for example, states that Marx's work serves to ". . . direct one to examine the relation between the interests of economically dominant groups and prevailing ideas of education as 'good' or 'worthwhile' in itself" (Young 1971: 28). In other words, the production of knowledge is not a disinterested process. This points the way to a class-based analysis. "Understanding the dynamics of class relationships is essential, we believe, to an adequate appreciation of the connection between economics and education" (Bowles and Gintis 1976: 67).

Scholars informed by Marx's work could be placed along a continuum according to the extent to which they embrace a structural perspective that emphasizes economic determination. Some see the economic "base" as determining the forms of "superstructure" (i.e., other social institutions, such as education); while others view the relationship as one of "conditioning" rather than determination (Blackledge and Hunt 1985: 113–114). Whether more or less "structural" in outlook, it is the *relations* linking social class, education, and the reproduction of the work force that interests all researchers inspired by Marxist thought. Further, they consistently insist that such processes be viewed largely through the prism of history. In other words, research must include a historical dimension if we are going to understand the connections between class, education, and the economy and how they came to be in the contemporary period.

Even theorists who take a relatively soft line regarding the relationship between economics and education do not grant full autonomy to the educational system. Antonio Gramsci's concept of "hegemony" is relevant here (see Gramsci 1971). For Gramsci, dominant social classes control education not just through their economic position but also by controlling the meaning of education. Michael Apple puts it this way: "hegemony acts to 'saturate' our very consciousness, so that the educational, economic and social world we see and interact with, and the commonsense interpretations we put on it, becomes the world *tout court*, the only world" (Apple 1979: 5).

Some critical researchers are interested in adding the dimension of "legitimation" to the idea of class reproduction (and thereby, in a sense, wedding Marx to Weber). Paulo Freire (1983), for example, suggests that education "rationalizes" class interests by legitimizing it through the myth of objective knowledge. This puts teachers in the position of being agents of legitimation for the class system in a modern society (e.g., Apple 1979; Bourdieu and Passeron 1977). In effect, these theorists are suggesting that student/teacher relationships inside the classroom reflect the dominated/dominating relationships that exist outside of schooling in a capitalist society. This brings us back to the concerns of Durkheim regarding teachers as moral authorities, though with a Marxist twist: "In deciding what is to be done about a pupil who does not learn or behave as required, a teacher not only brings her teaching skills and professional insights to bear but also makes judgments of an unavoidably moral and political nature; she adopts, albeit implicitly, an ideological stance which informs her understanding of the problems and justifies her response" (Chessum 1980: 116). Pierre Bourdieu and Jean-Claude Passeron have used the label "symbolic violence" to refer to the process of selecting meanings that benefit some students over others. They suggest an axiom: "Every power to assert symbolic violence, i.e. every power which manages to impose meanings and to impose them as legitimate by concealing the power relations which are the basis of its force, adds its own specifically symbolic force to those power relations" (Bourdieu and Passeron 1977: 4). In this theoretical position, teaching is assumed to largely represent the interests of the dominant classes and the children of those classes are therefore the ones most likely to benefit from the educational system. Children of the lower class, conversely, are the least likely to have the kinds of social and cultural skills necessary to coincide with the teacher's hidden social agenda and are therefore much less likely to be allowed to be "successful" within that school system.

Research that concentrates upon macro-level concerns alone is often criticized because "it tells us little about the richness and complexity of human life" (Blackledge and Hunt 1985: 233). In other words, it largely misses out on the cultural dimension of school life.

Some "macro" theorists do try to address this issue, most significantly in the literature dealing with student-led "resistance" to an unfair educational system. Peter McLaren suggests that "By the term resistance, I refer to oppositional student behaviour that has both symbolic, historical and 'lived' meaning and which contests the legitimacy, power and significance of school culture in general and instruction in particular (e.g. the overt and hidden curriculum)" (McLaren 1986: 143). While Henry Giroux adds that ". . . schools represent contested terrains marked not only by structural and ideological contradictions, but also by collectively informed students resistances" (quoted in Blackledge and Hunt 1985: 181). All this is to suggest that macro structures influence rather than fully determine school settings.

Perhaps the most complete statement in this regard by a Marxist influenced scholar comes in Paul Willis' book *Learning to Labour: How Working Class Kids Get Working Class Jobs* (Willis, 1981). In this book, Willis aims to explain the cultural process through which social reproduction occurs in a working-class enclave of a British city. In effect, Willis wanted to know how "the lads" he portrays talked themselves into living the same lives as their fathers, even though they understood, to a limited extent, the subordinate class position this entailed. Along the way, he shows us how resistance to school norms on the part of the lads partially reflects this class-based understanding and partially reflects the lads' sexism and racism (the latter forming the reasons why the lads can never fully penetrate the class-based ideology of the educational system and thereby doom themselves to repeating their fathers' lives). This excellent book opened the way for researchers to overcome the macro limitations of structural approaches to the study of education and bridge macro and micro levels of research while still maintaining a concern for the social reproduction function of education. More is said about this later in the chapter.

Micro Approaches to the Study of Education

Micro approaches tend to begin not with large-scale social processes but rather with considerations of childhood socialization as a form of cultural transmission.

In anthropology, this longstanding interest can be traced back to the first half of the 1900s and the emergence of the "culture and personality" or "psychological anthropology" school of thought, perhaps best personified in the work of Margaret Mead (e.g., 1975, original 1930). The concern was initially with the means that parents use to teach their children how to think and act in culturally prescribed ways, but later broadened out to include the role that schooling played in this enculturation process. Charles Harrington (1978: 139) has suggested that: "While many psychological anthropologists would argue over fine points, most would agree that education can only be studied as part of an overall socialization process designed to meet goals specific to the culture examined." This is a "micro" approach because the focus is upon the specific ways that children are socialized into adult roles (e.g., see Burnett 1978 for an overview of the field). This can be opposed to more macro approaches, in which socialization itself is more or less simply an artifact of relationships that are produced in noneducational social institutions such as the political economic structures of a society. Fundamentally then, education in micro theory comes to be about "all those ways that the human organism learns" rather than about the relationship between education and other social processes (e.g., see Harrington 1978, Kneller 1965, Kerber and Smith 1972). Here, other social processes (such as the economic structures that lead to social divisions) tend to be covered under the broader term "culture" and treated as background information rather than as the primary focus of study. They are not said to be unimportant, but receive very little attention in actual research projects. It is the specifics of cultural transmission that receive primary attention.

Psychological anthropology eventually joined forces with cognitive anthropology and both were used extensively in the study of education. In each, theory is focused upon the way that culture becomes replicated through the organization of individual human perception and experience, although in the case of cognitive approaches it is not assumed that perception is embedded within the individual's "personality" but rather that it is contained in the structures of the human mind (Harrington 1978: 136). Both approaches are often concerned with methods of measurement (using personality profiles, projective testing, and experimental design to study individual patterns of learning). Universalizing learning processes in this fashion and placing an emphasis on the "methodological rigor" of quantitative approaches meant that cross-cultural comparison became an acceptable option (e.g., Comitas 1978, Munroe and Munroe 1975). This suggests in turn that psychological and later cognitive anthropologists tend to locate their studies in aggregates of individuals (e.g., experimental work) or aggregates of societies (e.g., cross-cultural studies), but not in the historically contextualized, socially layered processes of social formation or reproduction.

An important theme in the "cultural transmission" approach to the study of education, one that parallels the Durkheimian functionalist approach written about above and that spreads beyond both psychological and cognitive perspectives, is the view that education serves primarily as a conservative force in society. Margaret Mead for example, stated in the context of her study about education in the Manus Islands, "As infants in the home, and later within the educational system of the wider society, child-rearing methods expose them thoroughly to the culture of their society, so that they perforce assimilate the values of that society" (Mead 1975: ix). While the "dean of anthropology and education studies," George Spindler, has stated that ". . . education is a process of recruitment and mainte-nance for the cultural system" (Spindler 1974: 77). There is agreement in these approaches then that education, both in terms of socialization and formal school-ing, is basically about cultural conservation. As among the functionalists, little concern seems to be expressed in much of this literature about the social ramifica-tions of education as a conservative force in a society. Perhaps because, as Harrington puts it: "The study of socialization is more than the study of how *individuals* learn particular ways of life but it is basic to our understanding of how *societies* perpetuate themselves by making particular kinds of humans as opposed to others" (Harrington 1970: 134). By focusing on the relationship between individuals and such reified aggregates as "society" or "culture," researchers in the cultural transmission perspective limit their ability to develop a more critical read-ing of educational processes and the social inequalities they help to engender.

Anthropological and sociological researchers focusing upon the process of cultural transmission have for the most part concentrated upon grounding them-selves within a concern for language and cognition. There are many names for this; some of the more common ones are cognitive anthropology, ethnoscience, ethnomethodology, and ethnosemantics. In all cases, they are concerned with the ways that people sort their world into a system of categories (which in turn, is assumed to reflect the way that human cognition works and how it may come to be expressed through language). Some scholars have been quite literal about the location of cognition: "Scholars generally agree that culture is in the mind of man. Any ideas are the foundation of culture and just as real as bricks" (Kerber and Smith 1972: 10). Others prefer to locate their work differently: "So, if one asks the question about where is the meaning of social concepts—in the world, in the meaner's head, or in interpersonal negotiations—one is compelled to answer that it is the last of these" (Bruner 1982: 835). All of the researchers agree, then, that cultural categorization is a key to the process of cultural transmission, but not necessarily about the exact process this key unlocks or even where the door is located.

One of the most important features of the above approaches is the focus upon language research. Language is where we, as researchers, can "see" categorization occurring. As Dorothy Clement (1976: 54) put it: "Cognitive anthropology exploits the relationship between language and cognitive systems to explain behaviour." We have to be careful, though, not to overemphasize the importance of words in the learning process. Kerber and Smith (1972: 21), for example, warn us ". . . formal education in Western culture has assumed that learning is nearly 100 percent through words." Jerome Bruner (1982) offers us a more balanced approach to the issue, suggesting that it is real "language in use" (i.e., language combined with action) that forms the basis of cultural transmission. This approach, which is common in sociolinguistics and performance studies, is very similar to what is often referred to in sociology and anthropology as an "interactionist" position. Kerber and Smith (1972: 9) suggest for example that: "For Man, the important arena of action is that of a symbolling social being responding to other symbolling social beings in a social situation." Anthropologists have long recognized that it is "symbols in action" that constitute the main micro arena of human behavior, but it is sociologists who have done the most to develop this concept in relation to schooling situations (usually under the general heading of "symbolic interaction" studies).

Blackledge and Hunt (1985: 238–249) have described this method in some detail. It involves the idea that when an individual enters a situation with another person s/he enters this situation with an already well developed notion of her "self" versus "the other." Since we tend to act toward "others" based upon our perceptions of them (versus the way "they really are"), this can lead to a number of confusing results. This occurs because we tend to know others largely as stereotyped players of social roles rather than as more complex and rounded human beings. This may be a key to understanding at least some forms of student and teacher interactions. To take one example, teachers may typify students in regard to whether they are "good" or "bad" students and act toward them in ways consistent with that typology—regardless of how pupils might conceive of themselves in a particular context. Pupils, in turn, type teachers (e.g., "strict" versus "friendly"). It is a truism that in situations that involve uneven access to power, as exists for example in teacher/pupil interactions, it is the person with the most social power who will ultimately be able to "define the situation" (e.g., control its outcome in the case of disagreement).

Frederick Gearing has suggested that it is crucial to pay attention to situations of cultural collision and how they become resolved in order to understand the micro activities of schooling (Gearing 1979a: 5). He believes that we need to study how people translate cultural categories into expectations about the social roles of others and also how these processes can "go wrong," for this will in turn help us understand both success and failure within school settings (178–179). Gearing has, in fact, attempted to create a total "cultural theory of schooling," based largely upon the importance of micro level interactions in this process. Notice that, as opposed to the more structural macro level researchers, Gearing seems to take inequality for granted in his theory of schooling.

> . . . the theory is intended to *explain* how it comes about that some members of certain, definable categories of persons predictably will, and all members of other categories of persons predictably will not, come competently to perform some complex task [such as learning mathematics], . . . The explanation of how such competencies predictably get distributed would entail the identification of those kinds of constraints that are interactional, and that are not mental and not motor in nature. (Gearing 1979b: 170)

We might ask where, exactly, these differences come from in the first place? Gearing promisingly suggests: ". . . one cannot adequately comprehend any one part of a system of education or schooling in a community unless one comprehends as well something of the variety of the other parts that coexist and may compete" (174). At first, it seems as though he is offering us a way to bridge micro interaction with macro structural constraints to form a holistic theory of education.

Unfortunately, he then goes on to suggest that we can locate these larger constraints by placing them within a good old-fashioned "structural-functional description" of the larger community. Such a description would include the basic social organization of a community, the kinds of jobs or work people engage in and the kinds of groups they gather into for social activities. Gearing defines these units "behaviorally" (177) and suggests that researchers can gain an understanding of the social context that informs micro interactions simply by focusing on the interactional behaviors of the members of a community.

It soon becomes obvious that most of the structural information that is deemed essential to a study of education by macro oriented researchers is left out of Gearing's orientation. For most macro researchers, societies cannot be narrowly defined by the easily observable limits of their communities; they are embedded within much larger socioeconomic systems (such as the world market system) and these too have to be taken into account (e.g., for how they affect local employment situations). To take an example from Papua New Guinea, a researcher could watch labourers planting coffee on a plantation and interview them to get their opinions regarding what they think they are doing, but without some understanding of where they stand as workers in relation to the larger market conditions of their region or even country and the ways these conditions are in turn affected by outside forces (such as the fluctuating world commodity market for coffee) only half an understanding will be achieved regarding why they continue to do what they do and how these actions affect their lives. In other words, many macro researchers would likely answer Gearing by saying that it is not enough to observe members of a community at work and talk to them about that work, it is also necessary to have some notion of why these particular workers are doing that particular job at this specific time and place. His theory attempts to contextualize the micro level of educational interaction, going so far as to acknowledge social inequalities and the fact that they may end up becoming reproduced within the classroom, but it largely fails to account for how these inequalities have come about and the role that education plays over and above classroom interactions in reproducing them.

For most contemporary ethnographic researchers, Gearing's ideas concerning the "structural-functional" contexts of constraint would never be sufficient for the simple reason that his notion of social context is largely ahistorical. If we think of "structure" as a snapshot in time, then it quickly becomes obvious that it is also necessary to have some knowledge of what went into making this picture the way it is at the moment it was taken. We also need to know about the kinds of forces that might alter this picture in the very near future. In other words, we need an understanding that can be reached only through a historical, rather than a functional, view of what constitutes an "adequate" context for educational research.

Developing a Personal Theoretical Orientation

Gearing's attempt in the 1980s at developing a coherent, holistic theory of cultural transmission that takes both larger constraints and immediate educational behavior into account is well worth pursuing as a goal. That was my opinion before I began my 1980s research and it remains my opinion today. It should seem obvious to the reader that a theoretical orientation that relies largely upon either macro or micro approaches to understanding education is inadequate for the creation of a methodology for educational research in developing countries. I would suggest that this is just as true for other ethnographic studies, regardless of the specific topical focus. What we need is something that ties the more socially "critical" (and not just functionalist) theories of macro processes to the more behavioral micro theories of behavior in order to form a larger research approach.

In my own case, I found just such a lynchpin in the work that Gearing and others have done on the concept of hidden curriculum (e.g., Postman and Weingartner 1969; Gearing 1979 and 1984; Gearing and Epstein 1982; Feinberg and Soltis 1985; Omokhodion 1989). Hidden curriculum, which might be thought of as the cultural organization of a specific school or classroom, normally becomes visible to the researcher through an investigation into the way education is organized and enacted within the daily context of school life. This involves the forms of interactions that are observable, for example, between teachers and pupils (or between pupils and pupils, teachers and teachers, and teachers and members of school administrations). It also includes the interactions of other members of the educational community, such as those between parents and members of the school's administration. However, it is not limited to direct interactions and can also be found in the decorations that appear on classroom walls, the spatial formations of a classroom or assembly area, the discourse surrounding what makes a good versus a bad pupil and what to do about them, and so forth. In short, hidden curriculum refers to all the ways that the verbal and physical organization of education affects the production of an ethos or form of cultural consciousness among students. It can be opposed to the overt curriculum, which consists of the content of education (such as the math or the science lesson that is to be learned).

To understand hidden curriculum properly, an analysis of it must include the macro-level political economy that impacts upon the local interactional context. How, for example, could we understand a primary school classroom in West New Britain that celebrated the "good things" of an urban, capitalist-based life on its classroom walls through the exclusive display of large numbers of consumer images involving items that were virtually nonexistent in West New Britain (such as sports cars, large modern brick houses, rock music concerts, etc.) without understanding something about the history of how an urban life based upon industrially produced objects came to be so important to the imagination of a nation of citizens who live largely in small rural villages?

It might be worthwhile to pause here and look back to see how the concept of hidden curriculum can help bring many of the diverse strands of theory together that have been presented so far in this chapter (as an example of how to weave your own theoretical position from the many strands available in the work of others). If micro levels of analysis are primarily about cultural transmission, then it should become immediately apparent that such transmissions will not always proceed smoothly. George Spindler has stated, for example, "Conflicts ensue when the school and teachers are charged with responsibility for assimilation or acculturating their pupils to a set of norms for behavior and thought that are different from those learned at home and in the community" (Spindler 1974: 74). In North America or Europe, this commonly involves situations of minority education or of working-class versus middle-class social conflicts. In developing countries such as Papua New Guinea, this often involves the imposition of a non-indigenous educational system upon groups of people who come from a wide variety of language and cultural backgrounds. Almost by definition, for example, the classrooms of developing nations will involve situations of inculcation in which the norms and values espoused by teachers will be significantly different than those of most of the students' parents.

Language has a critical role to play in this process. As Jerome Bruner reminds us ". . . the very medium of exchange in which education is conducted—language—can never be neutral, . . . it imposes a point of view not only about the world to which it refers but toward the use of mind in respect to this world" (Bruner 1982: 835). Gearing and Tindall have pointed out that educators are normally quite unaware of the ramifications of their use of language and of their actions and how these might "clash" with those of their students: "What in fact is happening is that society is reproducing itself—caste system, class system, sex roles, and all—and through actions which in some substantial part the actors themselves are only dimly aware of and actions which they in full awareness, would deplore" (Gearing and Tindall 1973: 103). One of the problems for education researchers in developing countries in relation to this kind of a statement is that it seems to presuppose an already fully created class/caste/gender system. In most developing countries, the social "system" is very much in flux. In one country, a class system may not yet exist by the standard definitions of the term. In another, a class system has already become firmly entrenched (though this of course does not imply that it is unchanging), but gender relations are still undergoing major upheavals. In my opinion, we can use Gearing and Tindall and others like them to point out to us the importance of looking at the hidden curriculum of classroom instruction (and I would add, of other educational practices that go beyond the classroom), but we cannot assume that education's main role is to "conserve" a specific set of social practices at the expense of others—not in situations in which even "dominant" social practices may be undergoing tremendous changes (e.g., contemporary South Africa or Iraq comes to mind; or in my case, a Papua New Guinea that had only been independent for just over ten years at the time of research). Hidden curriculum does, however, quite clearly bring many of the micro concerns of researchers regarding the use of both language and actions as forms of social and cultural categorization into an arena in which we may investigate its impact on educational practices. Do language categories, for example, influence the interactions of students and pupils in classrooms and thereby impact what students are able to learn there? Do administrators and teachers act out social differences through their interactions with pupils and parents and if so what effects do these actions have upon educational attainment? Hargreaves, Hester, and Mellor (1975) summarized the concerns of such researchers when they stated that for the most part they have been interested in finding out: (1) what the informal rules of interaction are in classrooms, (2) what becomes defined as a "deviant act" in a classroom, (3) who becomes defined as a deviant person, (4) how do teachers act toward those so labeled, and (5) what happens to the person labeled as deviant over time? By considering these questions, researchers are really trying to gain an understanding of how cultural categories are turned into meaningful actions within the schooling context.

These concerns link up quite well with the major issues pursued by researchers who are interested in the more macro aspects of education. Similar to Gearing and Tindall above, Paul Willis says for example that: "This study warns that disaffected working class kids respond not so much to the style of individual teachers and the content of education as to the structure of the school and the dominant teaching paradigm in the context of their overall class, cultural experience and location" (Willis 1981: 188–189). For many researchers who focus upon the macro aspects of education, the "structure of the school" is a direct reflection of education's role in the social reproduction of class systems or other social inequalities. As Michael Apple (1979: 8–9) tells us: "Social and economic values . . . are already embedded in the design of the institutions we work in, in the 'formal corpus of school knowledge' we preserve in our curricula, in our modes of teaching, and in our principles, standards and forms of evaluation." All this is to suggest that schools are never neutral—they always carry social and cultural baggage (this is of course just as true when they are transplanted to foreign shores, as is the situation in most developing countries). Bourdieu and Passeron (1977: 33) go even further when they suggest "The specific productivity of Pedagogic Work is objectively measured by the degree to which it produces its essential effect of inculcation, i.e. its effect of reproduction."

We might ask: the reproduction of what, though? In the case of class-based societies, it is the reproduction of a work force—which is supposed to make it possible to maintain relations between the social classes within their existing subordinate/dominant forms. Bowles and Gintis (1976) feel that schools are primarily organized to replicate relationships of dominance and subordination in the economic system. "Specifically, the social relationships of education—the relationships between administrators and teachers, teachers and students, students and students, and students and their work—replicate the hierarchical division of labor" (Bowles and Gintis 1976: 131).

Schools are often said to do more than prepare students for life in the workplace, they also legitimize the reproduction of students into the same economic class as their parents (a perspective wedding Marx to Weber). This of course can be seen in the hidden curriculum. "It is through the particular manner in which it [the school] performs its technical function of communication that a given school system additionally fulfills its social functions of conservation and its ideological function of legitimation" (Bourdieu and Passeron 1977: 102). This concern led Paulo Freire to attempt to create a whole new method of education, because he felt that in the most commonly used teaching methods we could see that "A careful analysis of the teacher–student relationship involves a narrating Subject (the teacher) and patient, listening objects (the students)" (Freire 1983: 57). This was said to replicate and legitimate the employer/employee relationship that most students experience when they leave school and take up economic life in capitalist societies—a "dialogue" between employer and employee that seldom takes the form of an equal exchange of ideas.

It is important to point out that researchers generally recognize that educators themselves seldom view their role as one of "reproducing" unequal social classes (or of other inequalities such as ethnic or gender stratification). The question of "consciousness" is a difficult one, but I think it is fair to follow Paul Willis here in thinking that "Certainly it would be quite wrong to attribute to them [teachers] any kind of sinister motive such as miseducating or oppressing working class kids. The teacher is given formal control of his pupils by the state, but he exercises his social control through an educational, not a class, paradigm" (Willis 1981: 67). That is, teachers tend to view their work through educators' eyes and not through the eyes of someone who is thoroughly conversant with the potential role of education in the social reproduction of society. We can expect, therefore, to see contradictions at the behavioral level between teachers' socially sanctioned role-playing and their "individual" styles of education. More is said about this contradiction and what it means for recording and analyzing information in chapter 5 of this book.

There are some things, then, that are held in common between micro and macro researchers in relation to research involving the hidden curriculum of education, as well as some differences. Micro researchers, for example, tend to be more concerned with what is occurring inside of the classroom or school in the form of personal interactions, while macro researchers would more often be interested in the outside forces that give shape to those micro interactions. As Paul Willis suggests, we very much need to bring these two concerns together to create excellent ethnographic studies of education in any context.

> In order to have a satisfying explanation we need to see what the *symbolic* power of structural determination is within the mediating realm of the human and cultural. It is from the resources of this level that decisions are made which lead to uncoerced outcomes which have the function of maintaining the structure of society and the status quo. . . . macro determinants need to pass through the cultural milieu to reproduce themselves at all. (Willis 1981: 171)

This leads us back to an issue that was mentioned earlier in this chapter. If both micro and macro researchers (including such "conservative" ones as those who follow Durkheim and more "radical" ones such as those who follow Marx and Weber) agree that the primary function of education is the conservation of existing social structures and cultural formations, then what do we do in the case of education in developing countries (and perhaps among indigenous populations or other "marginalized" peoples of industrialized countries)—situations in which education is defined as an agent for radical social change? This problem is, I think, primarily an artifact of most educational theory having arisen in the work of researchers who concern themselves primarily with largely urban-based and industrialized capitalist countries and who largely neglect the special circumstances of formal educational systems that do not exist in similar contexts (for exceptions to this trend, see the papers in Crossley and Vulliamy 1997). Scholars who work in developing countries or other "irregular" situations can make good use of the existing theories of educational processes (as my limited examples mentioned earlier should indicate), but they also must remain alert to the possibility that the "reproductive" role of education in a developing country or nonurban, noncapitalist social setting may be much more complex than it is for education in the urban centers of industrial countries.

In my specific project, both the long term and more recent history of Papua New Guinea *told* me that it was appropriate to use hidden curriculum as a focus for educational research in that country. The political economy literature, for example, let me know that there was tremendous concern on the part of educators, parents, and pupils about the assumed relationship that was "supposed" to exist between education and employment in the cash economy. It also suggested that there was a problematic relationship between rural and urban life in PNG. When I combined these understandings with the longer historical trends (chapter 2) that allowed me to see that substantial language and cultural differences had always existed in this region of the world and coupled this with the way that these intersected with historically increasing demands to "participate" in the newer political economy of "development" in Papua New Guinea, I became confident that these and similar trends would "show up" in the hidden curriculum of educational practices in the schools and classrooms of West New Britain. That this initial expectation turned out to be an accurate one is shown to the reader as we continue through the next several chapters of the book.

The important point here is that the researcher should be able to find a unifying theme or "location" for research if they: (1) read at least some of the secondary (and perhaps primary) historical sources available, (2) read some of the basic political economy literature about the last twenty-five or so years for a specific area, and (3) combine these with selective theoretical literature that both 1 and 2 above indicate is relevant for their particular project. Remember to take notes about the major information and ideas that leap out at you from these writings as you read through them. You might want to keep a small separate notebook just for the large thematic ideas that occur to you (especially those that show promise as overarching themes—ones that can potentially bring disparate levels of research and theory together into a single coherent direction for analysis).

Eventually, a single theme will emerge to guide your interests and your research work. It *emerges* not because there is anything magical about the process, but rather because we as researchers are already predisposed to be interested in some things more than others because of a combination of our personal backgrounds, educational training (including our fields of knowledge), and sensitivity to specific issues. These interests often unconsciously guide our reading and normally result in a perspective on the literature that leads to specific kinds of ethnographic research. I have already noted how my own predisposition, for example, to be concerned about social inequalities led me to concentrate upon writings centered around social and cultural issues that were associated with the issues of social inequality. If this approach to research strikes you as somehow "wrong" then you need to get rid of your idealistic notions about the objective social researcher—there is no such being. All researchers are positioned in relation to their social (e.g., class, gender) and cultural (e.g., religion, ethnicity) backgrounds and research agendas emerge out of a combination of the personal "needs" of a researcher to explore a particular topic and the social "needs" of a community or society to have certain issues explored. That is why we do all of the preliminary reading—so that we can combine our own emergent concerns with larger social issues in order to develop a topic for research that does justice both to ourselves as individuals and as members of larger social units (with responsibilities to help understand those units). The alternative to this approach cannot be gained by assuming the position of an "objective scientist" (in which the researcher does not seem to exist as a living human being). All that leads to is an uninformed solipsism—in which the researcher disguises his or her own selfish concerns as objective decisions that have not been "tainted" with the specific contextual knowledge that I call for above. "Objectivity," here, becomes another word for decontextualization and a lack of transparency about the purpose of one's research—a position that is unacceptable for ethically informed ethnographic research.

If no single theme has emerged at the end of the reading process I have outlined above, do not let it bring you to despair. It is perfectly possible (and some might even say desirable) for the theme to emerge out of the first few months of on-site fieldwork. Certainly, the researcher must be prepared to modify his or her guiding theoretical position as the work proceeds. Specific circumstances often create limitations in one area of research just as another (related) area opens up as an opportunity. The researcher's theoretical position guides the study rather than fully determines it. Without the preliminary background work that I have written about above, however, the scholar will be unprepared to take advantage of opportunities as they arise, to modify older concerns to fit new or unexpected situations, and to gather the kind of information that will eventuate in a holistic ethnographic account of a specific topic.

The rest of this book, then, is about how to take your theme and turn it into a methodology for guiding ethnographic fieldwork.

Newspapers and Government Documents: Popular and Official Sources of Information

In this chapter, we begin to consider how to collect information in the field. I want to start here by looking at some of the ways to make use of both popular and official sources of information that may be gathered during fieldwork that will help complete (along with your preliminary reading) your understanding of the macro context of education in specific region or country. In future chapters, I discuss how to compare macro information with the micro processes of human interactions in order to understand actual human behaviors in ethnographic settings.

Newspapers: Using Popular Sources of Information

Newspapers (magazines, web sites, and other locations for popular media) are sources of information that are often readily available in both developing and industrialized countries but that may be overlooked because of the bias many professional researchers have against "popular publications." A *serious* researcher, many seem to think, would never make use of information that comes from a mass media source (unless of course s/he was specifically carrying out a study of that mass media itself). It is true that great care must be taken when using popular media as a source of information. I would never, for example, use statistics that were quoted in a newspaper article without checking them first against a more reliable set of information (such as an official government publication), as journalists simply do not have the time to confirm their facts with anything approaching the accuracy that is expected from professional researchers.[1] Newspapers can however be excellent sources of certain kinds of information, specifically that which is concerned with wider public attitudes toward particular issues, rather than for more official data such as unemployment rates or how many boys versus girls attend primary school in different regions of a country.

In the case of Papua New Guinea, because my study was carried out largely in or around two of the most important towns of West New Britain (namely the towns of Kimbe and Bialla), it became possible to consistently collect newspaper articles, letters to the editor, and editorials. Over a six-month period (which I would recommend as the appropriate length of time for such information gathering) I systematically cut out newspaper articles that involved any of the following seven themes: (1) education, (2) domestic or other forms of individualized violence, (3) social disputes (e.g., fighting between groups), (4) gender issues, (5) government policies, (6) government or bureaucratic corruption, and finally (7) "development" (economic and social) issues. I collected information from newspaper sources about these issues because each of them is relevant to education. Violence and/or corruption, for example, are often behind school closings (which may involve temporary or even permanent closure) in both rural and urban areas (e.g., Fife 1992b). The intent in gathering information from newspaper sources is not to conduct a formal media analysis (which would lead us too far away from our specific topic of interest), but rather: (1) to gain a broader understanding of what is considered to be newsworthy and therefore of public concern in the country as a whole, and (2) to gain a background that would allow one to place the more parochial concerns of the local area that you are working in (e.g., West New Britain) against the wider social issues relevant to the country as a whole. To give an example of the possible uses of newspapers as information sources, I briefly discuss a small sample of the information that I was able to gather regarding the theme of "development" and suggest how this affected my overall study.

In the early stages of my fieldwork, while conducting informal interviews with parents (see chapter 6 on interview methods), it quickly became obvious that most West New Britain parents with whom I spoke viewed education as desirable *only* if it led directly to a job in the cash economy for their children when they grew into adulthood. If the child was going to make a living when s/he became an adult as part of the subsistence-based horticultural economy that dominated village life, as the vast majority of Papua New Guineans do, then most parents expressed a wish to pull their sons or daughters out of school after only a few years before it "ruined" them for the life of the village. The problem, as the parents generally saw it, was the decision about which one or two of their sons or daughters to invest in for the future good of the family (which would normally also include a considera-tion of the needs of a larger kinship group such as a lineage or a clan).[2] Children were not viewed as autonomous individuals in the sense of being seen as persons who were "free" to make the most out of their own lives through social agencies such as education, with no regard for the rest of the family (or lineage). Rather, they were seen as being but one member of a group who had collective responsi-bilities and if they were selected by the family for further educational training then they were also expected to "pay the family back" throughout the rest of their lives by continuing to contribute to the well being of the collective unit through group access to such "individual resources" as a wage. In a situation such as this, educa-tion "for its own sake" or even for the sake of an individual alone is an unthinkable proposition.

During discussions with parents, I found very few who understood the recent historical changes (see chapter 3) that made it possible for a small number of Papua New Guineans to gain well-paying jobs in either government or private industry positions immediately prior to and just after Independence was achieved in 1975, but that rendered it highly unlikely that any but a tiny minority would continue to have such opportunities for this kind of employment in the future. Newspaper reports verified my conjecture that a split was developing within Papua New Guinea in the late 1980s (the period of fieldwork) between the official government position of education for both rural and urban life and the overwhelming cultural projection among parents that education was to be seen as a form of "development" and therefore as something that "naturally" went along with urban life and a job in the cash economy. For parents, education as a form of development should by definition guarantee that a son or daughter graduating from secondary school or a higher level obtained a place within the cash economy. Newspapers were, for example, full of letters to the editor from disappointed parents and frustrated students or former students who lamented the lack of opportunity to participate in what they saw as development by participating in a direct wage-paying job, even though that person had become "educated."

A good example can be seen in the high school student from Chimbu (also referred to as Simbu) province whose letter appeared in the *Post-Courier* on August 15, 1986, complaining about members of the national parliament: "It is four years since the last national election, but Gumine is still underdeveloped . . . I am confused whether our MPs understand the word development. If they do, please implement it. They have promised that certain things will be done, but where are they?" Part of the "certain things" that are expected here would be a job for this soon-to-graduate student. A similar letter to the editor in the *Tok Pisin*[3] newspaper *Wantok* that was published on May 17, 1986 by a frustrated young man complains that high school and even university educated people are having difficulty finding employment in the government or with business companies. His solution was to suggest that (my translation): "The government must give a man or a woman ten years work inside of a company or the government. If a man or a woman is lucky enough to have this time, they must then resign so that a new man or woman can take their place."

In reply to letters such as these and in relation to the more general dissatisfaction expressed by many parents and students, elected government officials began writing newspaper articles or editorials of their own, in which they extolled the virtues of personal independence, hard work, and self-sufficiency. Then Deputy Prime Minister and Finance Minister Sir Julius Chan, for example, wrote in the *Post-Courier* on July 22, 1986 that Papua New Guineas were getting reputations as people who took the "easy way out" instead of "meeting problems head on with hard work and sacrifice." "Only hard work solve[s] problems—there is no one to blame for failures but ourselves." While a little over a month later on August 29, the Prime Minister wrote in the same newspaper:

. . . [I]t is now time to bury dependent thinking for good. We will restore confidence, respect the ethic of hard work, and renew the caring and sharing habits of our ancestors . . . Why should the tax money that comes in from those who are growing cocoa, and coffee, and oil palm go to help people who are not doing any work? Why should tax money of a few hard working people build schools and hospitals and roads for people who do not lift a finger to make any contribution at all?

Armed with this preliminary information regarding the clash between at least some of the parents and the government regarding the presumed relationship between education, development, and wage labor it then became possible for me to look to the community (or primary) schools in West New Britain to try to see where these attitudes were coming from and what lay behind them. Were students, for example, somehow being taught that life in a cash-based, urban-dominated economy was a "necessity" that must be provided for them by the government? If so, how was this related to emerging social inequalities in the country? These issues are explored further in the next few chapters.

Having taken a single issue and considered how information about it can be gleaned from newspaper sources, I would now like to show how a variety of newspaper reports might be used to build upon the prior knowledge that has been created through a reading of historic and contemporary sources prior to arriving at the field site. In other words, I suggest that contemporary newspaper information can be linked to the historic and contemporary sources discussed previously in chapters 2 and 3 of this book, using the specific example of emerging patterns of social inequality to illustrate this point.

Newspaper and other comparable news media sources are a good way to confirm that the larger-scale historical patterns that researchers have delineated through their previous readings are still important in a contemporary nation. Let's take the example of regional disparity, which was pointed to earlier in this book as a historic trend in Papua New Guinea before it became an independent nation. A newspaper article regarding "the islands region" (which included the smaller islands of PNG such as New Britain, which contains the province of West New Britain) in relation to economic and social issues confirmed that regional disparities were still very much a factor in the Papua New Guinea of the 1980s (as they are today). Under the heading "PNG's Most Prosperous Region," an article written by Bill Chakravarti appeared in *The Times* on May 17, 1986. He wrote that "Overall, the income level of the Islands region is over twice the national average . . ." He then went on to associate the long history of formal [missionary supplied] education in these regions with their advantage over other parts of the country; not only in terms of educational attainment, but also by correlating that attainment with healthier patterns of childhood nutrition, relative accessibility to health care, and lesser rates of out-migration from the region.

Other stories confirm an ongoing preoccupation by those who live in the more remote rural areas about gaining a place for themselves in the cash economy through education. A story by Anhwi Hriehwazi that was printed on August 27, 1986 in the *Post Courier*, for example, is about villagers who live in the interior part of Papua New Guinea, right next to the border that it shares with Irian Jaya. It seems that thirty-eight villagers crossed over from PNG into the other country, announcing that they "no longer wished to be Papua New Guineans." "Most of the crossers were young men who had completed formal education to grade 10 level. [Mr. Abel] said he was unemployed for four years after completing school in 1981. . . . Most of the 38 villagers were now working on a major highway." The article ends by noting that several hundred people from several border villages are said to have crossed over into Irian Jaya in search of employment. In a related fashion, another article by Graham Mills about "youth" and their search for a place in the new Papua New Guinea, printed in *The Times* on August 29 in 1986, suggests that "the youth problem is really a rural problem," noting that education has "drained an entire group of young men and women away from the village leaving a whole generation gap which distorted the traditional community way of life." In one of many such stories, Angwi Hriehwazi writes in the *Post Courier* on July 17, 1986 about the difficulties inherent in providing education at the Telefomin High School in West Sepik Province. Accessible only by air, all school supplies must be flown in at enormous costs. School teachers have a difficult time making their pay stretch far enough to cover the much higher cost of living in the area, and consider "giving up work sometimes." "All school classrooms are made of bush material, and look like little tool sheds in urban schools. . . . The school early this year was ordered shut down [for a time] because of poor facilities." In short, the experience of being a teacher or a student in schools located outside of the urban areas is quite different from those who are located in towns and cities and the implications are that such differences may lead to further educational and hence social inequalities. This leads to problems for both teachers and students. For example, Wesley Bunpalau reported in the *Post Courier* on August 8, 1986 that in West New Britain one school had to be closed and others left short handed as several teachers were pulled out of teaching in dangerous rural school situations. One school had been closed "for two weeks after a youth attempted to rape a female teacher." While another female teacher "had been recalled to Kimbe following another attempted rape on her by a gang." Furthermore, a male teacher "was pulled out [of the school] after his house was broken into and properties including a radio, a handbag and K50 [about US$50] were stolen." These reports confirm, then, the continuation of a trend that began as far back as a hundred years ago when missionaries began to set up shop in selected parts of the region. In chapters 2 and 3 we were able to see that the issue of social inequalities arising from urban versus rural opportunities and regional disparities has a long history in this country—a historical pattern that can be verified by a researcher as being of continual importance through the reportage available to us through newspapers.

The people committing the crimes that led to the withdrawal of the teachers from schools noted above are for the most part young male members of what are generally referred to in Papua New Guinea as "rascal" gangs. During the 1980s (and this continues into today) newspapers were full of the problem of "rascals" and what should be done about them. Many gang members were relatively well-educated and intelligent young males (gang leaders typically being high school graduates and members typically being middle-school or higher dropouts or even graduates), who were angry at having been "shut out" of the good life in the new Papua New Guinea in which they expected to receive tangible rewards for their relative educational attainments. Typical in this regard is a story about a once promising middle-school student by Therese Pirigi in *The Times* of May 17, 1986, in which she chronicles "The tale of a lost sheep: shot dead, aged 20." Raphael was said to have been a fun loving and intelligent boy when he was younger. He was a bright student and passed into secondary school in 1978. His father unfortunately died the next year and "This was a turning point for Raphael." Within months he was hanging around older boys and talking about a "style life." When he was fourteen years old he was involved in a car accident in a stolen vehicle, which left him in the hospital for three months. "He escaped from the hospital to do his [grade eight] exams." His teachers, however, wanted him to repeat the grade. He refused, as he didn't want to be separated from his school friends who would be moving to another school for grade nine. "Raphael became a grade eight dropout. Lacking the money to survive in his own his interest to join the rascals intensified." What follows is a litany of crime, culminating in being shot to death by a police officer at the age of twenty "for allegedly being involved in the robbery, abduction and rape of an expatriate woman." It is important to remember that such boys (and to a lesser extent some girls) are under tremendous pressure from their families to "succeed" in the educational system and help the family by finding wage employment (see Fife 1995a, for a discussion of education in relation to masculinity in the new Papua New Guinea). As was apparent in the historical trends reported upon previously, parents not only tended to view education as a road to a wage job but also to blame the person who could not obtain such a job to be a "failure," with no regard for the changing historical conditions that rendered such expectations unrealistic in the Papua New Guinea of the last few decades.

Using newspapers as a source of information makes it easy to see why there are so many angry young men in this particular country. Reporting on a key government document that outlined the national employment needs for the 1990s, an anonymous writer in the *Niugini Nius* of June 18, 1986 noted that while there would be very good opportunities for tertiary graduates in the near future, "a secondary education would no longer be a passport to formal employment and by the early 1990s there would be a considerable surplus of grade 10 school leavers. This was because the rapid growth of high schools had far outstripped the capacity of the formal sector to provided jobs."

The members of the various levels of government were not insensitive to these issues. As noted above, many of them began to write newspaper articles of their own in which they stressed the necessity for hard work and individual entrepreneurship (e.g., suggesting that school leavers use their skills to build up coffee or cocoa businesses in the rural areas and contribute to their home village economies rather than expecting to be "handed" wage jobs in the urban centers of the country). These issues could easily be discovered on the pages of various newspapers by a researcher who was monitoring this media as an information source. For example, in an article by Charles Adams that appeared on July 4, 1986 in *The Times* under the heading "The 90 per cent that misses out," he explored the implications of the fact that "Less than ten percent of last year's grade 10 leavers got jobs or further training offers after leaving school (it was only five per cent the year before)." He also delineated what the teachers at Tapini High School have been doing to try to lure "the 90 per cent" back to village areas after they leave school. They have, for example, begun to provide training at running a small trade store at school, so that those students could learn how they might run similar stores in their own home areas. Commercial market gardening was being taught in the school alongside of regular curriculum to show students the "healthy profits" that can be made by gardening for the cash market in rural areas. Two fishponds were also set up to teach former students about low cost aquaculture projects that could result in cash businesses. Further, chicken projects were created to facilitate learning about raising commercial stock. Tacked on to this story is an editor's note, which explains that the national government had in fact created a Secondary Schools Community Project (SSCEP) at ten schools throughout the country to try to provide secondary students with the kind of education that will make them want to return to rural areas after their education ends by introducing them to the kinds of entrepreneurial skills that will be necessary to "succeed" in the rural areas they will have to return to if they are not one of the lucky few to go on to a tertiary education or a wage employment opportunity in the new Papua New Guinea (on SSCEP, see Crossley 1981; Crossley and Vulliamy 1986; Vulliamy 1985). Such incentives were not limited to formal educational centers. An anonymous report in the *Post Courier* for October 12, 1986 noted that forty-six youth leaders (ten of them female) from various parts of Western Highlands province had recently completed a two week course to help them learn how to manage their own poultry farms, at a cost of K10,500 (about US$10,500) for the whole educational project. All of the youth who attended already had poultry projects funded by a national youth movement program.

What these newspaper reports tell the researcher interested in education is that he or she should expect to find issues of rural versus urban "development" and its relationship to cash economy employment to appear quite prominently in the hidden curriculum of the classrooms of West New Britain. It also suggests that many of the common themes that can be found historically in the region of Papua New Guinea have continued to be salient in the postindependence PNG of the contemporary period. The macro structures affecting social inequalities have specific histories and trajectories and newspapers can be of use in assessing to what extent these trends have continued into the present period. We should note as well that although I am not addressing the issue here, newspaper can themselves serve as historical information in many countries.

Contemporary newspaper sources (and of course other similar media) can be used to: (1) assess the contemporary saliency of historical trends and their relevance for on-site research, (2) examine the extent to which local social and cultural patterns associated with specific topics exist in other parts of the country outside of the actual research location, and (3) allow the researcher to gauge the relative public importance of specific issues associated with a topic (such as education's supposed linkages to wage employment or crime rates).

All of the material that has been presented in this chapter represents much larger sets of newspaper accounts about similar concerns. The scholar who wishes to make use of this valuable source is warned that the same questions of reliability that is met up with in chapter 5 regarding field observations is also relevant for the use of newspaper sources. An article or two, or even a series by one reporter cannot necessarily be taken to represent a large-scale concern in the country as a whole about a specific issue. Researchers will want to ask themselves how often this topic (or very similar ones) appears in the newspapers? How widespread (e.g., in terms of geographical coverage) does it seem to be? Does it engage the public's attention to the extent that it is associated with the writings of numerous letters to the editor from the public, or by follow-up articles from other authors arguing different points of view? Used with these caveats in mind, newspapers can prove to be a valuable source of information for the ethnographic scholar (for other writing on the use of newspaper sources, see Harber 1997).

Government Documents: Using Official Sources of Information

Most researchers who are not from the country in which fieldwork is to be conducted will fly into either its capital city or one of its largest urban centres in order to begin the on-site phase of field research (or at least have the option of so doing). I recommend that you allow for at least two weeks in the capital city (or its equivalent) upon initial entrance into the field and two weeks in the same city on your way out of the country. This will normally be necessary at any rate in order to secure the required long term visa and the research permit (or permits) that will usually be mandatory for an extended stay and also to allow for one or two meetings with interested government personnel at the end of your fieldwork so that you may briefly discuss your main findings with them (more is said about this issue in chapter 10). I suggest that you also use this time to gather as many government documents as possible (including local material associated with government sources, e.g., state funded university presses that may not distribute their publications outside of the home country). Most of this material will simply be unavailable to you once you return to your place of origin. Even if you are a researcher who lives within the fieldwork country, unless you also make your home in the capital city, many of these documents will be difficult for you to obtain after you leave the capital. If you are applying for a research grant, make sure to include money in your budget for the purchase of documents and books inside of the country (in my experience, very few researchers remember to do this). One thousand (US) dollars would not be too much, but five hundred (US) dollars would seem to me to be a minimum amount to allow for the purchase of at least the most significant of these extremely valuable sources of information. Many government documents will of course be available free of charge from specific government offices (e.g., basic economic statistics from the Ministry of Trade and Commerce)—though rising costs and falling economies are forcing many agencies to charge nominal fees for these documents now. Many other sources of information (e.g., an elaborate book of maps) will cost substantial amounts of money. Also, remember that you do not want to be carrying large numbers of books, monographs and papers around with you during your research. Some of the money, then, will be used to mail these materials back to yourself during the fieldwork period (secure a mailing address before you leave your home area or country; those employed in academic positions of course need only mail them to their home university departments).

Your first stop should be at the ministry or department of education (or health care, finance, rural development, or whatever ministry covers your primary topic area). They will, for example, normally be willing to provide you with a great deal of basic information about education in their country and government policy makers and others responsible for education will also normally wish to make contact with an incoming researcher so that they can discuss their plans with them. This is a good opportunity to set up several informal interviews with key education bureaucrats (see later in this chapter, and also chapter 6, for more about interviewing), as well as secure written sources of information. To give only a few examples, when I visited the federal Department of Education in Papua New Guinea, among many other documents I was able to obtain (either free, or for minor charges) were the *National Education Strategy* (for the period 1976 forward); a *Vocational Centres Manual*; the 1985 [most recent year available] *Education Staffing and Enrolment Statistics*; and the booklet *Growth of Education Since Independence 1975–1985*. The *National Education Strategy*, for example, outlined postindependence policy directions for education. The *Vocational Centres Manual* told of the vocational training centers in the country and their role as places for skilled training in nonformal educational settings. The *Staffing and Enrolment Statistics* gave detailed numbers regarding the enrolment of students by grade (and by gender) in each of the twenty provinces of the country and also statistical information about various kinds of teachers (including, for example, whether the teachers were nationals or expatriates).

We consider one of these sources in more detail in order to give the scholar an idea about what kinds of information will become available to him or her by collecting government documents. In order to do this, I use the 76 page report known as *Growth of Education Since Independence 1975–1985*, which was compiled by the Department of Education (i.e., what would be the Ministry of Education in many other countries). It should be understood that I discuss only a very small selection of the material from this booklet and that much, much more is available from this single source alone. Through a number of diagrams, for example, the booklet portrays the contemporary "chain of command" in regard to the hierarchical linkages of responsibility and decision-making between various departments of the government and separate levels of formal education (e.g., high schools, community schools,[4] vocational centers). The large number of diagrams used suggests that these hierarchies are very important to the current view of how education is "supposed" to function in relation to larger social structures within the country. In the booklet, the researcher can also see at a glance that while community school teachers are made up solely of native Papua New Guineans, high school teachers still remain 19 percent expatriate, while professors at teacher's colleges continue to be 56 percent expatriate in origin (primarily Australian). Teacher training itself, then, continues to be dominated by professors who are not native to the country of Papua New Guinea (all contemporary figures are of course for the period 1984–1985). A little further on in the document the researcher can find out that among seven year old children, 90 percent of boys are enrolled in school while only 76 percent of girls are so enrolled in the country as a whole. However, this can also be compared with province by province figures that are given a few pages later in order to discover that in the province of West New Britain the gap is less pronounced, with 86.7 percent of boys and 79.7 percent of girls enrolled (this particular graph also tells us that West New Britain has the fourth highest overall enrolment rates for the country as a whole). Despite government control of the educational system, this booklet further informs us in a graph format that 56 percent of the schools in the country are still run by specific churches and that only two out of the ten teachers colleges are truly "government" colleges (with the rest being church run colleges that exist under government rules).

Form this one government source alone, the perceptive researcher will see that many of these issues are connected with patterns of education and society that come from the history of the region prior to the emergence of the independent nation of Papua New Guinea. The current reliance on church run schools in a "government" school system, for example, reflects the missionary history of education in the area. The differential rates of male/female enrolments at various levels of education are related to many other issues, including the historic circumstances that led large numbers of parents to view education as a form of "development" and therefore as more suitable for boys rather than girls because of the general perception that girls will only grow up to be childbearing women anyway, which might interfere with their ability to "pay back" their families through wage labor employment. The relatively high enrolment rates for West New Britain reflects the information that we learned earlier from both newspaper sources and historical records about the uneven development of various parts of the region because of previous missionary and colonial patterns in relation to the provision of social services in the country. The tremendous concern for diagramming the "chain of command" resonates with a neocolonial legacy of viewing government services as a set of interlinking hierarchies that reach outward from the urban centers and into the rural areas of the provinces or the country. And, that is only a small fraction of the relevant information that is available within one government document.

Collecting as much government published information as possible will allow the scholar to check evidence from more than one source. In the examples given above, a researcher could cross check the statistics and graphs given in the *Growth of Education* booklet with the more detailed numbers provided in *Education Staffing and Enrolment Statistics*, as well as in the *National Education Strategy*. Since there are many difficulties associated with the use of statistics in many developing countries, for example, it is important that the researcher avoid whenever possible an overreliance upon a single source for statistics. It is also important to avoid over determining which material might eventually prove to be of use to a researcher a year or two later when she or he is writing articles or books based upon the study. My simple rule of thumb is this: If the source looks like it has interesting information about some aspect of my topic (e.g., education, tourism, or aging) and/or the larger social milieu that informs it, collect it (especially if it is free). You may never come this way again.

Other government departments and agencies will also prove valuable sources of information. Generally speaking, the researcher should visit those departments or agencies that are most directly concerned with the issues that s/he has previously identified as of concern in their pre-fieldwork period of reading. Certainly, for example, someone following a similar agenda to mine would want to visit the various departments that have to do with the political economy of the country.

The Law Reform Commission of Papua New Guinea, for example, had a number of useful publications regarding such issues as domestic violence (e.g., Toft 1985; Toft and Bonnell 1985). In an article in one of these books, for example, Anne Chowning writes in relation to the Kove people of West New Britain that "Children were rarely beaten by their true parents, but since so many were orphaned, they were not always treated so well by others" (Chowning 1985: 87). Statements such as this would of course alert an educational researcher to a consideration of the schooling attainments of orphans versus others in the West New Britain region, especially in relation to the Kove people and other cultural groups with similar patterns of interfamily violence.

At the time of my PNG research The Institute of Applied Social and Economic Research in PNG also published a number of books and monographs about contemporary political and economic issues, such as monograph number twenty-six: *Decentralization and Development Policy: Provincial Government and the Planning Process in Papua New Guinea* (Axline 1986). In it, for example, we find out that many provincial education ministers and bureaucrats see themselves as just as "important" as their counterparts at the national level (despite the differences in population size and budgets); that the education departments were quite willing to cooperate in the "decentralization" movement of the 1980s, but with their own specific agendas about the meaning of that term (one that did not necessarily reflect the understandings of other government departments); and that provincial departments of education often have the only true "planning" capacities in a province and therefore normally capture more than their fair share of provincial government resources (which of course would add to the feelings of "importance" noted above) (Axline 1986: 26, 42, 173). Some of this information resonates with more personal research experiences. I was *warned*, for example, by educators when I was in the capital city of Port Moresby to be careful to be very *low key* with provincial government officials from the department of education in West New Britain and to make sure that it did not look like I was "some guy from Port Moresby" or "some guy from the United States" (many Papua New Guineans confused Canada with the United States) who was out to "teach the locals how to do education." The monograph above and its report about the feelings of "self-importance" among provincial educational bureaucrats suggest at least some reasons why I was warned in this fashion.

The researcher should also be sure to check in with academics at the local university (virtually all capital and most large cities have at least one). Scholars at the education department at the University of Papua New Guinea, for example, put me onto the series of low cost reports that they published, with such titles as *Factors Affecting Standards in Community Schools, Factors Affecting the Enrolment and Retention of Girls in Papua New Guinea Community Schools*, and *Papua New Guinea National Inventory of Educational Innovations*. In all, I bought over three-dozen reports, at a cost of between (US)$2.00–5.00 per report. Today, similar material might cost the equivalent of (US)$5.00–10.00 each. For any scholar who thought that I was exaggerating the need for setting aside money for the purchase of government and government related documents it becomes quite obvious from the above that it is easy to spend between

(US)$200–300 on reports alone, and this does not include the costs of mailing them home.

It should be clear by now that it is well worth spending some weeks in the national capital city (or its equivalent) to secure the above types of documents for your research. A scholar who wished to conduct even a preliminary search of primary historical sources (e.g., so that s/he could know whether or not they would be worth a follow-up research trip in a future period) will also want to schedule an extra week for that work. Most archives will be connected to the university or government offices located in the capital city, or at the very least in an archive located somewhere else in the city (e.g., perhaps at the national public library) and it is therefore quite convenient for a quick reconnaissance at the beginning or closing stages of your field research.

Talking to Government Workers and Academics

While the researcher is taking advantage of government documents, s/he might as well make use of the situation to informally interview several people involved with her/his specific topic in the capital city. I would suggest one or two government bureaucrats, as well as the director and one or two members of the relevant government departments (e.g., education, tourism, economic development) and/or a special research unit attached to the university (e.g., an educational research unit or a rural development research unit). In developing countries at least, these individuals are likely to seek you out rather than the other way around. If you make it known that you are in the capital upon your arrival (e.g., by immediately visiting the relevant ministry or the university) you can be sure that active individuals involved in your topical area will hear about you and make it their business to see whether your research is relevant to their interests. A member of the government, for example, might ask if you could conduct a small survey for him or her while you are in a specific area, or a scholar might ask you to keep your eyes open for examples of certain kinds of information while you are doing your own work. Such requests are very common and reflect the desire of responsible bureaucrats and researchers to make use of all available "resources" to add to their fund of information about a field of knowledge in their country in the face of restrained financial conditions. Doing these sorts of small favours is part of the way that you can *pay back* a developing country or a relatively poor region in an industrialized country for hosting your research. When speaking with these local experts you may wish to use a semi-structured interview format similar to the kind that I recommend for interviewing members of a provincial government (see chapter 6), but I would instead suggest that you will have a better response to a "conversational interview" format—in which you simply ask questions as part of the regular ebb and flow of the overall discussion. What will you ask? It depends upon your specific interests. If education is your topic then you might be interested in some or all of the following issues. Is there a large problem in the country with the equality of opportunity for female versus male students? What is the official government position in terms of the relationship that is assumed to exist between education and employment? Do you think that education contributes to political unrest or to stability within the country? In other words, ask questions that center around the themes that your prior reading has led you to focus upon—ones you hope to pursue on the micro level of research now that you are about to begin field research. Be sure to also include a few general questions that will allow you to take full advantage of the person's local knowledge. For example, instead of inquiring about something specific, try the following type of question: What do you think is the single biggest problem affecting primary schools (health care, small business, an aging population) in the country today? Or alternatively, what is the single biggest educational (business, urban renewal, forestry) success story of the last decade? By not specifying the topic, you will allow the interviewee the freedom to educate you about a topic that they think is particularly important (and one that you may have previously either overlooked or not understood to be of such importance). Above all, be willing to be guided and show that you have an open mind. Whatever you do, avoid sending the message that you are an *expert* about a particular topic and are there only to confirm what you "already know" about the country.

Be prepared to change you mind about the direction of your research in relation to what you learn during the first few weeks in the field. By changing direction, I am referring here to changing the content of your study as opposed to the overall theoretical orientation. A specific example, elaborating on a situation that I mentioned earlier in this book, explains this point better than an abstract statement.

Several days after I arrived in the capital of Port Moresby in Papua New Guinea, I went to the educational research unit at the University and met Dr. Sheldon Weeks, the director of that unit. I gave him the research proposal that I had prepared back in Canada as part of my Ph.D. studies. He told me to have a seat and disappeared into his office to read it. Fifteen minutes later he came out, looked me in the eye, and said "You can't do this. There is already a sociologist in West New Britain right now who is studying the high schools and there is no need to duplicate his research."

My original proposal called for a study of two primary schools (one urban and one rural) and a high school in the same area, so that I could follow the "hidden curriculum" from grades one to ten (the highest standard grade at the provincial high schools) and consider the effects it might be having on various categories of students (such as males versus females, or students from rural versus urban backgrounds). The fact that the sociologist was in West New Britain for only a few months and spending literally a few weeks at each high school (while I would be there for a year and expected to study only one high school for several months) and that the other researcher was utilizing primarily a quantitative approach while I would be working out of an ethnographic tradition made no difference to Dr. Weeks (who was both a highly respected educational researcher and in a position to decide whether or not I would be granted a research permit to pursue educational research in the country). It "was being done" and that was all there was to it. On the other hand, Dr. Weeks suggested, there was a tremendous amount of work that needed to be pursued on primary (i.e., community schools) and why didn't I concentrate on that? Sheldon (as I later got to know him) disappeared into a computer room, emerging a few minutes later with page after page of printouts that listed community schools in West New Britain and such important facts as drop out rates, success rates in grade six examinations (the key to achieving entrance to secondary school) and attendance rates. Why didn't I take these with me, study them, and think about a plan to do research in some of the community schools of West New Britain? Come back in a couple of days with a new proposal, I was told (a daunting task, as the first proposal had taken several weeks to write).

As it turned out my preliminary reading (most of which was listed on my proposal and could therefore be utilized for my new plan) served me well. I was able to figure out that my basic theoretical orientation—centering on hidden curriculum and its potential relationship to various forms of social inequality—remained viable. If the researcher has read carefully prior to coming to the field this will almost always prove to be the case. What I would have to do was change the content of my research (since high schools, at least those in West New Britain, were now out of bounds). I considered various possibilities. The print-out suggested that there were tremendous differences between "success" rates in rural versus urban schools and I briefly considered a study in which I would compare urban and rural community schools. However, there was a fatal flaw in such a proposal. As explained in chapter 3, Papua New Guinea has many different languages and hence cultural groups. West New Britain was no exception to this pattern. As a single researcher, how could I possibly study a sufficient number of schools to ensure a "representative" sample of the rural situation? The answer was that it was impossible to study a sufficient number of schools using a basic ethnographic approach (which requires that vast amounts of time are spent at each single school) in order to do a rural/urban comparison. Since I had no intention of abandoning my basic research orientation, my solution was to focus upon three community schools. Two would be in the largest urban areas (Kimbe and Bialla, which are towns rather than cities) and one would be a school in a rural situation outside of Bialla—a school that took in students from several nearby villages but which also had a reputation (confirmed by Dr. Weeks) of being very "successful" in terms of student achievement. In other words, I would study "successful" schools to see what hidden curriculum could tell me about educational processes within them. This project seemed to me to be a good compromise between my own academic interests and the more pragmatic interests of the country of Papua New Guinea as they were represented in the person of Dr. Weeks (and others associated with educational analysis and provision in the country as well). At the very least, I would be able to delineate how hidden curriculum worked in the "best" primary schools of West New Britain. The advantages of this was that when I discovered "problems" in the schools (e.g., patterns of hidden curriculum that in all likelihood made it more difficult for students to succeed in achieving the goals of education as they were set by the government of Papua New Guinea) they could not be dismissed as something that existed only because the school was in a remote part of a rural area in WNB. If they existed in the *best* schools, then the patterns probably existed in all schools of WNB to a greater or lesser extent and that would make my research relevant to the province as a whole.

Sheldon thought that my plan was a good one. He expedited my research permits, introduced me to people he thought I should know, arranged for me to have the use of an office while I was in the capital, and in general did everything humanly possible to allow me to proceed with my work.[5] Sheldon, in fact, turned into as valuable a colleague as I have ever had once he was assured that I was not just another researcher from a rich country who wanted to make his own career on the backs of Papua New Guineans without conducting a study that would be useful for local purposes. I promised to give a seminar when I returned to the capital after my fieldwork and write a report of my findings for them to use. A scholar who is coming into a developing country (or even a relative poor region of a heavily industrialized country) from elsewhere often needs to be prepared to align his or her own interests with those of local researchers and/or government bureaucrats in such a way that the project ends up being both "academic" and "practical" at the same time. If I were doing a study of tourism in Tonga, for example, I could not expect to simply focus the fieldwork on some relatively obscure theoretical point in order to help create a name for myself as an academic researcher. In all likelihood, I would be expected to have something useful to say at the end of my study about how well local tourism projects and policies were succeeding if I wanted the ongoing cooperation of indigenously located researchers and government bureaucrats. This not only seems to be a perfectly reasonable trade-off to me but also the only ethical position to take if one wants to conduct research among relatively disadvantaged populations of human beings. I would also contend that if s/he has done her preliminary work properly, as outlined in chapters 2, 3, and now in chapter 4, the researcher will be able to adjust to these kinds of situations with a minimum of time and trouble.

Part B

Methods for Micro-Level Research

5

Participant-Observation as a Research Method

Participant-observation is the most basic ethnographic research method. Similar to playing the guitar, it seems simple at first but it takes years to truly master. However, even inexperienced researchers will be able to use this method effectively to generate large amounts of useful information if they follow the guidelines laid down in this chapter. Chapter 5, then, begins part B of the book, which is concerned with methods for conducting research at the micro-level of human behavior.

Participant-Observation Explained

In his now classic methods textbook, James Spradley declared: "The participant-observer comes to a social situation with two purposes: (1) to engage in activities appropriate to the situation, and (2) to observe the activities, people, and physical aspects of the situation" (Spradley 1980: 54). David Fetterman (1989: 45) adds:

> Participant observation combines participation in the lives of the people under study with maintenance of a professional distance that allows adequate observation and recording of data. [P]articipant observation is immersion in a culture. Ideally, the ethnographer lives and works in the community for six months to a year or more, learning the language and seeing patterns of behavior over time. Long-term residence helps the researcher internalize the basic beliefs, fears, hopes and expectations of the people under study.

In the time-honored phrase of Clifford Geertz, ethnographers try to learn "the native's point of view" by both participating in behavior from within and observing it from without (Geertz 1976). Natives, in this case, refer to anyone who has grown up within a specific cultural milieu rather than specifically referring to a concept of aboriginality. Everyone is a native in his or her home environment. The trick, then, is to learn what it might be like to inhabit a native's life world, to take his or her common sense for our common sense, and to learn to solve existential problems in locally appropriate ways (Jackson 1989). "Participant observation involves establishing rapport in a new community: learning to act so that people go about their business as usual when you show up; and removing yourself every day from cultural immersion so you can intellectualize what you've learned, put it into perspective, and write about it convincingly" (Bernard 1994: 137). Along with this "intellectual" understanding, most ethnographic researchers would agree that an emotional empathy for the people with whom we work is also necessary for good ethnographic research. This does not mean that we agree with everything they do or with everything that they believe in, but it does mean that we should move beyond a merely cerebral relationship and develop more intuitive or gut-level feelings about what it is like to be "a native" in this particular time and place.[1]

Generally speaking, we learn how to do these things by making mistakes and by figuring out how to correct them, as well as by learning how to observe people closely. Long term observations are necessary in order to gain some understanding of the unwritten "rules" that govern human interactions among a specific group of people, whether this involves working with Papua New Guinean educators and students who have come together for the purposes of "education," or with a population of Canadian Cree hunters who are at a lake in northern Quebec hunting ducks. We learn though observation and analysis; then we test these analyses out by attempting to participate in the life world that we are currently studying. For example, if most people present at an event begin to laugh at my behavior, or a room is suddenly filled with shocked faces in reaction to me, then I can assume that I have misread the social and cultural patterns of behavior that I thought I had understood from my observations. As researchers in such situations, we ask those present what we did wrong, we spend more time observing, and we try to gain a better understanding of the behavior under consideration. It should be apparent that the key to this process is good observational skills. I propose to teach those skills in this chapter.

As an experiential method of research, participant-observation can of course only be taught through specific research situations. That means that it is best to turn to examples from my own research in order to consider how to conduct participant observation methods in the field.

General Methods of Observation

As I suggested in chapter 3, my basic theoretical orientation during my period of Papua New Guinea research involved viewing hidden curriculum as a key to understanding the processes of education in the community schools of West New Britain and focusing on how this was related to issues of social inequality. In my opinion, the best way to begin to understand education in the field is by attending classes in schools as a general observer. The researcher should obtain permission from the educators involved to simply sit down at the back of a different classroom every day for a minimum of two weeks for each school in the project (in my case, six weeks in total). The research goal during this general observation period is to record as fully as possible the micro-level context of schooling inside of that classroom. This will include detailed descriptions of the physical environment of the room as a whole; the spatial arrangements of objects, educators and students; and the ongoing verbal and nonverbal interactions of teachers and students, as well as students and students. Of course no one can actually compile a record that fully records everything actually occurring within the micro context of even a single classroom or school, but even new observers are soon surprised by how much detail can be recorded and the extent to which notes can accurately reflect the minute by minute interactions that take place within a school room (or other micro situation). The goal at this stage is to make the best record possible about what is occurring inside of real classrooms for several weeks *before* the observer begins to analyze these patterns of behavior in order to make decisions about narrowing the ethnographic focus to accommodate his or her more specific research interests. Be prepared for surprises at this point of the work. A constant pattern of behavior may appear, for example, that prior reading has not prepared the researcher to be able to "see." An open mind will reveal new and interesting avenues to add to your more macro-based assumptions about what is important in relation to a topic in a given location or it may reveal patterns of interaction that you did expect to find in a new and often more complex light. I can illustrate this issue by taking an example from tourism research I have conducted that partially involves primarily middle-class, urban visitors to Gros Morne National Park in Newfoundland, Canada. My early reading on tourism involving national parks in general and about "nature" tourism in Newfoundland in particular did not prepare me for the extent to which many visitors that I spoke with in Gros Morne have a strong sense of "postmodern reflexivity" about what it means to be a contemporary tourist in a national park. Some visitors that I spoke with displayed a very self-conscious sense of being a relatively privileged tourist in this area of high unemployment and about the kind of problematic relationship this creates between them and the local workers who "serve" and "entertain" them. Other visitors showed no such reflexivity or postmodern self-knowledge about tourism as a quintessential service-industry and the kinds of class-relations that it helps to engender. The literature that I read had not prepared me for this contradictory consciousness among visitors for the simple reason that most writers assumed either a resolutely modernist or postmodernist theoretical stance in their studies and therefore failed to acknowledge the complex human reality that prevailed among today's national park visitors.

A warning before we continue considering the example of educational research in Papua New Guinea and what it can tell us about participant observation as a research method. Wherever they might do their fieldwork, I strongly suggest that researchers write their work out in a notebook that contains duplicate pages that can be ripped out of the book (a carbon copy is fine). More than a few ethnographic scholars have lost their notes in the field. It is therefore imperative that the researcher periodically mail the duplicate notes back home on a regular basis. Whether using a pen and pads of paper or the latest in portable computers, make sure that you duplicate notes daily and send them home no less than once a month. If you are using a word processor, then it becomes possible to simply add each day's notes to an email attachment and email them home to oneself or to a friend on a regular basis. I personally know several researchers who for one reason or another (such as robbery or catastrophic weather) lost virtually all of their research notes because they failed to send copies back home to themselves. Some of them (at the end stages of their Ph.D.) abandoned their chosen profession all together because of these disasters—they simply couldn't face the thought of beginning their work over again. At the very least, the project itself is likely to be abandoned after considerable time, money, and other forms of personal sacrifice have already been put into it.

Inside the School

Classrooms

How, then, would a researcher record "everything" that is found inside a classroom during the first couple of weeks of observation? To begin with, remember that you have more than the sense of sight. Don't forget to record what you hear, smell, taste and feel, as well as what you see (see Paul Stoller for the argument that we often neglect our nonvisual senses in ethnography [e.g., Stoller and Olkes 1989; Stoller 1989]). Although much of what you record *will* be focused upon what you hear and see, a good exercise that often reveals surprising patterns of behavior involves taking one morning or one afternoon (or even one hour) of general observation time and only recording what you smell, or only recording what you touch (which of course can best be done in an empty classroom), or what you taste (best done in a school cafeteria or other similar venue). Sitting on a hard wooden chair inside of a cramped desk (or on a bench "chair" that has no back) and recording your sensations of touch can forcibly remind you later when you are writing your notes into publishable material how physically difficult it is not to "move around" on what are often very uncomfortable and confining material objects. This in turn may cause you to ruminate about what confining active young bodies to such physically uncomfortable constraints is really about (e.g., creating a disciplined social body as opposed to allowing "natural" bodily movements), or why so many students "disobey" teachers and physically leave their desks during the first few years of schooling (behavior that is normally viewed by teachers as a character flaw or a manifestation of a psychological state rather than a response to physical discomfort; as in a teacher suggesting that "this child is hyperactive" rather than saying that "these chairs/benches are really hard and uncomfortable, no wonder the children can't sit still").

When you are recording your observational notes, you will want to remember to leave space for coding the information at a later point in time. This is true no matter what your ethnographic work is focused upon. The simplest devise is to leave a wider than normal margin along the left hand side of your notes. This margin can then be used to write later commentaries about the patterns of behavior that seem to be emerging in your observations. I suggest that you use pencil in this coding process, as the categories that you use for this coding will often change over time (i.e., you will readjust them as you record more observations and/or reconsider the analysis from a larger perspective). The point of the coding is twofold: (1) It creates an initial analysis that will allow you to decide on how to focus later classroom (or other) observations, and (2) It allows you to glance down the left-hand side of your notes and find relevant examples for specific kinds of behavior or other forms of evidence when you are writing your thesis, book, or article. If you have forgotten to leave a space for coding on the page itself, or if you wish to code the notes in a more temporary manner (e.g., to write a specific article about a particular topic) rather than in a more permanent form, then the widely available Post-It Notes (smallest size) can be used as a handy tool to affix categorical codes onto the page along the left hand side of the page (and they lift right off the fieldnotes after you are finished with your temporary project). These notes have the added advantage of being available in numerous colors and can therefore be used to create a very visible coding procedure if you wish to do so.

Take a few days and code all of your notes after you have completed the initial weeks of general classroom observation. The categories that you use to code the notes will depend upon a number of factors. The first one is the theoretical orientation that you have brought to the project. For example, because I brought a general orientation that involved searching for the effects of hidden curriculum upon various forms of social inequality, I was theoretically predisposed to coding categories of behavior or evidence that pointed to anything that might be related to larger issues of social inequality (such as differences in the treatment of boys versus girls in the classroom, or differences in the ways that urban versus rural lifeways were discussed by teachers and students). What you are looking for are repetitive themes that you believe are likely to have important effects upon the lessons that students are learning in classrooms settings, whether these themes involve manifest or hidden curriculum. The second factor that influences how you categorize your fieldnotes, then, is the amount of thematic repetition that you find in these notes. Patterns of interaction (or other forms of evidence) that constantly recur in your notes (and remember that you were not initially looking for any specific patterns when doing these recordings) are likely to be of the greatest significance and therefore should become the patterns that you focus upon in this coding process. The way that you code them depends upon the eventual goal you have for this evidence. For example, a first coding might simply record "gendered behavior" every time that you come across something in your notes that seems to be about differences in the ways that boys and girls are treated in the classroom. After the first coding is completed, you may wish to return and reconsider this single category, recoding it with more a fine-grained analysis in mind. For example, you could decide to differentiate evidence concerning "gendered disciplinary actions," "gendered math lessons," and "gendered language instruction." The extent to which you continue to differentiate more general categories of evidence into finer categories depends upon the third factor influencing the categorization of fieldnotes—what this analysis will be used for in terms of the creation of an end product. If you want to write a very specific journal article that focuses exclusively upon gender issues in the classrooms of West New Britain, for example, then you will want to impose a very fine-grained set of categories on your research notes. If you are going to write a Ph.D. thesis, on the other hand, you will not want to limit your themes too early in the process and therefore will likely find larger categories more useful to you (at least during this initial stage of the research process). After all, you can always go back and recategorize the material (e.g., after you decide which themes to turn into chapters or sections of your thesis or book and therefore require that categories be broken up into smaller pieces of discrete information).

To help the reader visualize this process of analysis, here are a few samples of raw fieldnotes and some of the ways that I chose to categorize them.

Coding	Fieldnotes
Competitive Individualism	As the students finish the writing assignment, each takes his/hers up to the front for the teacher to check. "Eh, that group of boys there. What are they doing? Girls, why are they spying? Peter! You should be using your own head—shame on you!" (Writing Class, Grade 2, Bialla)
Competitive Individualism	She [the teacher] is doing question and answer, where each student has to put the right answer down on his paper in response to her oral question. . . . "And make sure you cover your work from your friends." . . . Something that I see. Boys think this is a game. They see their friends and help them. I caught a few today. Next time you do it, I'm going to put you in a different place." (English, Grade 2, Kimbe)
Cooperative Individualism	The kids are doing math problems. "Alright, when you finish, I want you to change [papers] with a friend." She has to leave the class for a minute to check on some noise outside on the grounds. There is more talking now, moderately loud. They pass papers back and forth. Some of the kids begin checking their answers against each other. (Math, Grade 4, Ewasse)
Cooperative Individualism	When the teacher asks Matias a question he can't answer, his two friends look through their books to help him find the answer. They find it before he can think of it and tell it to him, which he then gives to the patiently waiting teacher. This seems to be acceptable, since it is done openly. (Spelling, Grade 4, Bialla)

When I took these initial sets of notes, I was not looking for "competitive individualism" or "cooperative individualism." These categories came to me as I read and reread my initial observation material and kept noticing that there seemed to be two very different messages given out to the students by the teachers about whether or not schooling was to be thought of as a place that rewarded individual competition (as, for example, the tough examination system seemed to imply) or a place that allowed for cooperative peer learning. Because I had done my homework (as outlined in chapters 2, 3, and 4) I was able to "recognize" that the contradiction I was observing in the classrooms in many ways replicated the broader social struggles then present in Papua New Guinea between the desire to shift to a "modern" political economy based upon capitalistic principles of individual competition (e.g., in regard to competitive access to well paid wage work as well as privately owned means of production) and at the same time a desire to maintain many of the principles of older cultural values that universally stressed (despite cultural differences among populations) that individual efforts had to benefit the group as a whole (e.g., the family, the lineage) if they were to be socially acceptable. Coding my notes in this fashion also allowed me to see that while there were many examples of each kind of hidden curriculum situation, the evidence coded as "competitive individualism" occurred in far greater numbers and with much greater frequency (e.g., in the duration of a single lesson) than the evidence that I coded as "cooperative individualism." Eventually, I noticed similar patterns of dominant/subordinate pairings of coded material for several themes and this became part of a larger analysis that suggested to me that hidden curriculum in West New Britain could be divided between what I came to call primary forms of hidden curriculum versus secondary forms of hidden curriculum (e.g., Fife 1992b). The primary form was tied to a dominant theme of social change that was itself linked to the emerging political economy of capitalistic social relations, while the secondary form was tied to the desire to hang onto values that resonated with the customary concerns of village Papua New Guinea. This understanding allowed me to see why some teachers, at least some of the time, allowed or created these secondary forms of hidden curriculum in their classrooms—as a kind of nostalgic expression that gave a certain emotional satisfaction in the face of the overwhelming educational messages that they were expected to project regarding the "need" for a new kind of Papua New Guinea, one that was rooted in competitive social relations, a neocolonial form of bureaucratic government, and a market-based economy. It is through coding our notes that we can see that what at first seems to be individual differences in specific teacher and student performances or even simple idiosyncratic behaviors can actually often be tied to much larger social and cultural patterns affecting the educational process. Again, this method of coding notes and building a theoretically informed analysis that is tied firmly to the information that you collect during fieldwork can be used for any kind of ethnographic subject.

The School as a Whole

I would suggest that a somewhat shorter period of time (approximately one week for each school being studied) be spent doing initial unfocused observations in relation to the school as a whole (i.e., outside of individual classrooms). What happens at recess, for example? How do students interact with each other and with educators in corridors, hallways, or along school paths that lead to and from classrooms? Describe the school setting itself. Is the schoolyard fenced in? How many buildings are there and how are they arranged? Are there external and/or internal signs, decorations, notices, and so forth on or in the school building(s)? Try to look at the school with new eyes. How might a teacher, or a pupil, or a parent view it? Try to put yourself in the place of one of these categories of persons and then reconsider what the school might look like from that perspective. This kind of a "step" system of observation, in which the researcher moves from the smaller to the larger context within the micro level of field research, can also be used in virtually any kind of ethnographic field situation. For example, when conducting fieldwork in a home for the aged in Southwestern Ontario, I began my observations in the individual rooms that two to four seniors shared, moved on to public spaces such as the recreation area and hallways, and finally considered the rest of the institutional home (including the outside grounds). Most research spaces can be divided up into an imaginary set of boundaries, moving from the most individual and intimate of places to the most public—and hence conceptualized in this manner for the purposes of an initial set of general observations.

Why would a researcher want this kind of general information (e.g., about the school as a whole)? Again, I prefer to answer this type of a question with a specific example. I have already noted earlier in the book about how the regimented ways in which students were "assembled" prior to the beginning of each day reminded me of earlier archival evidence concerning missionary and militaristic styles of school formations. In this fashion, I was able to suggest a linkage between contemporary "secular" schools in West New Britain and much older forms of missionary-run schools in relation to the use of bodily discipline exerted on the students—even though the teachers themselves expressed no awareness of the origins of this continuing pattern of behavior. I did not, of course, base this conclusion on only one or two contemporary observations. Because I had relegated a certain amount of time for the general observation of school life, my notes were full of similar observations regarding this missionary/militaristic style of disciplining students, as in the following notes:

> Outside Assembly. The students begin by marching around the flagpole, led by a senior female teacher. She gives orders as they go: "Left, right, left, right, left . . ., about turn, left, right, left . . ." The children march by classes and rows. "Alright, by this time there should be no talking. Fall in behind your markers please." The children bunch up into squares behind previously fixed rows. "No talking, I haven't said you could talk! Okay everybody, mark time. Stop and fold your arms. Bow your head. Alright, let's say your morning prayer." (Morning Assembly, Kimbe)

The actual fieldnote in which the above excerpt is based upon goes on for pages, as do many other similar descriptions of not only assemblies but also other forms of similar behavior, such as physical education classes that are held outside in the schoolyard. Each of these descriptions is not necessarily important in and of itself. What makes this kind of behavior important, for example, is: (1) that many examples combine to show a repetitive pattern of disciplinary behaviour, (2) that this pattern of educator/student interaction has a long history in Papua New Guinea (going all the way back to the first missionaries who began the school systems), and (3) that this pattern has important parallels to patterns of behavior that can be found inside of the classrooms of West New Britain that involve teaching content. In regard to the latter point, take the following excerpt from my fieldnotes regarding a language class as an example:

> The lesson is about forming sentences using certain types of construction. "Okay, this week we are practicing using don't and doesn't. Who can give me a word we can use to start our sentence for don't?" She accepts various words from the class. "What about doesn't?" Again, the same thing happens. "Yes, alright. Group leaders stand up at the front." Two girls and three boys move up to take their places at the front of the room. "Okay, those people at the front when you are talking, stand still. Speak up." Each group leader takes turns forming sentences using the words for the week. The teacher drills each of them several times. "Alright, stop. Go to your places (meaning move back into the groups sitting in lines on the floor). Okay, start. Group leaders make sure you listen carefully to what your group says." She goes around [the room], checking and listening as groups practice under the direction of the group leader. (English, Grade 2, Bialla)

Notice the very strict lines of hierarchy (with group leaders acting as a kind of classroom "sergeant") and the importance placed upon uniform and disciplined actions. Again, my research notes have many similar examples from the classrooms of all three of the community schools in the study. As in the grade six Expressive Arts teacher at Bialla community school who was teaching his students how to "make a flower" by marking a starting point on the paper and then tracing around the bottom of a bottle that had one edge placed upon the point. "There are two rules," he told the class, "always moving anti-clockwise [to trace around the bottle] and stick to the starting point." Walking around the classroom, the teacher told several students that they were "wrong" and made them erase their work and begin again because they had not traced in an anticlockwise direction—even though the final results in relation to the "drawing" were exactly the same. This example is very similar to the grade three expressive arts teacher at Kimbe community school who told her pupils that they were going to draw a tulip. She began by strongly emphasizing to the children how to do each step "in order" on the chalkboard and then told them that they had to copy her exactly, stating "two leaves, not one leaf and not three leaves. When you are finished, you can color it. But remember, what color are leaves?" The class responded with a loud "GREEN!" "That's right, not purple, not yellow, eh John?" The class laughed loudly at this reference to John's propensity for not following instructions exactly and for apparently not knowing the "correct" color of leaves.

The above examples are especially important as they indicate that students are subjected to strict intellectual discipline (parallel to the fashion of subjecting their bodies to strict, almost militaristic discipline in morning assemblies) even in classes that are not considered to be of primary importance, such as expressive arts class. My research notes for lessons in mathematics, language arts, and science are bulging with similar examples of strict hierarchies and rigid notions of "correct" forms of learning behaviour. Most language arts teachers, for example, seemed to believe that the only "correct" form of interpretation regarding short stories were the ones printed in their teaching instruction manuals. Novel interpretations from students were usually labeled as being incorrect and not accepted as having any validity. For example, I watched on several different days in a single math class as one particularly gifted student was told over and over again by his teacher that his math answers were "wrong," because the student had worked out his own method for arriving at the correct final answer for the math problems and had not strictly followed the methods set out by the teacher on the board. The teacher often embarrassed this boy by referring to him as a "bighead" and quite forcibly erasing the answers from his sheet of paper and telling him to "do it again correctly."

It should be clear, then, that observations made in the school itself, such as those I made above regarding the militaristic nature of morning assembly, can be combined with observations inside of the classroom to form a more comprehensive analysis (in this case, one about the importance of the hidden curriculum of bodily and hence intellectual "discipline"). In a similar manner, the researcher also needs to move outside of the school to take broader educational contexts into account.

Outside of the School

Parent–Teacher and Other Extracurricular Venues

It is common to have meetings between teachers and parents, between teachers and teachers (e.g., from different schools), between Head Teachers (also known as Head Masters or Principals in some places) from different schools, between teachers and/or parents and school board members, and between all of the above and representatives of the provincial (state) or federal Ministry of Education and other similar offices. It is important to conduct participant-observation at as many of these venues as possible. Meetings may be about obvious educational issues, such as the annual parent–teacher assembly, or they may involve less formal events such as an Intra-School Sports Day or a day of Cultural Celebration. Wherever educators meet with other members of society, the researcher can learn something of value about educational issues and relate this new knowledge to what he or she has been learning about the more direct aspects of education as it occurs inside of classrooms and schools. Of course, similar relationships and meetings are equally relevant to a project when studying a hospital setting, a local small-business voluntary association, or an indigenous activist group. In this period of general observations, the focus is upon the kinds of relationships that exist between those involved at the most basic level of the local group (e.g., teachers and pupils or the members of a local naturalists club) and others who, though not involved with the group on a daily basis, remain critical to it.

As usual, a specific example will best illustrate the value of participant-observation involving nonschool educational activities (or other similar situations). This example comes from my attendance at the annual board of management (what might be called a school board in other countries) meeting between board members, teachers, and parents of the children attending Kimbe community school. The meeting took place on a Friday afternoon and involved between eighty and one hundred people—occurring in the open air of the schoolyard itself (in which parents and teachers sat on the ground, while the board members sat on chairs at a small table while the chairman used a microphone especially set up for the occasion). Among many other issues was a consideration of whether or not to raise school fees (fees paid by parents for each child attending the community school) for the next year. One parent, dressed only in a ragged pair of shorts and no shirt, which was in sharp contrast to the "Sunday best" clothes worn by most of the other parents, stood up to speak on the issue.

> He tried to explain to the school board, using only Tok Pisin, that he had a number of children in school and lived in a village just outside of Kimbe. He did not have a job in the cash economy and it was hard for him to pay for school fees. Some parents objected to his use of Tok Pisin, and shouted out "use English, use English." He asked that the board consider cutting all school fees because parents like him, who had no job, couldn't afford to pay them. This was greeted with a lot of angry shouting by other parents: "Go back to the village!" "Bush Kanaka!" "How can we have a good school then?" He sat down quickly and looked quite shamed. The chairman who was running the meeting quickly passed onto voting whether or not to keep the fees as they were, or to raise them, ignoring the villager's suggestion to abolish them. The majority voted to keep them as they are for another year. (Board of Management Annual Meeting, Kimbe C.S.)

This and many other examples of hostility being expressed toward what are thought of as "village" values as opposed to "modern urban values" as they are displayed at public meetings can be compared quite easily to similar attitudes presented daily by school teachers inside of the classrooms of West New Britain concerning the supposed "backwardness" of rural peoples versus the "modern" outlook of urban groups. Often specific cultural groups, such as the Nakanai of West New Britain or the Simbu of the Highland areas of the country, are implied to be exemplars of "primitive, rural thinking." A few examples of how these dichotomies unfold in the classroom are as follows.

> The teachers sometimes begin class in the morning by asking the students if they've heard any interesting news items in the last few days. This morning a girl got up and gave the news that a Simbu had attacked and killed a boy with an axe at Mosa [an oil palm project area in the province]. The teacher responds by saying: "Yes, this is stupid! Only stupid primitive people do such things, hurt others. Is that good?" The class responds by shouting a very loud "No!" (News, Grade 4, Ewasse C.S.)

In another school, community life classes make use of kits that contain a series of pictures and category headings. Students are divided up into "ability groups," given a kit, and attempt to match pictures to category headings (e.g., Town Area, Coastal Area, Swampy Area, Mountain Area, etc.).

> The kids in all of the groups match the picture of a Simbu male to "Mountain Area," even though many Simbu live in Highland towns [i.e., Town Area] and in the flat coastal oil palm areas of West New Britain. They match a picture of a car, as well as a picture of a newer style house, to "Town Area." Even though some villagers who live along the rural north coast Kimbe to Bialla road area also have cars. The teacher and a group of students argue about where to put a picture of a large ship. Students say the "Coastal Area," but the teacher demands that it be placed under "Town Area." Town Area also has all of the factories, large stores, and banks put under it. (Community Life, Grade 4, Bialla C.S.)

Notice how what most Papua New Guineans view as the "good things" of "modern life" are generally associated with urban areas above, as well as how the Simbu (notoriously thought of by non-Simbu as a "primitive group") are resolutely associated with the rural mountain areas. Researchers who have done their homework should not be surprised in finding a strong split between the portrayal of "urban" versus "rural" life, as such a dichotomy would have been prefigured in a reading of the historical literature about the creation of Papua New Guinea as a nation and the emerging distinctions between what is increasingly assumed to be the good life of "modern, urban Papua New Guinea" versus the backward life of what is increasingly thought of as "traditional, primitive, rural Papua New Guinea." Given the vast majority of urban parents' attitudes, as they are displayed at such venues as board of management meetings and teacher/parent meetings, it is not surprising to see similar attitudes displayed by teachers inside of the classrooms. Both of these trends are, as noted above, linked with much larger historical patterns in Papua New Guinea. The importance of the urban versus rural (often couched as modern versus traditional) issue will be underlined as it reappears later in this book. Suffice to say here that it appeared constantly in both school and nonschool settings in West New Britain (see Fife 1992). One of the more extreme examples of it, and behavior that suggests how serious an issue this is in contemporary Papua New Guinea, came in the school fights between rival high school groups that often occurred after school dances. At one fight that I witnessed from a distance, a small group of local boys (who were actually from several different cultural groups who lived in and around the Kimbe area of the province) rushed another group of boys as the first group's leader shouted "Fucking Tolai, think they're so smart!" As the group of visiting high school students (who were also actually from a variety of cultural groups) from the neighboring province of East New Britain counterattacked the local group, one of their members shouted "Fucking Nakanai, know they're so stupid!" As a small number of teachers were nearby, this fight was quickly broken up—though many other similar fights have had much more destructive consequences. The Tolai people come from a historically missionized area of East New Britain and are associated by many Papua New Guineans with very successfully adapting to "modern urban ways" and to the cash economy. The Nakanai are in some ways seen as the local West New Britain equivalent of the notorious Highland Simbus (also known as Chimbus) and both groups are associated by many Papua New Guineas with being "backward, primitive, violent, lazy, traditional villagers." These are of course stereotypes, but they remain powerful symbols of contemporary life in the country and, as we saw above in the extra-school situation of a dance, become played out in the educational experience of West New Britain children.

Focused Methods of Observation

After researchers have completed the initial period of evidence collection and analysis, they will want to move into a more advanced period of focused participant-observation. This is most important in terms of the classroom observations, though focused observation may also be used both in the school as a whole and in the content of other educational events as well. In this section of the chapter, I concentrate upon showing researchers ways to do focused note-taking for the classroom, as well as how to deal with the reliability issue in qualitative research through the use of counting schedules. These methods can be adapted by the researcher for focused note-taking on other occasions such as meetings (whether a parent–teacher event or a local political rally) as well.

Focused Note-Taking

Once a researcher has isolated what seems to be a widespread pattern of behavior he or she will wish to confirm the importance of this pattern through classroom observations that focus upon only one or two specific types of interaction at a time. This form of observation is done in order to obtain a much greater number of examples of similar forms of behavior so that the researcher may: (1) saturate this category of behavior by recording samples that show the widest possible variety of interactions that occur within that single category or pattern of action, (2) record behavior that originally appears to be similar but upon later analysis may turn out to be different from the "type" pattern itself, and (3) determine how frequent and widespread the behaviors are and in which contexts these patterns tend to appear in the classroom. The importance of this list of reasons becomes clearer when the reader reaches part C of the book, which deals with ethnographic analysis and writing. All the researcher needs to consider at this point of the book is the importance that focused observations have for the question of ethnographic reliability. The earlier form of participant-observation that I taught the reader contains no means by which to judge the relative importance of the specific patterns of interaction that s/he has isolated in the initial coding of her general ethnographic observations from the classroom. In order to provide yourself with such material, the researcher needs to begin by selecting a specific pattern of behavior that s/he wishes to investigate, decide upon a specific time period (e.g., two hours per classroom) for focused observations, and do these observations in every school within the study. I would also suggest that each pattern is checked for a variety of grades (e.g., grades two, four, and six) at each school and for a variety of subjects (e.g., Language Arts, Math, Community Studies). In my experience, patterns often vary between grade levels and between different subjects.

A specific example of focused observation will help explain this method in more detail and illustrate the advantages of it. Because it takes a considerable amount of time to do focused observations (so many hours in each classroom, of each selected grade, in every school) I often chose to focus upon two patterns or categories of classroom interactions at the same time, especially if I thought that these two patterns were closely related to each other. I, therefore, use this method of dual focusing as my example—although the individual researcher may choose to focus upon one pattern at a time in her own work.

In my initial coding of my general classroom observations, I created a category that I referred to as "hierarchy" and another category that I referred to as "authority."

Hierarchy, I defined as the overall effect of organizing education along a system of ranking that extended from the federal Minister of Education to the provincial and local authorities responsible for individual schools, to teachers, and finally to the students themselves. Schools in West New Britain, for example, are each divided into a hierarchy that includes the head teacher, senior teachers, junior teachers, and students. Students are themselves commonly further organized into "ability groups" within the classroom, each group having its own student leader.

Authority, in turn, refers to the assumed naturalness of this arrangement. In a particular situation, an individual will be given (or will take) the "authority" that is "due to" him or her because of the position s/he plays in the organization of schooling rather that because of any specific personal ability. In a sense, this is what Pierre Bourdieu and J.C. Passeron (1977) refer to as "pedagogic authority"— the unquestioned place or social role that receives respect due to its placement in the educational system.

How, then, did my two sample categories become manifested in the classroom? After I became aware of the categories through my initial analytical coding, I initiated a period of time at each of the schools in which I specifically looked for examples of "hierarchy" and "authority" in the classroom. Let's begin with an example from the category of hierarchy. Many classrooms in West New Britain community schools are decorated with magazine cutouts depicting scenes or items from the "modern world," such as automobiles, airplanes, professional soccer or rugby teams at play, and so forth. Along with these, it is also common to see visual representations of social organizations such as the educational system and the various levels of the government upon on the walls of the classrooms. For example:

> Classroom description. On the front wall there is a large blackboard, with ruled-off sections for "Teacher's Corner," "Notices" and "Policies." There is also a "Duty Roster" printed on cardboard paper taped up on the wall [for student duties]. A similar poster shows the "supervising Structure" of Kimbe Community School (from headmaster down to junior teacher). Class rules and rules for marking are on paper above the blackboard. [O]n the left hand side of the front wall there are the Provincial Governments and the Premier of each Province. Beside that, the teacher has put the members of the West New Britain Provincial Government, with cabinet ministers clearly indicated. Beside that, on the left wall, is another chart that outlines the structure of the WNB [West New Britain] government. (Grade 4 classroom, Kimbe C.S.)

These are common "decorations" in classrooms in West New Britain (for example, I recorded intricately detailed handmade charts of every level of the educational system in several classrooms during my focused observations—information that I overlooked before I began specifically searching for it). Other classrooms had posted all of the levels of government, from national to local levels, and the relative rank of office holders in each system. The overall collective message embedded in these practices seems to be quite simple: contemporary Papua New Guineans live in a county and in a social world that contains an intricate series of hierarchies and they therefore "need" to know how to recognize and deal with them.

These are not empty forms, put there solely to appease school inspectors or local government officials. My focused notes also include numerous examples of students memorizing these lessons as a normal part of Community Studies. A surprising number of students were amazingly adept at reeling off the intricate authority structure of the local government, for example, often including the names of each office holder and his[2] place of origin on the island of New Britain.

The lesson of hierarchy, however, is most forcefully brought home to the students in the form of the everyday authority lessons taught in the hidden curriculum of classroom instruction. It is at this level that they most strongly experience the lessons of going along with, or fighting against, pedagogic author-ity. The most important lesson of course concerns the assumed relationship that is supposed to exist between the teacher and the students in the classroom. The fact that the teacher has a "right" to constantly correct both the pupil's work and the pupil's behaviour, while the student has no similar right in relation to the teacher, repeatedly reinforces the idea that an order-giving/order-taking hierarchy is part of the "natural order of things," as in the following two examples.

> The students are working in what is called the "Pre-Writing Activity Book," put out by the Department of Education. [T]he book begins by having the students trace pictures, then colour them in. Eventually, more abstract patterns are traced, moving left to right. And then eventually they move on to tracing out the alphabet. Today, the students are working on a pig. In response to several students, who finish early and ask: "Can we do more," the teacher says: "No, trace the pig, that's all." As the children are colouring the pigs in, the teacher stops and stands up from looking at a pupil's work and says in a loud voice to the entire class: "Eh, have you ever seen a red pig!" Students laugh, and several call out a loud "NO!" (Pre-Writing, Grade 1, Kimbe C. S.)

> She [the teacher] is teaching the class how to pronounce certain sounds: fun, run, sun, etc. She will say a word out loud, such as "run," and then ask "What sounds the same?" Individual children often call out a correct answer, but she persists in waiting for the person she herself chooses to answer "correctly." (English, Grade 2, Bialla C.S.)

My notes are full of examples of teachers refusing to accept any initiative for learn-ing if it came from the pupils themselves. During one particularly memorable Math lesson at Kimbe community school, the children were learning how to do basic arithmetic by arranging sticks and stones according to a pattern laid out by the teacher on the floor. Each pattern represented a counting problem that the students had to solve. While walking around the room to check how her students were doing, the teacher came across a boy who was making up "extra" problems for himself with the sticks and stones. "Eh, what are you doing. These aren't the problems." The boy explained that he was finished and showed the teacher the neatly arranged sticks and stones that he had compiled for the assigned problems. "I'm finished," was all he said. "No, you're not," replied the teacher, while erasing the assigned problems by scattering them with his foot. "Now you have to do them again, bighead."

By this point, the potential researcher might be wondering "but, how does one know when to record information during focused observation?" That is, how can we possibly know ahead of time that a behavior is going to be an example of a spe-cific category? The answer of course is that he or she could not possibly know the significance of a set of behaviors ahead of time. Recording occurs in two ways. The first and most common method is to record the information immediately after observing the pattern of behavior—when it becomes obvious that this may well be an example of category X type of interaction. This is not as difficult as it sounds. With practice, most people can become quite adept at recording detailed descriptions, including direct quotations, only minutes after something occurs. Because the researcher is no longer recording almost everything that she notices in the classroom, as was done during the general observation period of the research, s/he is free to observe classroom behavior in a much more concentrated fashion. Details that went unrecorded because of the original emphasis upon writing while observing now come into a more complete relief through focused observation. The result is normally a more detailed set of evidence for eventual analytical use.

The second method for recording involves what we might think of as researcher's intuition. I found that after I began my focused observation on a specific pattern (or pair of patterns) for a while, I often intuitively knew as a pattern of interaction began to unfold that it might turn out to be something that I wished to record. In order to make use of a more focused method of recording, researchers need to learn to trust their own abilities to "recognize" significant evidence as it unfolds before them. A scholar who is uncomfortable with the idea that research intuition will often tell one when to begin writing notes during focused classroom observations need not use this method of recording and is of course free to remain solely with the first method of note-taking (what we might identify as the slightly-after-the-fact method). Was I always correct in my suppositions about what might prove to be "significant" information as it began to occur before me? No, of course not. But, I was correct the vast majority of the time—certainly often enough to come to trust my own judgment about when to begin recording during interactions as opposed to waiting for them to completely end before my note-taking began. The worst that can happen is that you spend some time recording material that is not strictly necessary. A few extra notes will not hurt you and you never know what interesting patterns you might reveal at a later period in these "useless" notes as you reread them.

Rather than offer more analysis here of the importance of the focused observation of such categories of behavior as "hierarchy" or "authority," I prefer at this point to move on to a consideration of counting schedules and the role that they can play in ensuring the reliable collection of ethnographic data. Much more is said about the analysis of focused information in chapter 8.

Counting Schedules (the Question of Reliability)

Focused note-taking is itself one way of checking how reliable one's initial analysis of educational patterns are during the opening stages of general participant-observation. It will soon become obvious when the researcher returns to each school to conduct focused note-taking about a specific pattern whether or not that behavior is as significant as s/he first thought. If the category of behavior only appears once or twice more then it is likely of no great significance; if it shows up regularly over a wide variety of contexts then it is likely a pattern of major importance. The art of analysis comes into play when patterns show up sometimes (but not other times), in some places (but not other places). When in doubt, keep recording and leave the analysis for later.

Even with focused note-taking I was not always satisfied that I was able to answer the question of whether a specific type or pattern of behavior was of true significance. This is a standard problem among qualitative researchers—it might be thought of as the reliability issue. How do we know when behavior forms a significant social or cultural pattern? We cannot fall back upon the same tools used by quantitative researchers (i.e., the use of statistical tests to tell us whether or not a pattern is statistically "significant"). However, we can follow the advice that the well known Canadian anthropologist Richard Salisbury often suggested to his listeners: "When in doubt, count." Counting does not of course provide us with the same kind of statistical assurance that some quantitative researchers obtain from their use of true statistical testing (counting, for example, does not imply random sampling), but it does provide the qualitative researcher with yet another check on their ethnographic reasoning and is therefore a useful (and easy to use) technique for qualitative research. As before, I of course illustrate the use of this technique with specific examples from my own work.

In order to try to confirm my suspicions about what I considered to be important patterns of ethnographic evidence that I had gathered during both generalized and focused note-taking in Papua New Guinea, I created a technique that I refer to as "counting schedules." This method is quite time consuming and should only be used to answer important ethnographic questions. For example, I had three questions that I wanted to try and answer through the use of counting schedules. The first one involved the issue of whether there was a substantial difference between the use of Tok Pisin by teachers in rural versus urban schools, and whether that difference changed from the lower to the higher grades. My confusion in this case stemmed from having witnessed very few instances of the use of Tok Pisin during my generalized period of note-taking. Focused note-taking did not turn up many more examples of teachers using the *lingua franca* Tok Pisin (as opposed to the official language of education in Papua New Guinea, English), which was officially forbidden for use inside of classrooms. I became puzzled by this, because my notes did not coincide with the information that I had previously been given by several very experienced field researchers (who had worked in both West New Britain and/or in other parts of the country). They assured me that Tok Pisin was used widely for instruction in rural classrooms. In order to try to answer the question of the rural versus urban use of Tok Pisin inside of classrooms, I selected one of the two urban schools (Kimbe) to compare to a single rural school (Ewasse—a collector school which serviced a cluster of several villages located within a few hours walk of the town of Bialla). My plan was to sit for several hours in at least three grade levels for each of these two schools and simply record (i.e., count) every use of Tok Pisin by either the teacher or the pupils. I soon abandoned this work, as it very quickly became apparent that Tok Pisin was seldom used by teachers or students at any grade level in either school. I decided to quit this work after spending two full days on it at each school, as it was obvious that there was no need for further confirmation—a near zero count after approximately 12 hours of observation at each school in different grades was more than sufficient. Either my colleagues were mistaken in their observations at their own field sites (none had specifically conducted educational research at their locations), or my rural school was not sufficiently "rural" enough to register this language pattern. Negative confirmations are of course just as important as positive ones, and by sitting down and counting Tok Pisin language usage in these classrooms I was able to put to rest (at least as far as my own research area was concerned) an issue that was taken to be "common sense" by most noneducational ethnographic researchers who worked in that region.

Two other ethnographic questions for which I used counting schedules resulted in very positive results. One question involved the issue of student "discipline." I had recorded quite a few examples of disciplinary behavior in both my generalized and focused observation periods and was eager to answer the following two questions: (1) did students internalize these disciplinary actions in such a way that they did not "need" to be disciplined as frequently in the higher grades as in the lower grades in the community schools? and (2) were there any substantial differences between teachers in their preference for disciplining individual students versus the class as a whole? Both of these questions came from a careful reading and preliminary analysis of the results of the generalized and focused periods of participant observation. The third major issue that I wished to investigate involved questions about gender inequality in the classrooms. In particular, I wanted to know the following: (1) were there any differences between the ways male and female teachers interacted with their male and female students? (2) were there any differences in the ways boys and girls were treated during instruction in specific subject areas (e.g., Math versus English classes), and (3) was there a general pattern of favoring boys over girls in the classroom? Each of these issues turned up interesting patterns. The gender issue, however, involved somewhat complicated numerical "corrections" due to the different enrolment rates of boys and girls at each grade level and I would like to offer the reader a more straightforward example of how to construct a counting schedule here. I have, therefore, chosen to focus in this section on the example of constructing a counting schedule for the issue of disciplinary actions inside of classrooms (for the gender issue, see Fife 1992).

In order to answer the questions about discipline in the classroom that I asked above, I first had to define what "discipline" meant behaviorally so that I could count occurrences of it being applied. Because I had no video equipment with me, I decided to exclude the nuances of bodily corrections (e.g., a teacher subtly leaning into the back of a boy to signal him to stop talking) and instead concentrated on the much easier to record examples of verbal corrections. For my purposes, I defined what I came to call "disciplinary action" as any verbal command, instruction, or response by the teacher that indicated a negative evaluation of a student's or students' behaviors, which also in turn led to a relatively immediate response by the student or students (i.e., a response that indicated that an effective communication had taken place).

Given the nature of classes in community schools it was not possible to hold observation times perfectly even across schools or even across different grades in the same school. As you see in the tables below, I therefore chose to ensure that each grade in every school was observed for between seven and eight hours. This requires strictly recording the periods of observation within research notes. What keeping time does is allow the researcher to even out the differences in classroom observation times by dividing the disciplinary actions by the actual observation time in order to arrive at a figure that yields actions per hour for each classroom (see the tables 5.1 and 5.2). This makes these actions more comparable with each other, both inside of a school and across schools.

In order to actually do the counting, I simply sat in the back of each classroom with two sheets of paper. One sheet had the heading "Disciplinary Actions— Class," and the other the heading "Disciplinary actions—Pupil." I made single strokes for each action observed, arranging the strokes in groups of five for easy addition. As in the following example of twenty-three disciplinary actions involving individual students.

Disciplinary Actions—Pupil

Time Observation Began: 1:15 p.m.   Time Observation Ended: 2:18 p.m.
Disciplinary Actions: IIIII   IIIII   IIIII   IIIII   III

In the table that lists results below, "class" refers to the number of times the class as a whole is disciplined (e.g., "There is too much noise in here!"); while

Table 5.1   Disciplinary Action in the Classroom

	Grade Two		Grade Four		Grade Six	
	Class	Pupil	Class	Pupil	Class	Pupil
Kimbe Community School						
English	39	31	11	10	10	12
Math	12	10	0	9	1	0
General	23	22	5	3	2	5
Total	74	63	16	22	13	17
Bialla Community School						
English	25	80	20	24	3	1
Math	11	28	3	4	0	2
General	7	32	4	8	1	1
Total	44	140	27	36	4	4
Ewasse Community School						
English	45	68	9	8	7	5
Math	6	13	0	4	2	3
General	7	8	2	1	1	1
Total	58	89	11	13	10	9

Table 5.2   Disciplinary Actions per Teaching Hour

	Total/Grade	Observation Hours	Actions/Hour
Kimbe C. S.			
Grade Two	137	7.6	18.0
Grade Four	38	7.8	4.9
Grade Six	30	7.9	3.8
Bialla C. S.			
Grade Two	184	7.8	23.6
Grade Four	63	7.3	8.6
Grade Six	8	7.3	1.1
Ewasse C. S.			
Grade Two	147	7.9	18.6
Grade Four	24	7.8	3.1
Grade Six	19	7.9	2.4

"pupil" refers to the number of times individual students are disciplined (e.g., "John, stop that right now!"). "English" refers to English Language Studies; "Math" to Mathematics; and "General" refers to General Studies (a mixture of community studies, history, and other forms of "social" studies at the various grades). "Total" of course refers to the total of all of the subjects together for that grade.

This table of results allows me to answer the second question that I asked myself earlier: Were there any substantial differences between teachers in their preference for disciplining individual students versus the class as a whole? The answer to this question is "yes," there were substantial differences between individual teachers in this regard. For example, the table shows that the grade two teacher at Bialla Community School strongly favored disciplining individual students rather than the class as a whole, the grade two teacher at Ewasse Communty School moderately favored disciplining individuals over the class, while the grade two teacher at Kimbe Community school actually slightly pre-ferred to discipline the class as a whole over disciplining individuals. In this way, the researcher can make qualitative comparisons (remember, these are not "statis-tically valid" numbers, but rather further confirmation of the patterns of behavior found through ethnographic research) between the same teacher for different subjects, between teachers in different class grades within the same school, between teachers in the same grades in different schools, and so forth. What we are doing in this kind of analysis is looking for the ways that smaller patterns combine to form larger patterns. For example, how the category of "disciplinary actions" can be expanded beyond an individual teacher or student's configuration to form more collective configurations. Again, substantially more is said about building analytical levels in this fashion in chapter 8.

The next table combines information from table 5.1 in a new way in order to answer the first question about disciplinary actions asked earlier in this chapter: Do students internalize these disciplinary actions in such as way that they do not "need" to be disciplined as frequently in the higher grades as in the lower grades in the community schools? In table 5.2 "total/grade" equals the total number of disciplinary actions by a teacher regardless of the subject these occurred in or whether or not they were directed at the class as a whole or to individual students; "observation hours" refers to the total number of hours for which I observed this particular teacher (grade); and "actions/hour" equals the total number of disciplinary actions divided by the observation hours in order to give the average number of actions per hour. Note that I decided not to divide "observation hours" up into both hours and minutes, but instead converted minutes into a percentage of an hour. For example, 7 hours and 54 minutes of observation would become 7.9 hrs. of observation time. Minutes are rounded to the nearest tenth (e.g. both 54 minutes and 55 minutes would come out as 9/10 of an hour when rounded). This is desirable to keep the figures relatively simple and permissible because absolute numbers have no special meaning in a counting schedule (remember, this is a qualitative check on ethnographic evidence, not a statistical test). What we are after here are relative numbers (i.e., numbers that can be compared to each other in a relative manner). Given the difficulty of gaining completely accurate figures for observation times (the most conscientious researcher is likely to be off a minute or two in recording his or her observation times) rounding numbers off likely gives just as accurate a picture of the situation as dividing hours into smaller fractions. For the same reasons, "actions/hour" are also rounded to the nearest tenth.

We can see from table 5.2 that the answer to the question posed above is "yes." Students as a whole do receive much less overt verbal "discipline" by their teachers as they move upward in the grades. This consistent and dramatic reduction in disciplinary actions would seem to indicate that students in some sense internalize this "discipline" in such a way that makes it less necessary for teachers to verbally discipline them in the higher grades. It can be suggested that it might not mean this at all, but could simply be an indicator that teachers (for whatever reason) lose interest in disciplining students in the higher grades. As will become clear in chapter 6, which deals with interviewing, teacher interviews indicate quite clearly that this is not the case and that grade six teachers are just as likely as the earlier grade teachers to feel that discipline is a primary consideration when evaluating student performances. In fact, teachers are often rewarded with assignments to teach grade six classes because of their reputations as disciplinarians. As usual, it is important to remember that it is this wider context of ethnographic knowledge that allows the researcher to carefully interpret results gained from such techniques as the use of a counting schedule, rather than something "inherent" in the data itself. This is equally true of information gathered through interviewing techniques.

Again I would like to remind the reader that, with a little imagination, the technique of counting schedules could be used to check ethnographic results in a wide variety of situations. In a study that involves tourists who visit national parks, for example, the researcher might find that his/her general fieldnotes seem to indicate that there are decided gender preferences in relation to specific hiking trails in the park. In order to check this observation it would be a relatively straightforward matter to set oneself up in a specific location along a trail and count the number of male and female (and perhaps adults versus children) who make us of a particular trail over a specific time period. These figures could then be compared for several trails that the researcher has identified as being "different" from each other (e.g., relatively level versus climbing trails; forested versus coastal trails; scenically diverse versus homogeneous trails that have one spectacular sight at the end; and so forth). The results of these counting schedules would, in turn, give new insight into the gendered use of park trails and suggest specific questions that could be explored further with individual tourists during formal and informal interview situations—which leads us to the next chapter of this book.

6

Interviewing

The Basics of Interviewing

Along with an eye for observation, it is necessary for an ethnographic researcher to develop an ear for interviewing. It is probably easiest to divide interviews up into three main types: structured interviews, semi-structured interviews, and unstructured interviews. Structured interviews, also commonly known as formal interviews, most often involve sitting down with an individual in order to elicit answers in such a manner as to render them translatable into numbers for the purpose of quantitative comparison (for good examples on how to do this see Weller 1998). As Fetterman (1989: 48) suggests, such interviews are "verbal approximations of a questionnaire with specific research goals." As such, fully structured interviews are not of any real interest to us here, as this book is concerned with the use of non-positivistic ethnographic research methods. I (along with most other ethnographers) do not agree with the falsely scientific agenda of forcing those with whom we do research to "answer" questions in such a way as to suggest that complex lives can be understood through a multiple choice questionnaire format (or its analog). Another way to think about this issue is to understand that the questions used during interviews are also some-times divided between what are called closed-ended questions and open-ended questions. Closed-ended questions give the person being interviewed only a very limited number of choices. An example of a closed-ended question might look like this: Which of the following best describes your reaction when a teacher openly corrects you in the classroom: (1) you become very uncomfortable, (2) you become somewhat uncomfortable, (3) it does not bother you at all. As you might expect, closed-ended questions are the kind of format that is nor-mally employed in structured interview situations. As I suggested above, ethno-graphic researchers are seldom interested in limiting the responses of the people we do research with in this manner. Ours is the art of the open-ended interview, or of asking questions in such a fashion that the person being interviewed has the "right" to interpret the question and take it any place he or she pleases. It might even be suggested that if the researcher comes from a developed coun-try such as Canada, the United States, or France, then the extensive use of closed-ended, structured interviewing methods in a developing country is in some ways a replication of the colonial or oppressor/oppressed relationships of the past (for a parallel argument regarding the methods of school instruction, see Freire 1983). Setting oneself up as an "authority" and suggesting that all research needs to consist of is a few weeks of structured interviewing in which a captive set of interviewees (such as school teachers or students) merely need to say that "Yes, a, or b, or c, or d, or e response captures my feelings, thoughts, and experiences exactly," is surely little different than former colonial administrators saying: "Yes, we know what is best for the indigenous population—all they have to do is agree to abide by our rules." It hardly seems worth doing the study if we are already assuming that we know so much about the research situation before the actual fieldwork that we can reduce the potential results to a handful of possibilities in preformulated interview questions. In other words, if we are already so knowledgeable that we can reduce answers to virtually yes or no formats, then why are we spending all of this money and our precious time in research? There are exceptions to this situation, such as when the researcher wishes to gather a basic demographic profile of a village or community, or when s/he wishes to conduct a household survey (e.g., recording the basic membership of each household). In cases such as those, a closed-ended structured interview can be a useful research tool.

Generally though, ethnographic researchers will prefer to make use of open-ended semi-structured or unstructured interview methods. Taking each of these in turn, we can begin to explore how they can be used in qualitative research. Before we do so, however, I want to remind the reader that these research methods are to be taken as examples and suggestions, rather than as a set of objective rules that, if followed, automatically result in "good research." Robert Levy and Douglas Hollan suggest that we should think of both observation and interviewing as akin to engaging in the performing arts. The relationship between a researcher and a book of research methods is, according to them, rather like that between a musician and a musical score. "This means that none of what follows is to be followed mechanically. It is rather to be taken as a series of examples . . . [T]hese methodological prescriptions are no more mechanical and positivistic than is a musical score for skilled performers" (Levy and Hollan 1998: 335). This chapter (and this book) is an attempt at helping the researcher become a skilled performer. Much like a musician, this will require hours, weeks, months and even years of practice. Methods are simply a place to begin that practice.

Semi-Structured Interviewing

In a sense, semi-structured interviews are an attempt to capture something of the "control" of structured interviews without the need to use closed-ended questions or force people into the role of a "respondent" rather than that of an "initiator" of information. Typically, such interviews involve a mildly formal setting (in the sense that the interviewer and interviewee sit down together in a quiet place and attempt to work their way through a specific list of questions brought by the interviewer to the situation). Semi-structured interviews are a chance to develop a conversation along one or more lines without most of the usual "chatter" (i.e., extraneous information) that accompanies such talk. At the same time, through the use of open-ended questions, the interviewee is given the opportunity to shape his or her own responses or even to change the direction of the interview altogether. The conversational metaphor (in the sense of a two-way dialogue rather than a one way interrogation) is so important to both semi-structured and unstructured interviews that Lynn Davies (1997: 135) prefers to use the term "structured conversation" rather than divide interviews up into their usual tripartite division (see earlier). As usual, the reader should get more of a sense of what this means through the use of specific examples, beginning with the use of semi-structured interviews.

As private conversations circumscribed from other social interactions, semi-structured interviews will not work with every type of person in all research contexts. For example, in my own work in Papua New Guinea I soon discovered that it was useless to attempt anything like a semi-structured interview with the young students who attended community schools in West New Britain. They were far too shy to say anything other than "yes," or "no" to an adult in a one-on-one formal situation (or at least to a strange, white researcher from a country that most of them had never heard of before). What did work with such children were group interviews, in which I might sit down at recess with a small group of playing or better yet talking children and begin to ask them (as a group) several contextually relevant questions. For example, "what do you like to do most during the recess period," or "what is your favorite subject in school?" The children were much less shy in a group and one child's answer would often set off the other students—who soon wanted to tell you why little Adam was either "right" or "wrong" about what he had just said. Group interviews have their own charm and often elicit information that is more social (i.e., shared) than the information that flows from one-on-one interview situations. At the same time, group interviews seldom result in the discussion of strongly held minority viewpoints and have a tendency to move toward consensus after an issue has been bandied about for a while. In short, group interviewing can add a new dimension to the more often used technique of interviewing individuals and in certain situations (such as that involving children, or in countries or areas in which it is inappropriate for a male/female researcher to be alone with a female/male interviewee) it may be the only way to conduct semi-structured interviews with members of specific social groups within a community. Many of the points that I am about to make with regard to specific research situations involving individual interviews can be modified and applied to group interview situations as well. One important issue, however, is that group interviews seem to work best with fewer questions. If a "typical" semi-structured interview with an individual involves ten to twelve questions, then four to six questions would work best for the group interview situation.

In chapter 4, I suggested that the researcher should think about conducting some brief interviews with politicians, government bureaucrats, and academics before proceeding to the actual field site itself. In many ways, unstructured interviews (see later) would work best at that preliminary stage. However, there may be reasons why the researcher decides to conduct semi-structured interviews with some of these individuals. One such reason would be that the scholar knows that s/he will not have time for interviews on his or her way out of the country and wishes to ask a specific individual about particular aspects of education while there is a chance to do so (e.g., officials of the ministry of education or high ranking educational bureaucrats might only be available to the researcher once because of their busy schedules and it might be necessary to make the most efficient use of this time through the device of a semi-structured interview format, followed by a little informal discussion if the situation permits). In any case, once a researcher arrives at the field site proper, there are sure to be government officials, upper level educational officials (such as Inspectors), headmasters, teachers, and perhaps parents and other community members that s/he wishes to interview more formally. It is best to attempt to construct a standard interview schedule, which can then be modified as needed for each type of social group being interviewed. For example, it is often possible to either re-use or simply modify a question that is appropriate for one group into a question that is appropriate for another group. This has the added advantage of gathering information on themes that may prove to be comparable between social groups. For instance, one question that I asked each community school teacher was the following: "Why do you think more male than female students continue on in their education, both in community schools and beyond them?" The exact same question could be and was used in my construction of an interview schedule for parents. The same or a similar question could also be used when interviewing government officials, and so on. Certain core questions should have broad applicability, while specific additional questions can be either deleted from or added to the interview schedule as needed for a specific group. To use another ethnographic example, in a study that I conducted in a home for the aged in southwestern Ontario, a question such as "What do you think is the main job of someone who works in the home" could be profitably asked of residents, part-time or full time staff, senior administrators, and even community volunteers. Whereas a question such as "Describe a typical day of living in the home," that was originally created for a resident interview, could very easily have the last part of the question retranslated as "working in the home" for a staff member, or "volunteering in the home" for a volunteer. However, a question such as "What is it like to share personal living quarters with a stranger" makes sense only for an interview with a resident of the home.

I would suggest that the standard interview schedule not be constructed until the scholar has spent at least several weeks in the field doing preliminary research. Ideally, the schedule could be written around the same time as the researcher finishes the period of general observations and is ready to move on to a more focused period of study (see chapter 5). To give the reader an idea of how to construct a standard interview schedule that is applicable for a wide variety of interviewees, here is the actual schedule that I used (and modified as needed) for research in West New Britain with school teachers, school administrators, government officials, and parents:

Standard Interview Schedule
Background Information
Name:
Education:
Home Village:
Job Title:
Married/Children:

Goals for Education
1. What do you think is the main purpose of community school education?

Problems in Education
2. What do you think is the biggest problem with community school education right now?
3. Many children leave community school before finishing grade six. Why do you think this happens?
4. Why do you think more male than female students continue on in their education, both in community schools and beyond them?
5. Many children who finish community school do not go on to high school. What chance do these children have for getting the kind of jobs they would like, or for living in the places where they would like to live?

Participation in Education
6. Who do you think should be most responsible for looking after the community schools, the government or the members of the community?
7. Do you think that community members, especially parents, should help decide what curriculum their children are taught in community schools? Why/Why not?
8. Is it important that parents pay school fees for their children? Why/why not?
9. Which courses do you think are most important in school? E.g. Science, Community Life, etc.?
10. Could you briefly describe what a good pupil is like? What about a pupil who is not very good?
11. Could you briefly describe what a good teacher is like? What about a teacher who is not very good?
12. Suppose your children have to make one of two choices. They can stay in their home village and live a more traditional way of life *or* they can go live in a town a long way from their home village in order to get a job in the cash economy. Which of these two choices would you want them to make? Why?

Extra Comments
Record comments that were made during the interview that are useful or interesting, but do not fit under any of the question headings above. Make sure to ask: Is there anything that I have forgotten to ask you that you think is important for me to know about education in West New Britain?

It is impossible for me to demonstrate to readers the many kinds of valuable information that can become available because of the use of semi-structured interview schedules. One small example will have to suffice. During the interviews that I conducted, a significant number of teachers indicated to me while answering question number four above (concerning why fewer females than males continue with their education) that many parents were concerned about the possibility of their daughters becoming pregnant by boys who were not of their parents' choosing and that they would not therefore be in a position in the future to "payback" the parents for their education. Here are two responses that touch on this and other issues:

> What I think is, their parents—think of their traditional customs. That they don't want girls to continue in school. Parents say they get married and then they don't payback their school fees. Even though they pass grade six [i.e., at a high enough level to enter grade seven], they take them to stay home [in the village]. Boys continue and girls stay back. [T]hey think boys will finish and girls won't. They don't trust their daughters. (Teacher, Bialla Community School)

> I can give you the reasons around here. Most parents—they rely on males only. They go and they train and later on—they complete the work properly. Say ladies, they don't know the type of course they are doing. Make friendships and spoil their course of study. That one is a fact. Course, sometimes when ladies go to university, we had one in our area, they come back with a child and no father. That is a problem parents don't want. To get a job, they rely on the male. (Teacher, Ewasse Community School)

Such interview material of course not only provides us with specific information, it also opens up new avenues for study. The quotes above, for example, tell us much about why teachers think that parents often pull their girls out of school earlier than their boys. In order to find out whether this is in fact what parents think, we as researchers of course need to go on to ask parents similar interview questions. As it turned out in West New Britain, parents were much more reticent than teachers in suggesting that they were afraid that their daughters might get pregnant by a boy not of their choosing (e.g., often a boy from another cultural group in the country) and were more likely to suggest more general reasons such as "boys are more trustworthy than girls," or "boys are stronger and can work harder later on and pay the family back more," or "I've got four boys, so I am keeping two in school and two at home, but I want all my girls [two] at home so I can watch out for them." None of these answers of course precludes the reasons that teachers gave in relation to parents above. They do suggest at the very least that parents are not comfortable with talking about this issue to a stranger and that they have other important reasons for not wanting to send many of their female children on to higher education.

As I indicated earlier, in many instances questions such as the ones listed in the schedule above can be used as a kind of "stock" from which to create an alternative set of interview questions for a specific social group. For example, in West New Britain a set of government bureaucrats existed within the provincial department of education, each responsible for specific duties (e.g., supplying the schools, maintaining school property, assigning the teaching staff, etc.). Because of this, I added the following two-part question to the schedule above: What specific job do you do here in the government? How does this differ from what other people who work here do?

New researchers are often worried about how they will decide on which questions to ask—and may become even more anxious if they are faced with creating a standard interview schedule that will form the basis for the interview portion of the study (e.g., a common academic requirement when creating a project proposal). Though not always possible, this is one reason why I suggest that ideally you should wait at least several weeks into the field project before attempting to write semi-structured interview questions. The questions themselves often come from both this preliminary phase of information collecting (many issues will become apparent to the researcher after the first round of review and analysis has been completed), but they may also come from the preparation carried out prior to the research situation (the historical, political economic, and popular media preparation spoken of in chapters 2, 3, and 4 of this book). For example, the question "Why do you think more male than female students continue on in their education, both in community schools and beyond them" was suggested to me by my prior reading of both historical trends in the country and statistics available in contemporary government documents (which were also extensively reported on in newspaper sources on a periodic basis). While the question "Who do you think should be most responsible for looking after the community schools, the government or the members of the community" primarily came from conflicts that had shown up during the initial conversations that I had with teachers, government education workers, and parents in the opening weeks of my research.

The biggest advantage to using a basic interview schedule and adding or subtracting from it as needed involves the opportunity to compare answers from the members of different social groupings in relation to the same issues. Two examples from the above schedule should suffice to show how this advantage actually worked in the West New Britain situation. For example, in regard to the question above concerning who should be most responsible for looking after the community schools most parents leaned strongly toward an answer that implicated the provincial government as being primarily responsible, adding commentaries such as "I have no money, what can I do," or "this is why we have them—they must give us school and things like that." Answers obtained from various educational workers in the government (from educational bureaucrats to school teachers) were more mixed in tone, but on the whole gave parents much more "responsibility" for "their" schools than parents gave to themselves. These answers coincided well with the kinds of informal issues that continually cropped up concerning community school responsibility when I was talking to parents, teachers, and bureaucrats during standard participant-observation opportunities. These latter conversations, however, normally occurred in reaction to specific school situations, such as who should keep the school yard clean, help repair the sagging school fence, or ensure that students got to school on time each morning. In this way, semi-structured interview material can offer a check on the more ethnographic information that is coming to light, in much the same fashion that counting schedules can be used as checks on the ethnographic study of classroom interactions.

In question number twelve above in the standard interview schedule, I asked adults which of two choices they hoped their children would make when they grew up: to stay in their home villages and live a more traditional life or to go to live in a town a long way from their home village in order to get a job in the cash economy? Urban-based bureaucrats and cash economy workers, such as government workers, bank workers, or school-teachers, overwhelmingly stated that in one way or another they expected their children to pursue a job in the cash economy no matter where it took them in the country. These answers were often modified, as in the following fashion: "I will miss my son very much if he has to leave us, but I want him to get the best life he can—so he should leave us if he has to." Parents who were currently living in villages themselves (e.g., near one of the towns in which their children were attending schools) or who expected themselves to "retire" (often as early as age forty or forty-five) back to their home village, often gave much more detailed and complex answers. These answers were related to issues brought up in other interview questions, such as questions number two, three, four, and five. What these answers told me was that many parents thought long and hard about issues of education. Who should be "invested" in as a child? Who might continue through the educational system and eventually land a good job in the cash economy? And, who might be "needed" back home for horticultural work, to look after aging parents, or to provide the next generation of villagers? Parents who themselves maintained a strong commitment to village life offered strongly contextualized answers to these issues, involving the total number of children they had, how many were boys and how many were girls, their judgment about the relative talent of each child and that child's chances of obtaining a wage job after education, and their own and their kin's ability (and willingness) to pay school fees and living expenses for the higher educational credentials that would be required to make the child employable. Many parents, for example, felt that if they did not think that a specific child was worth the investment then it was important to pull him or her out of the school system while still of community school age (e.g., generally before the child got much older than ten or eleven years of age) so that s/he would not, as one parent put it (echoing the sentiment of many), "become a bighead and ruined for life back home."

Only two or three community school-teachers that I interviewed out of a total of twenty-seven such teachers gave answers that could be interpreted as favoring the village option. Most, in fact, gave very positive accounts of life in urban areas and made it plain that they wished nothing more than to have their own children follow them into an urban way of life. These attitudes coincided very well with the ethnographic observations made in classrooms that indicated (see chapter 5) that many teachers displayed a considerable bias in their classrooms in favor of an urban way of life at the expense of a life primarily based upon subsistence horticulture in a village setting. Given that the towns of Papua New Guinea were already overcrowded with unemployed want-to-be workers and that the cash economy was structurally incapable of providing more than 15–20 percent of those who wished for such work with wage labor jobs, this pervasive attitude (as shown in both interviews and in their classroom performances) by community school teachers in favor of urban versus rural life did not, in my opinion, bode well for Papua New Guinea as a developing nation. In addition, it directly contradicted their own federal goals for education in PNG, which included a desire that education help to create a new kind of citizen/entrepreneur who was willing to live in the rural areas of the country. In chapter 8 we return to the issue of the analysis of semi-structured interview material.

Notice how semi-structured interview material can be related to other information gathered in the ethnographic situation and utilized to strengthen (or of course to question) an analytical perception that the researcher may have about a specific educational trend in relation to larger social issues. Relationships are what we as ethnographers are primarily interested in finding out about in our research and discussing in our written work. We are interested in relationships between one piece of information and another (e.g., information variously gathered through interviews, counting schedules, or general observation), or between one social institution and another (e.g., education in relation to economic opportunities or political trends), or between one time period and another (e.g., early missionary run systems compared to contemporary government controlled systems). The eventual goal is to combine more circumscribed patterns of information into broader patterns of analysis and embed these within appropriate political economic and historical contexts in order to arrive at satisfying ethnographic products. More of course is said in this regard later in the book. At the moment, let's turn to a consideration of unstructured interviews and how they differ from semi-structured interviews so that we can think about the role they might play in the ethnographic process.

Unstructured Interviewing

In its purest form, unstructured interviewing is best thought of as a virtually invisible part of participant observation. In chapter 5, I emphasized the observational aspects of that research method. Here, we can consider how these observations may be complemented by the kind of interviewing that occurs primarily in the form of true conversations. Unstructured interviewing does not involve the more formal question/answer format of semi-structured interviewing—backed up by the use of a standard interview schedule. In its simplest form, unstructured interviewing occurs every time a researcher participates in a conversation and, upon hearing a subject come up that interests her/him, decides to try to keep that particular conversation alive for a period of time. As an example, we can consider what might happen if the researcher is standing around a schoolyard at the end of the day, talking informally to teachers about no topic in particular. One of the teachers in the conversation brings up the issue of student discipline and states "it is really up to the parents to do more about getting the children to obey school rules." The researcher can then take this opening and turn it to his/her own advantage, saying, for example, to another teacher present "what do you think about that Mary," or even a more generically "really, do you think most teachers feel that way?" The first type of question is directed at another specific teacher in the group, while the second question is sure to provoke a more collective response from those teachers present as to whether they agree that most educators think that way about this particular issue. In either form, the researcher should be able to gain more information about the specific topic. This kind of unstructured interviewing can be thought of as fortuitous interviewing; that is, as a kind of directed conversation that takes advantage of the topics initiated by those with whom we are doing our study. Stated another way, this method makes use of the "lucky breaks" that occur in naturalistic conversations and turns them to our own advantage as researchers. One of the benefits of this kind of unstructured interview is that it can help lead us to topics that we might not have thought of before but which teachers, parents, students, and others think about and discuss at great length amongst themselves. This should allow us to discover not only new areas for study but also to confirm whether or not we have been correct in our assumptions (gleaned from ethnographic observation and the use of both contemporary and historical sources) about the key issues of education in this particular social setting.

Despite the many uses of the above form of interviewing, we often have a need for a more directed or topically specific type of unstructured interviewing. In this situation, the researcher approaches the conversation already armed with two or three particular subjects that s/he would like to discuss further with a specific group of people. For example, at one stage of my work in West New Britain I was very interested in coming to a better understanding of the role that discipline played in the educational system. As has been mentioned before in this book, I had already recorded numerous examples of various forms of disciplinary actions inside of classrooms and had also elicited a number of very interesting answers involving discipline issues as open-ended responses to questions number two, ten, and eleven in semi-structured interview situations. At the same time, I had also analytically linked aspects of both classroom behavior and interview answers to the historical issue of the almost militaristic style of discipline used in missionary education in many schools of the past. I therefore became interested in obtaining more information through the use of informal methods on the following issues involving discipline: (1) was a "good" teacher necessarily thought of as a "strict" teacher? (2) was a "good" pupil necessarily thought to be an "obedient" student? and (3) did people other than myself see a linkage between historical forms of missionary-run education and the specific kinds of disciplinary methods used in the government-run community schools of West New Britain? Rather than formulate specific questions around these three issues, I simply kept these topics in mind and went out in search of "conversations" with teachers, parents and other community members—during which I could bring up these issues in whatever seemed to be the appropriate wording of the moment. In my experience with carrying out several quite different research projects (and I have had this opinion confirmed by a number of colleagues), three issues (preferably centered around a single theme) seem to be the limit for single conversations. Any more than that number appears to "force" the conversation and create a situation in which the researcher dominates the situation to such an extent that either the other participants become uncomfortable and refuse to continue to engage in the discussion or else clam up and begin to issue only "yes" or "no" answers to our by now very obvious questions. In other words, the situation becomes too much like a formal interview and loses the conversational quality that we value most about this type of interview. If you sense this happening at any time during the conversation, simply "back off" your attempt to direct the discussion in a specific direction and let the natural flow re-enter the situation before (if you deem it prudent to do so) attempting another redirection.

I want to emphasize that none of this is done in a clandestine fashion. It is true, for example, that the researcher is not standing around with a clipboard and asking questions but it is also true that s/he is not in any way trying to "hide" the fact that s/he is doing research in these conversations (to do so would of course be a serious breach of ethics). If you feel that the people you are speaking with may have "forgotten" that this too is a part of your research project, then you can always overtly remind them of this fact by pulling out a small notebook and begin making notations as the conversation proceeds. Normally, this interrupts the flow of talk and most researcher choose to make their notes as immediately after the ending of a conversation as possible. However, many researchers will purposely make a few jottings in a notebook from time to time in order to remind those we are talking with that we are not just "having conversations" but are rather "conducting research" and what they are saying might go down in our notes as part of the information we are gathering about education (or any other topic) in their country.

The primary disadvantage of the more directed form of unstructured interviewing involves the loss of spontaneous information that might have come the researcher's way if s/he had not directed so much of the conversation. This can partially be compensated for by limiting the amount of questioning that one does in any single conversation situation and also by remember that these are, after all, open-ended questions and any tangents the conversation evolves into may prove to be as interesting as the topics we had in mind in the first place. The great advantage of this more directed form of conversational interviewing (which again can be utilized in either a group or in a one-to-one situation) is that it allows us to collect on a much more informal basis a variety of responses to issues that have been raised in more formal research settings such as those of semi-structured interviewing or focused classroom observations. As an example of the kinds of material that might be gleaned in this fashion, let's briefly reconsider the topics that I mentioned above concerning the overall theme of discipline. Whether I was having discussions with head teachers, government officials, or parents there was a very consistent agreement that a "good" teacher was in fact a "strict" teacher. Certainly, variations existed in exactly what individuals meant by the term "strict." In one informal conversation with a group of parents that I met while I was standing around a store front in the town of Kimbe, for example, some of the parents suggested that "strict" meant that a teacher would not be reluctant to use a strap or other form of physical punishment if necessary, while others in the same group believed that firm verbal discipline should be enough to keep students along the right path for learning in a classroom.

Alternatively, I experienced much more varied conversations around the issue of whether a "good" student was necessarily also an "obedient" student. Teachers overwhelmingly agreed with this maxim (in keeping with their more formal comments during semi-structured interviewing on the same issue), as did most other educational workers (e.g., government officials). Some officials and many parents (and virtually all children), however, disagreed with this concept and often suggested specific examples to show that a "good" pupil might in fact be a "big-head" on occasion and still be a good student overall. Many individual parents, in particular, brought out examples of their own male children in conversations and described how they "got into trouble" with school authorities for "doing normal boy things," going on to point out that "smart boys" in particular were much more likely to get into a bit of trouble than boys who were not as bright. The same was not generally said to be true of girls and parents were much more likely in conversational interviews to suggest that to be a good student a girl had to indeed be an obedient pupil. These viewpoints were very much in keeping with the various cultural traditions of West New Britain, in which boys were generally expected in most cultural groups to be much more aggressively active than girls.

During my research in West New Britain, unstructured conversational interviewing really proved its worth when I directed conversations to the potential connection between historical forms of missionary style educational discipline and contemporary disciplinary styles in the government run school system. Virtually no one saw this connection as being particularly valid and many even challenged this analytical interpretation. Government personnel, teachers and parents alike regaled me with tales of "what real discipline is like" by telling specific horror stories about what missionary style discipline "used to be like" before the government took over the system as a whole and made corporal punishment in the classroom illegal. Many of these stories came from their own experiences, such as the following one that was told to me by a young male neighbor of mine in the town of Kimbe, who had gone to a school run by United Church missionaries from the United States in another part of West New Britain. During a long conversation one afternoon, Mark (who has also been reported upon in Fife 1995a) told me a brief history of his life, including many things about his educational experiences. He had been an excellent pupil in grade school, eventually passing into one of the few elite high schools in the country (at the time, only a very small number of students attended grades eleven and twelve in Papua New Guinea, at special high schools that were aimed toward preparing students for a tertiary education and hence positions of leadership in the country). He emphasized that he had always been a very "obedient" pupil and never made trouble, enduring beatings by the missionary teachers in silence. "I just kept to myself. And I think that's one thing that makes me want to try, to correct all my mistakes myself, you know." It is worth noting here that both of Mark's parents were Nakanai people from West New Britain and that like many other cultural groups in Papua New Guinea, the Nakanai highly prize a boy's ability to endure hardship in silence. The worst beating occurred one day, Mark told me, when he had climbed up into a tree to sit and think by himself for a while. Tree climbing was forbidden and a teacher found him and made him come down. Mark did not see why he could not climb a tree and so when the teacher told him to hold his hand out for a strapping he made one of his rare protests and refused to put his hands out in front of him. Infuriated, the teacher forced Mark (who was nine years old at the time) to kneel down and place his hands on a wooden board on the ground. "Then he took a chunk of cement and, yeah, started cracking me on the hands!" "My God, I said, did you get hurt badly?" "No," he replied, "I kept my hands in a fist and wouldn't put my fingers out as he wanted me to. But, I was bleeding pretty bad." He told no one of the event. "I kept my hands like this [he tucks his hands up out of sight underneath his armpits] for the next days and nobody really noticed."

When even young adults (e.g., Mark was in his early twenties at the time of the above conversation) were asked about a possible connection between the kind of discipline that occurs in the schools in contemporary Papua New Guinea and the kind that used to occur in nongovernment organized missionary schools, they almost invariably stated that no, there was no connection between the two situations and that things were very different "now." What they seemed to be primarily referring to was the fact that it was now illegal to use corporal punishment in education in Papua New Guinea. Although I can say from personal observation that this rule was not always obeyed, it was quite true that I had no evidence that anything like the above type of event (or many other similar stories told to me by other former pupils) occurred on a regular basis in the contemporary schools of West New Britain. People such as Mark, then, emphasized the literal difference between the overt forms of heavy physical punishment used in the past missionary schools and what they saw as the much lighter forms of largely verbal discipline used in the missionary and government schools of the late twentieth century. The more analogical connections that can be made through metaphorical analysis meant nothing to the adults I had conversations with, even when I pointed out the more literal physical similarities between the forms that morning assembly and other situations involving organized lineups took in the past in mission schools and the way such things continue to be done in today's schools. As one parent put it: "No, no, this is really more like the police, or something. Anyway, how else would they do it? That is the way it has to be. Students have to be told what to do." Answers such as this were extremely valuable in showing me the extent to which such historically engendered educational practices had become naturalized among the contemporary populations of Papua New Guinea.

The disagreement above, then, between the researcher and most of the adult citizens of West New Britain that he spoke with in regard to a possible "connection" between older forms of missionary discipline and newer forms of educational discipline reminds us of the power of hidden curriculum. It works precisely because most people, even those who are perpetuating it, are normally quite unaware that there is a "pattern" to their interactions and that this pattern puts forth an educational message in and of itself. This is why the researcher has to remember that s/he is ultimately responsible for the final interpretive analysis of the educational patterns (or tourism practices, or women's organizations) that s/he is doing research about. It is nice when the people we do research with "recognize" or agree with our interpretations. Such recognition makes us feel good as researchers and partially verifies that we are "on the right track," but it cannot be allowed to fully determine our role as critical scholars doing an ethnographic study in a specific country. We alone are responsible for what we say about a topic and must realize that we may well "see" things that others, even those who are otherwise most intimately involved in particular social behaviors, will not see. This difference is largely due to our ability to devote ourselves full time to ethnographic projects. Along with this privilege goes the responsibility of bearing witness to what we find out to the best of our abilities—even if that means being disputed or even criticized by others because no one else seems to "see" things in quite the same way. At the same time, researchers often do change their own perceptions of situations or events because of the insights that we glean from how others see things—we are certainly not infallible interpreters of information.

Having said that, one of the most valuable results of unstructured interviewing is that it allows us, as the field research progresses, to gain a sense of what local people think about various parts of our ongoing analysis. In the above cases, for example, material gathered in semi-structured interviews from teachers were verified by unstructured conversational interviews with members of the same social grouping in regard to the supposed relationship between good and obedient pupils. Conversely, I was able to find out that most adults with whom I spoke interpreted discipline quite literally and therefore emphasized the difference between educational discipline in the new "modern" Papua New Guinea versus that of the older, missionary dominated Papua New Guinea school systems. That is, in contrast to the researcher, they emphasized a "break" with the past. This, of course, is valuable information that did not show up in any of the other research methods utilized by myself in this educational study.

There are other ways to get unique kinds of information. One of these involves self-reported information, which is the subject of chapter 7.

7

Self-Reporting

Research methods that utilize self-reporting can yield extremely useful information. Self-reporting can come in many forms. For example, if a researcher were conducting a study about education in a refugee camp, s/he might request a camp teacher to ask each of her students to draw a picture about what everyday life is like in the camp. The pictures that would result from this kind of exercise are a form of self-reporting and would contain many clues as to the kind of social and cultural consciousness the child is currently experiencing while living in this camp situation. If many children drew pictures, for example, that involved the procurement of basic sources of nourishment, such as standing in line to obtain a meal or a ration of rice for the family, or carrying water from a communal watering truck or well, then it would be reasonable to conclude that children in this camp spend a great deal of their time worrying about having enough to eat or drink. The researcher can then take this bit of information and expand upon it. Is food and water actually a problem to obtain in this particular camp? If not, why do the children seem to be so preoccupied with the issue—does it, for example, relate to other anxieties that children have about their own futures and whether or not they feel that as they in turn become adults they will be able to provide the basic things of life for themselves and their families?

In a less dramatic situation involving a different kind of a camp, children who are tenting for one or two weeks with their families in a national park might be asked to draw pictures of or write a short story about their favorite park activity. These visual or verbal representations could then be used to engage in discussions with the children and other adult members of their families concerning the park and the relative popularity of various park activities.

Insights gleaned from self-reported material can often be effectively used to expand topical areas for discussion within a research project. They can also, and this is perhaps the most common usage, be utilized as a technique for gathering more subjective information on a topic that has already come to light during a period of prior research. Self-reporting methods, then, are an area limited only by the researchers own imagination and, if used properly, can add immensely to an ethnographic study. As usual, a more detailed and specific example of using self-reporting is probably the best way to explain the potential utility of the method.

Remember as you read through my example that ethnographic research is a creative endeavor and not simply a product of a specific technique that can be counted upon to yield such-and-such results with a mathematical type of precision. Don't be afraid to experiment with this research method in your study— adapting the basic idea for your own specific ends.

Essay Writing as a Form of Self-Reporting

As the reader is by now aware, in my own work in West New Britain Province, I was most interested in issues of social inequality, including inequalities that occurred because of differences associated with the opportunities of rural-based versus urban-based ways of life. Having gathered a considerable amount of information from a variety of sources that indicated that students in the three community schools which I was studying were receiving consistent messages that urban life was far superior to more customary forms of rural-based life, I was curious to find out to what extent the students themselves might have internalized these messages. The question that I wanted to answer was this one: To what extent did students at Kimbe, Bialla, and Ewasse community schools accept and internalize the message that it was "good to be modern in a modern urban world" and to what extent did they reject that message. My solution to this question came in the form of a self-reporting exercise. I reasoned that if I asked students to write a short essay on the topic of "My Future Work," I would gain some idea of how their fantasies concerning their own future lives related to the urban (modern) versus rural (traditional) dichotomy that was being played out in their school classrooms.

I asked teachers in grades five and six at each of the three community schools to have their students write a short essay on the theme "My Future Work" as a normal part of their written composition assignments. Students were very familiar with writing these kinds of essays in their ordinary class periods and I requested the teachers to give the pupils the same kinds of instructions that they would normally give them during similar exercises. I was purposefully not present in the specific classroom when each exercise was carried out, as I did not want the assignment to be associated with me. The word "work" was chosen quite carefully rather than the word "job" in the essay title for this exercise. In Tok Pisin, the word "wok" (work) refers to just about any active endeavor that can lead to a practical result. This is also the way that, in my experience, most Papua New Guineans understood the English word work—as something that could refer equally to planting a crop, conducting a community meeting, organizing a ritual feast, or engaging in a wage labor job. Work, in this context, was a far more neutral term than the word job—which was associated by most Papua New Guineans quite specifically with wage economy situations.

Findings from the students' essays can be broken down and presented in tables for each community school, as seen in tables 7.1, 7.2, and 7.3. Note that the term D.P.I. Worker refers to a government job in the Department of Primary Industries (i.e., resource industries such as copper and gold mining). I have chosen to list each type of work in relation to its overall popularity (after adding both grades five and six results together in each school), with the most popular choice coming first and the least popular choice coming last in each table.

Table 7.1   My Future Work: Kimbe Community School

Work	Grade Five			Grade Six		
	Male	Female	Total	Male	Female	Total
Teacher	0	11	11	1	4	5
Mechanic	2	0	2	8	0	8
Village Agriculture	4	0	4	2	3	5
Nurse	0	2	2	0	6	6
Pilot	5	0	5	1	0	1
Doctor	1	1	2	3	0	3
Clerk	0	3	3	1	1	2
Police	3	2	5	0	0	0
Air Hostess	0	2	2	0	2	2
Armed Forces	2	0	2	2	0	2
Typist	0	1	1	0	3	3
Carpenter	1	0	1	2	0	2
Store Owner	2	0	2	1	0	0
Rugby Player	0	0	0	2	0	2
Printer	0	0	0	2	0	2
Electrician	0	0	0	2	0	2
D.P.I. Worker	1	0	1	0	0	0
Engineer	0	0	0	1	0	0
Parliament	1	0	0	0	0	0
Astronaut	0	1	1	0	0	0
Radio Announcer	0	0	0	0	1	1
Architect	0	0	0	1	0	1
Ship Captain	0	0	0	1	0	1
Building Inspector	0	0	0	1	0	1

Table 7.2   My Future Work: Bialla Community School

Work	Grade Five			Grade Six		
	Male	Female	Total	Male	Female	Total
Teacher	0	7	7	0	10	10
Mechanic	10	0	10	3	0	3
Doctor	3	0	3	1	0	1
Nurse	0	3	3	0	1	1
Police	1	2	3	1	0	1
Clerk	0	3	3	0	1	1
Typist	0	1	1	0	2	2
Armed Forces	1	0	1	1	0	0
Carpenter	1	0	1	1	0	1
Pilot	1	0	1	1	0	1
Village Agriculture	0	1	1	1	0	1
Driver (Taxi)	0	0	0	2	0	2
Sister (i.e., Nun)	0	1	1	0	1	1
Priest	0	0	0	1	0	1
Lawyer	1	0	1	0	0	0
D.P.I. Worker	0	1	1	0	0	0
Fisheries Department	1	0	1	0	0	0
Businessman	0	0	0	1	0	1
Engineer	1	0	1	0	0	0

Table 7.3   My Future Work: Ewasse Community School

| | Grade Five | | | Grade Six | | |
Work	Male	Female	Total	Male	Female	Total
Teacher	3	9	12	0	1	1
Nurse	0	4	4	0	3	3
Mechanic	3	0	3	2	0	2
Doctor	4	0	4	0	0	0
Store Owner	0	1	1	1	0	1
Armed Forces	2	0	2	0	0	0
Police	1	0	1	1	0	1
Carpenter	0	0	0	2	0	2
Pilot	0	0	0	2	0	2
Geologist	0	0	0	2	0	2
Engineer	0	0	0	2	0	2
Dentist	1	0	1	0	0	0
Typist	0	1	1	0	0	0
Boat Captain	0	0	0	1	0	1

It is worthwhile noting that there are many different ways that this same information could have been presented to the reader other than the one I chose to use above. I prefer to lay it out in this manner because I think that it offers the most straight-forward and fullest presentation of data, in a fashion that allows the reader not only to follow my own analysis that stems from this presentation but also to develop his or her own separate analysis through their own use of the material. An alternative format, for example, might have lumped grades five and six together for each school and presented the schools side by side in a single table. Or, I could have ignored the fact that this evidence comes from three different schools and simply presented it by grade number and occupational type alone. Try presenting the table(s) above in these or other alternate formats, show them to people and ask them which ones they prefer (and why) and you will soon discover that each form of presentation has a very different impact upon potential readers. The presentation of information is not a neutral process and decisions that you make about how to reveal specific pieces of data are really decisions about two other invisible agendas: (1) your basic research philosophy, and (2) aesthetic decisions that you reach as part of the process of writing ethnography as opposed to the ethnographic research itself. See chapter 10 for more comments on the second issue. In terms of the first issue above, my basic philosophy of research includes the concept of reflexivity and the notion that a certain openness of presentation is desirable. This contains the viewpoint that at least some of the research process should itself become evident in the way that we write our ethnographies and also the idea that the reader should be given enough information in as "raw" a format as possible that s/he can use it to both consider the validity of my own analysis and at the same time formulate a potentially different analysis of his or her own. Another researcher might choose to present only fully "finished" (often called "cooked") information (e.g., using paraphrases rather than direct quotations taken from research notes, or tables that offer conclusions rather than information that can be subjected to different interpretations by both the author and the reader). Because of my basic philosophy of research, which is part of a much larger critical agenda that rejects giving all of the authority to the author and leaving the reader with little to do but nod his or her head in agreement, I personally reject the slicker forms of writing that are implicated through the use of more "finished" information. This of course is a point of judgment. In its fully raw format, I might simply have presented every single essay that I received from students and allowed the reader to make his or her own charts to organize the material. However, this would very quickly lead to ridiculous situations, such as a fifteen-hundred page book for a single ethnographic account (without the analysis). So, we have to cook the information to a certain extent, while also serving up material that remains at least partially raw so that the reader has some chance to consider the validity of our interpretations. Again, this is why ethnographic research remains an art form as much as a science, equally at home in both the humanities and the social sciences.

In keeping with the above ideas, it should be obvious that the tables presented above contain the possibility for many types of interpretation. I illustrate only a few of those possibilities in this chapter.

To begin with, tables with this kind of information often open up new avenues for research. For example, the reader might have noticed that at Ewasse community school, which is the most rural of the three schools, only fourteen different types of work were mentioned by the students; while at Kimbe community school, the most urban of the three schools, no less than twenty-four different types of work were mentioned in the students' essays. The immediate interpretation that comes to mind is that students who live in denser urban environments have a larger number of work models to choose from than students who live in more rural communities. The problem with this perfectly plausible interpretation is that it may not take into account that the data we are dealing with is an ethnographic and not a statistical form of information. It is easy to lose sight of this fact, especially when pieces of this evidence are presented in the format of tables or graphs. However, we have to keep in mind that this information was collected in the ethnographic tradition of "as much as we can get, from whomever we can get it," rather than in the statistically justified manner of quantitative information. The latter would have required random sampling and a weighting process, for example, that corrected for the fact that ninety-four essays were collected at Kimbe community school and only forty-six were collected at Ewasse community school. In other words, the large difference between the number of work types mentioned by students attending each of these two schools could potentially be accounted for by the very substantial difference that exists between the number of total submissions completed at one school versus the other school. More children thinking about their futures might simply lead to more diversity in thought. Does this mean that the rural/urban interpretation made above is necessarily invalid? No, of course not. It simply means that it is necessary to give more than one possible explanation for the same material if more than one explanation seems reasonable. It may well require more research to sort out which explanation is the preferable one. Meanwhile, there is nothing wrong with giving readers open-ended forms of analysis when such seem called for, rather than pretending that there is really only one plausible interpretation of the evidence that we present in our ethnographic products. Some readers of our ethnographic work will be future researchers, and they may well take our explanations and test them further, either in new ethnographic venues or through the use of quantitative methods of research and analysis. This is one of the ways that knowledge moves along, becoming transformed through the work of new researchers in new situations.

One of the patterns that does come through quite clearly in the tables presented above is the tremendous bias that these grade five and six students have toward a desire for urban employment in the cash economy (remember, this was in a country in which less than 20 percent of the population had such employment at the time of the research and in which there were severe structural limitations for the possibility for growth in wage labor jobs). Only eleven out of the total two hundred and seven students (or slightly more than 5 percent) participating in this essay writing at all three schools said that they wanted to make their future work in village agriculture. Ironically, not a single one of these students came from Ewasse, the community school that serves the needs of seven rural villages located near the town of Bialla. Some of the occupations mentioned by students, such as teacher or member of the police force, can of course be practiced in rural areas of the country. However, these are not in any sense "traditional" rural occupations and owe their existence primarily to the urban-based cash economy and its support of the "modern" bureaucratic nation-state of Papua New Guinea. To become a school teacher, for example, requires that a student spends long years in both secondary schools and in one of the teacher's colleges— the vast majority of which are located in or near one of the main towns in each province.

What is important here is not that grade five and six students in West New Britain have unrealistic expectations regarding their personal futures (it is quite probable that most students at similar levels of education anywhere in the world hold such unrealistic expectations), but rather that so few want to participate in the agriculturally based rural economy that is the mainstay of life in Papua New Guinea.

After I had completed my research in PNG, I was lucky enough to stumble upon a study originally conducted in the late 1960s by J.D. Conroy (1977), who surveyed 819 primary (grade six) children who were about to discontinue their education. In this study, he also asked them about their future occupational expectations. Despite the fact that just under 60 percent of these pupils were the children of village horticulturalists, only 8.7 percent of the boys and 2.2 percent of the girls saw agricultural work as an "ideal" career choice. Conroy's project covered seven different school districts on the mainland and despite the differences between his study and my own, it suggests a remarkable continuity of student expectations over the last few decades in Papua New Guinea. It is my suggestion that these remarkable expectations are directly linked to the hidden curriculum of classroom interactions and the consistent messages that teachers give in the classrooms of community schools in places such as West New Britain concerning the superior status of a life in the urban-based cash economy versus one created largely in the context of a rural-based subsistence agriculture economy. I would not be surprised, for example, if similar results could be found today not only in other regions of Papua New Guinea but also in other developing countries in which most of the population continues to make their living in rural agricultural pursuits.

Many more things can be said about the information presented in the tables above. There are both interesting gender stereotypes visible in occupational choices, for example, and cases of cutting across these stereotypes. Being a teacher, for example, is largely seen as work suitable for female students to aspire toward (which may in turn be related to the large number of female teachers at the primary school level in Papua New Guinea). Being a mechanic, on the other hand, is viewed exclusively as a male type of work. At the same time, a grade five girl at Kimbe wanted to be an astronaut and while seven boys wanted to be in the police force, so did four girls. In short, there were consistent patterns of gender stereotyping, such as boys wanting to be doctors and girls wanting to be nurses in their future lives, but there were also some surprises that suggested that these choices were not simple reflections of hidden curriculums that promoted gender stereotypes. Even though teaching was largely seen as a female profession, for example, no fewer than nine boys in a grade five classroom at Ewasse community school wanted to be teachers. I would suggest that this is most likely a direct result of the fact that these boys were in a classroom taught by a very dynamic male teacher, whereas most of the other students in the self-reporting exercise were taught wholly or primarily by female teachers. In other words, we cannot assume that the gender patterns that can be found in these self-reporting essays *necessarily* reflect something specific in the hidden curriculum of classroom instructions. Again, this is ethnographic information and it should be interpreted in the context of other ethnographic information, such as the evidence that boys in grades five and six have very limited access to male teachers as role models and females have a great deal of access to female teachers as role models. The "mixed" results of the self-reported essays in terms of gender patterning is also paralleled in other ethnographic information gathered during my study, such as the counting schedule that was used to investigate gender patterns of pupil-student interactions in the classroom lessons as conducted by male versus female teachers (as previously mentioned in chapter 4 of this book, and more fully reported on in Fife 1992). The results of the counting schedule were also mixed, showing that some male and some female teachers favored boys over girls during specific type of lessons, but that other teachers showed either no pattern of favoritism or actually showed slight preferences for girls over boys. Clearly, the hidden curriculum of gender interaction and the expectations they might create in students is a complex process and not something that can be reduced to a simple bias in favor of boys over girls, despite both long term cultural traditions in the area and wage-economy opportunities that would seem to strongly favor males over females in contemporary Papua New Guinea. Such complexity may actually be taken as a sign that many West New Britain teachers are making substantial efforts to overcome both customary and "modern" biases that differential preferences for boys over girls in terms of wage work and in other aspects of individual's life choices.

As important as the information reported in the form of numbers in the tables above is, it only tells half the story of the self-reported essays. Just as telling is the tone of expectations that were reported by the grade five and six students of these three schools in West New Britain. Reading through the paragraphs provided by the children, for example, left little room for doubt in my mind about whether these students preferred an urban or a rural-based way of life in their future. In the examples presented below, all grammatical, spelling, incorrect tense use, and other language errors were in the original documents themselves.

> When I finish my grade 6 I join the vocational school and when I grow big I join the Machine [the mechanics school in the capital city of Port Moresby]. I will know how to fix truck or car, bicycle and I stay on, e.g. one time a man came to see me and I fix his car. Then I finish, they'll give me money and I become rich and stay happily in my home in Moresby. (Boy, Grade Six, Kimbe C.S.)

> My future work I want to be a teacher at Bialla community school. I want to teach all the children, I want to help them to learn the words. I want to be a FUTURE in Bialla. Everyday I want the children to know the words in the school ground, to respect the teacher. (Girl, Grade Five, Ewasse C.S.)

> In My Future Time
> I will be an Engineer, for overseas ship. Because I want to see other countries. And the salary is very high and the life is good. And I want to pay back [his parents for his education]. When I am small my parents look after me at school and at home. (Boy, Grade Five, Bialla C.S.)

Even when students mention the possibility of living in villages, they usually do so only as a very secondary choice—one they would make only if they "fail" to be what they truly want to be.

> I'm thinking that I will go to my village and carry on my father's bisnis [Tok Pisin for business] if I drop out of school. My father has a trade store and a big place. We are very lucky people in the village. But if I am lucky and pass my school I'll become a Government clerk and try overseas. I really try hard in school. (Boy, Grade Six, Kimbe C.S.)

There are some students who indicate a willingness to work in the rural areas as their first choice, though they do not necessarily wish to participate directly in the way of life commonly associated with those areas. Examples include a grade five student in Bialla, who wanted to train in the fisheries so that he could get a job with the Shell Oil Company, or the Ewasse boy who wanted to be a geologist.

> Well in my future job I will become a GEOLOGIST because I want to study about rocks and to find minerals like gold, copper and oil in the ground. Because at this moment I heard people become Geologist they get a lot of money in that job that's why I want to become a Geologist and also enjoying myself patroling in the bush looking for minerals. (Boy, Grade Six, Ewasse C.S.)

For this boy West New Britain, and I would argue for increasing numbers of students from the schools in and around town areas, the "bush" or rural areas are starting to be seen as a "resource" that town people wish to exploit but do not necessarily desire to live in.

These few examples from the actual self-reported essays entitled "My Future Work" completed by grade five and six children from three community schools in West New Britain are sufficient to illustrate the very strong desire on the part of the vast majority of pupils to participate in an urban, cash based economy in their adult lives in at least this region of Papua New Guinea. They also suffice to give the reader an inkling of the complexity of material that may easily be gathered in as simple an exercise as the one proposed in this chapter. For example, the inclusion of such material in our ethnographic writings allows us to go far beyond the bald statement that "most children clearly want to grow up to live in urban areas and gain good jobs in the cash economy" and shows some of the nuances of these desires. In this way, presenting actual excerpts from written self-reportage (or visual representations if a pictorial form of self-reportage is used) adds greatly to the drier tables or other forms of presenting information that we also include in our work. The passion with which the children express themselves, as when the grade five girl from a village in the Ewasse area unwittingly states "I want to be a FUTURE in Bialla" or when the grade six boy from Kimbe declares with great simplicity "they'll give me money and I'll become rich and stay happily in my home in Moresby," is heart rendering when we understand from our reading of both the historic and contemporary political economy of the country that such jobs and such lives will remain elusive for all but the very few in Papua New Guinea. This is ethnography at its best—putting human faces to structural inequality in a developing country and showing readers that an institution such as education can both help and harm students in these countries—depending upon how it is delivered and whether it promises a life in sympathy with the social, historical, and environmental realities of the country in which it is taught or whether it promises a life that cannot be fulfilled for the vast majority of students it purports to serve.

Researchers can modify the method that I have outlined above to gather a wealth of self-reported material for use in their own studies. For example, although I have focused on children in this chapter, it might be just as useful to take advantage of this kind of method to collect some short life histories of adults in order to find out if the desire for wealth, position, and authority in relation to the cash economy is also deeply rooted in adults in a given country. In some parts of the world, children and adults may share their "future hopes," while in others these values may be at cross-purposes. Self-reporting diaries, essays, or other forms of writing; artistic activities such as drawing or painting scenes of "home life," "school life," "work life," "play life," or even dramatic presentations of "scenes from our history" or "scenes from our future lives" can all be very effective tools for learning about what both children and adults are thinking about a specific topic. It often yields material that cannot be garnered in any other fashion. As a method it is limited only by the researcher's imagination and budget. Remember that most people who live in developing countries or in poor areas of industrialized countries have little or no money for such "extras" as artwork or diary keeping. It is necessary (and only fair) that the researcher provide each family, school, or other institution, such as community club or voluntary association with the tools necessary to carry out any form of self-reporting that he or she may ask individuals to do. Crayons and paper for drawing, small blank books for diary writing, or even a school, community, or library prize offered for the best essay explaining "what life is really like in the city" or "what life is really like in the village" will go a long way toward ensuring the cooperation of those we wish to involve in our self-reporting projects.

Part C

Putting the Ethnography Together

8

Analysis

Many researchers find that the end of the fieldwork phase of the project is not the end of their questions about how to go about completing the study. The research project should be thought of as something that includes both the analysis of the information gathered during fieldwork and a consideration of its theoretical implications (the subjects of this chapter and chapter 9). What good is all of this evidence if it sits on a shelf (or in a drawer) collecting dust? The scholar must analyze the material and eventually turn it into various kinds of anthropological products if he or she is going to successfully complete the work. In this chapter, we concentrate on how to analyze the information that was gathered during fieldwork, including both preliminary and secondary forms of analysis and the issue of what to do when we find contradictions within a pattern itself.

Earlier in the book, I told the reader that a convenient way to conceptualize a study was to divide it into macro versus micro levels of research. In my study of education in West New Britain, for example, macro research focused upon the larger historical and social context—of which education was merely one part; while micro research focused upon the actual experience of education in a particular time and place. At the same time, I noted that these are relative terms. For example, in a historical study of a specific high school, primary archival material that contained direct evidence about that high school would then become the micro level of the study. I want to remind the reader here then that micro and macro levels of analysis are relative terms and have to be conceptualized in relation to the specific project under consideration. For the purposes of this chapter, I utilize these two terms in relation to the specific case study material that I use throughout this book in order to illustrate how to proceed with the analysis of ethnographic information. For the sake of simplicity, I often refer in this chapter to "macro data" or "micro information" in order to place the specific material within the relevant analytical context for the reader. I would ask, though, that the reader remember that these are heuristic devices only and that whether specific kinds of information "belong" to the macro or micro level of analysis in any given study depends upon the particular project that is being carried out. Knowing this, the reader can adjust the lessons of this chapter accordingly for use in his or her own research project.

In a sense, the project as I outlined it here took the scholar from the understanding of broader contexts to the gathering of more and more detailed information. The time has come to reverse the process. The point of analysis is to build up an ethnographic picture that links human behavior in specific human environments to larger patterns of social, cultural, and historic importance. We will now work from the micro to the macro, or from the detail to the big picture, in considering how to put an analysis together. The goal will be to learn to draw upon that analysis in order to create written ethnographies of education in developing countries or other topics (the subject of chapter 10).

It is common to feel overwhelmed when faced with the idea of writing a thesis, report, or book from the material you have gathered over a period of many months or years. The piles of notes and papers look too daunting to even think about tackling. Luckily, if you have followed this guide to any extent, you will already be a fair way toward creating an analysis of your material. Much of the preliminary analysis, for example, will already have been completed. The best way to decrease your anxiety about the total project is to divide the task of analysis up into specific bite-sized pieces of work, combining them together as you go. On a daily basis, you will be so concerned about analyzing a specific pile of evidence or tracing a particular thematic linkage between categories of evidence that you will forget about the task as a whole. Proceeding in this fashion, large amounts of information will soon become "analyzed" and you will be surprised at how rapidly you are able to move on to the next pile of information. I do not mean to minimize the analytical task here—it takes courage to create an original analysis, relate it to larger theoretical issues, and finally to put it "out there" for all to judge in a published format. However, following a systematic approach to this task will make it easier to complete then simply proceeding with the usual helter-skelter method that many researchers rely upon to "somehow" get their ethnographic data to fit together. There are reasons why some scholars publish a lot more, and a lot better, pieces of writing than other scholars. The way you choose to approach the analysis/theory/writing task is one of them.

In this chapter, I first outline how you should proceed in each section of the analysis and then take examples from my own West New Britain research in order to show you how such analysis can move forward in reality.

Preliminary Analysis of Information (Creating Concepts)

In chapter 5, I suggested that the reader do a preliminary analysis of the notes that were written during the general observation period of research in the classroom. This basic method of coding your notes can be used for any information that you have gathered (e.g., in relation to micro or macro forms of analysis). For example, self-reported writing (whether in the form of diaries, essays, or other writing) can be coded in the very same way—looking for preliminary themes that seem to stand out in the material as you read it. The same thing can be done for interview material (whether these notes were gathered as a part of unstructured or semi-structured interviewing), for both observational and interview material gathered at parent-teacher and other meetings, and so on. If you have notes about anything, gathered by virtually any method, you can do a preliminary coding of them in this way. This process is actually cumulative and you will have to take this into account as you proceed.

You will soon find that every time that you begin to look through a new pile of information in order to give it a preliminary coding, you will be influenced by the coding already completed on earlier sets of evidence. Because of this, I suggest that you proceed with the analysis in a very specific order (though it is quite conceivable that a scholar may wish to reverse or otherwise modify this order to suit his or her own requirements). I have found it best to begin with the micro information that I judge to be the most "basic" or important, move on to other micro levels of evidence, and finally consider the macro material in the light of my completed micro analysis. I prefer this approach as it feels to me as if I am building an ethnographic case from "the ground up," linking it to larger issues as I go but always remaining firmly grounded in the primary material of actual human behavior that forms the core of my participant-observation fieldwork.

It was no accident, then, that I suggested in chapter 5 that in a study such as the one I conducted in West New Britain the first analysis to be undertaken should involve coding the general observation notes regarding classroom behavior, as I regard this material as the core of any good ethnographic study of education in a developing country. In a project involving residents in a home for the aged in southwestern Ontario, on the other hand, I began my preliminary coding using the transcripts for interviews that I conducted with residents in the home—as I considered those to form the core information of that particular study. Where you begin the coding, then, depends on the ethnographic grounding of any given project.

Returning to education in PNG as the example, I would suggest that the researcher then move on to do a preliminary coding of the focused note-taking for classroom observation, the materials regarding schools as a whole, and finally the notes about educational events outside of the school (such as meetings). Counting schedules are in a sense a form of analysis in and of themselves—as they are an attempt to take a coded theme that has been identified as important and "test" it through minutely focused observations in the classroom. Preliminary analysis for counting schedules consists of deciding how to present the results in a table (or graph, or other summary format) and then checking over that type of presentation for basic thematic patterns (such as how male versus female teachers treat male versus female students in terms of discipline).

Only after the micro level analysis has been completed would I then do the same preliminary coding for material collected from newspapers and government documents, writings about the contemporary political economy of the country, or writings from primary or secondary historical sources (I am referring here to analysis that occurs over and above what you have already done in your first reading of this material—a reading that was carried out to sensitize you in a general sense to the themes you might come across in the period in which you are primarily conducting micro research). What you will end up with after all of this preliminary coding has been completed are a large number of conceptual themes, many of which immediately seem to be related to each other. It is these relationships that form the basis of the next step in analysis. Before we move on to consider secondary analysis, however, let's consider some specific examples from my own work in order to illustrate not only how this preliminary analysis functions on the ground but also how it tends to become a cumulative process.

I have already given some examples of coding classroom observations in chapter 5 when I showed the reader how concepts such as "competitive individualism" versus "cooperative individualism" emerged out of reading my observational notes. Another good example, this one involving the issue of private property, can be seen below. One example comes from my observational notes from the classrooms and the other from observational notes about other behavior in the schools of West New Britain. The theme here involves situations in which students are taught through the hidden curriculum of classroom instruction that specific items "belong" to particular individuals. Teachers assert this as being part of the "natural order of things" rather than as acknowledging it as one among many possible forms of social construction.

Coding	Fieldnotes
Private Property	"Okay, come and get your books." The teacher hands booklets out at the front of the room. Each has blue pages, with designs on each page (fish, trees, an axe, etc.). As the children flip through them I can see that some of the designs have been coloured in. Each book has the student's name clearly printed in large letters on top. This clearly "says" that these books are individual property, individual work. (Pre-Writing, Grade One, Kimbe C.S.)
Private Property	Morning Assembly. The headmaster is holding forth. "Good morning children." "Good morning Headmaster," they reply. "Okay, just one announcement. Don't forget to come early and don't wait for us to tell you not to go all over the place. A policeman will come and shoot you with a gun." (There is some laughter at this, though he seems serious and does not laugh.) "You leave rubbish all over the place! Don't think someone else is responsible for things. And don't take pencils or things." His voice becomes increasingly louder, until he is shouting. "That's stealing! Or taking betel nut or stuff from the garden. I am looking after that, you must come to me. That's stealing! People come and ask for it, but it's not theirs. You must ask me. So be careful." (Assembly, Ewasse C.S.)

Once a specific category of behavior has become identified in a particular set of material, such as the observational notes for classroom behavior, the researcher will begin to automatically search for this category among each new data set as s/he proceeds in the analysis. This is why I called the preliminary analytical process cumulative—there is a tendency for the same coding categories to come up again and again as each new pile of information is analyzed because the researcher is now predisposed to be aware of the potential existence of that pattern of behavior. For example, having already identified the theme of "private property" in general observational notes for both the classroom and the school as a whole during an earlier period of fieldwork, my eyes woke up as I went over notes involving a lunch that I had with two men in their twenties who had recently graduated from the University of Papua New Guinea and who were launching their careers in engineering and business. "I will tell you what is wrong with our country," said one of the men. "We need to have land in the hands of the people. This old fashioned thing of group ownership is no good. How can a man make money properly if he can't buy land?" His friend agreed wholeheartedly with this point, adding his own comment: "Yes, how can a man get rich?" "I don't want to be rich," corrected his friend, "but how can we develop this country properly without individual ownership." Similar themes could be found in newspaper articles and in the public statements of many people involved with "business" in Papua New Guinea. In fact, there *is* individual ownership in the country, but the vast majority of land remains firmly under the collective ownership of kinship units such as lineages or clans. What the two men were really lamenting about was that the alienation of land from kinship units had not proceeded to any great degree and that they did not know how they could be considered to be a "modern" country until it had done so. My own comments during lunch about how the continued collective ownership of land helped ensure that (barring natural disasters) few Papua New Guineans went hungry held no weight for them. "No, no," one of them declared, "everyone will benefit if they own their own land. Then they can do what they want on it, or sell it, or whatever."

This whole discussion could be coded as "private property" in my fieldnotes. In addition, we can immediately see that it is strongly related to the same theme of "private property" as it exists within the classrooms of West New Britain.

Secondary Analysis (Seeing Patterns)

In the second part of analysis, the goal is to begin cementing together the various levels of data collection so that we can form a larger analysis of the patterns of human behavior. I refer to this kind of analysis as secondary because it involves putting together already analyzed bits of information to form larger conceptual patterns. In a sense, this type of work involves the analysis of analysis. The researcher is no longer working directly with his or her notes but is now concerned about the potential relationship between one analytical concept and another. Again, I suggest that we begin using my own research as an example by proceeding from the smaller to the larger, or the more detailed to the bigger picture.

There are two main types of linkages that the researcher wants to look for when considering broader patterns of analysis. The first involves drawing conceptual linkages between the same types of evidence (e.g., a linkage between the concept of "competitive individualism" and "private property" in notes about classroom behavior). The second type of linkage can be sought between concepts that emerge from different kinds of information (e.g., a linkage between the concept of "competitive individualism" and related concepts that were present in published secondary sources on the political economy of wage labor jobs and/or certain aspects of colonial history). As usual, specific examples will help draw this distinction in a cleaner fashion.

As you are analyzing a specific pile of evidence (e.g., all of the research notes involving classroom observations), it should quickly become apparent that some of the concepts seem to be both separate from each other but at the same time closely related as analytical themes. A good example comes from work that was previously presented in this chapter and also earlier in the book. It seems to me that the hidden curriculum of classroom interactions concerning "private property" and those involving "competitive individualism" are closely related analytical concepts. Competitive individualism is ultimately built upon a European tradition, stemming from the Enlightenment period and running throughout the philosophy of Humanism. This thought system is not indigenous to Papua New Guineans and here, as in may other parts of the world (such as among the indigenous peoples of Canada), was imposed on a colonized people through colonial forms of government, religious institutions, and schools. Basically, this mode of thought views the individual, as Stuart Sims tells us, "as a unified self, with a central 'core' of identity unique to each individual, motivated primarily by the power of reason" (Sims 1999: 366). He goes on to further suggest that the social condition of modernity also encouraged the notion of the "entrepreneurial subject"—a person who exploits the natural world and subjects it to his dominion (the masculine bias in this paraphrased sentence is retained here on purpose). In relation to this and simply put, my concept of competitive individualism can be thought of as referring to the celebration of forms of competition that justify individual differences in access to both natural and social resources—with the assumption that the outcome of competitions are decided because of inherent or innate differences in the "abilities" of the autonomous individuals competing for resources (such as educational attainment). Compare this kind of thought to the classroom material presented earlier in this chapter regarding the individual "ownership" of books, or pencils, or plants growing in the garden (a type of "ownership" at odds with the customary practices of the many cultural groups that live in Papua New Guinea). After this, think about some of the material presented in chapter 5, when we saw teachers emphasizing that each student must do "his own work" alone and that most forms of cooperative learning were to be viewed as "cheating." To me, these are all related concepts. In fact, after I made these analytical linkages I was even able to return to my notes regarding classroom observations and find further incidents that showed students learning that "knowledge" itself is a kind of private property that individuals compete to obtain, as in the following examples.

> The teacher in this classroom rewards students who finish assignments quickly by letting them go and get a storybook from the shelf to read while they are waiting for the rest of the class to finish. This is clearly popular with the students, and they run to the shelf to grab the "best" storybooks as soon as they are finished. There are not enough to go around and a few are clearly favorite books, so there is quite a bit of grabbing and mild pushing going on. (English, Grade Four, Bialla C.S.)

> Okay, I want three people to come up and put three words down in the right place [on the board]. The kids are quite enthusiastic: "Excuse, excuse" [the equivalent of

saying "pick me, pick me"], they call out. One girl shouts out "Whoopee!" as she is picked, which makes the teacher smile. (English, Grade Two, Kimbe C.S.)

There is much to learn then by a straightforward comparison of the concepts that you have created in your codes for each specific type of information. There is, however, even more to learn when we take these understandings and begin to look for linkages across categories.

Take what I have just recorded above, and compare it to the statements of the young men mentioned in this chapter who did not think that Papua New Guinea would ever be truly modern without the dominance of private property. In doing this, we link concepts from one set of material (classroom observations) with concepts from another set of material (unstructured interviews). When I did this kind of cross-material comparison it became quite clear to me that a number of concepts were closely related and that this material would allow me to write a section about the theme of private property and competitive individualism in a thesis, book, or article.

The best way to illustrate the strength of this method of analysis is to take a single concept and trace the ways that it can be linked to related concepts that arise from material gathered though the use of other specific methods during the study. Since I have introduced the notion of competitive individualism in this chapter, let's remain with that concept and consider what other linkages we can find between this concept as it was first delineated from classroom observations and compare it to other forms of research data. Again, I would suggest that in doing this form of analysis the scholar begin with concepts that are tied closely to other forms of micro research before proceeding to concepts that can be gleaned from more macro sources of information. The reader should note that I am not presenting an exhaustive list of the linkages that I found between even these limited conceptual categories, but rather simply offering an illustration of the usefulness of this type of analysis for the reader's consideration.

In chapter 5, I presented a counting schedule involving the theme of disciplinary actions inside classrooms. I would like to suggest that there is a very strong linkage between these forms of disciplinary action and the idea of competitive individualism. How, for example, does a human child come to think of him or her self as an "autonomous being," unique and separate from family, kinship group, and society (and remember, this kind of thinking is quite "foreign" to the non-westernized customs of the cultural groups of Papua New Guinea)? The answer seems to lie in the concept of discipline—the kind of discipline that occurs everyday in the classrooms of West New Britain and that show up in the counting schedule presented in chapter 5 of this book. The fact that students very quickly learn to internalize disciplinary behavior is strongly supportive of the idea that they are learning to become autonomous individuals in keeping with enlightenment/modernist notions of the "free and independent" person who "decides" through rational choice how best to make his or her own way in the world. In this case, the "rational" choice is for a student to learn to conform to norms of classroom behavior and to "decide" to act in ways that teachers find appropriate to reward. Such decisions are not unimportant. Teachers, for example, discuss the behavior of students when deciding which ones to put on the list for moving from grade six to grade seven (i.e., from elementary to secondary school). Students (and there are substantial numbers of them) who pass the grade six exams but who do not have marks high enough to automatically qualify them for the move to grade seven have their futures decided by headmasters and teachers. Those school authorities differentiate, for example, between little Johnny, who was always getting help from Tommy with his homework and constantly getting answers off of Mary in class, versus Mark—who all might agree is not really as bright as Johnny, but who "does his own work." In this way, a student who does not learn the lesson of competitive individualism by accepting the inculcation of "self discipline" is put at a tremendous disadvantage for chances at gaining further education. One of the ironies of competitive individualism is that is it only encouraged to exist within parameters that are firmly established by higher authorities (such as the teachers and the other educational workers of the state). More will be said about this in a moment.

I have already mentioned how the theme of competitive individualism can be tied to material gathered through unstructured interviewing (the two young men having lunch with me that were spoken of above), and I would like to turn now to a consideration of related themes that were found to exist by me through semi-structured interviews. Using the interview schedule presented earlier in this book, I interviewed twenty-seven teachers (the total number available at the time) from all three community schools. Below, I present some of their answers in regard to question number ten: Could you briefly describe what a good pupil is like? What about a pupil who is not very good? These results can be quickly summarized in the following table, which categorizes statements by teachers concerning "good" versus "bad" pupils. I have only included answers that were mentioned by two or more teachers. Characteristics are recorded in diminishing order of response and the number listed beside each "characteristic" equals the number of teachers who described "good" versus "bad" pupils in a particular way. As you can see by the total numbers, most teachers offered more than one characterization.

It is very instructive to compare some of this semi-structured interview material with the material from classroom observations for what the two categories of information tell us about the concept of "competitive individualism." This is also a good point to note that one of the benefits of comparing concepts across material gathered through different research methods is that it often enlarges our understanding of the concepts that were coded during the initial period of the fieldwork. These categories or patterns of behavior have a tendency to become transformed during our analysis when we add new examples or parallel concepts to them. For example, I briefly noted above that one of the ironies of competitive individualism as it is performed in the classrooms of West New Britain is that it only seems to be encouraged to exist within very strict parameters. As table 8.1 shows, six teachers noted that a good student was by definition self-reliant and disciplined and they and other teachers gave alternate examples of this self-discipline by suggesting that such a student reads a lot and studies at home, knows how to behave outside of the classroom when no one is watching, and so forth. This would seem to coincide very nicely with the idea of a self-disciplined competitive individualism that contains the modernist notion of an autonomous

Table 8.1   Teachers' Perceptions of Good Versus Bad Students

Good Students		Bad Students	
– listens to the teacher/obedient	(13)	– a bighead/shows self pride and disrespect	(19)
– behaves well in the classroom	(12)	– plays up in the class/disturbs the class	(13)
– concentrates/quiet	(11)	– never listens to the teacher	(9)
– is self reliant/disciplined	(6)	– can be bright	(7)
– asks a lot of questions/talks at the right time	(6)	– doesn't ask a lot of questions/and is lazy	(6)
– is neat and tidy/good manners	(6)	– lacks concentration/is noisy	(5)
– early to school/starts to work straight away	(4)	– lacks manners/swears	(4)
– reads a lot/studies at home	(3)	– does not do homework/lags behind the class	(3)
– also behaves outside of classroom	(2)	– is not independent	(2)
– doesn't hit his friends	(2)	– does not look after books and things/untidy	(2)
– must show love to others	(2)		

individual making rational choices for his or her own benefit. At the same time, the three most common answers from teachers in regard to what makes a good pupil were all variations on the same theme: (1) is obedient and listens to the teacher, (2) behaves well in the classroom, and (3) is a quiet person who concentrates well. In other words, these three characteristics of a good pupil all point out that these teachers expect the "autonomous" child to "decide to behave properly" in the face of the state sponsored authority of school teachers. As seems to be true of all forms of modernist notions of competitive individualism, this idea does not include the notion that an individual can do whatever he or she likes, or be totally self-directed and make autonomous decisions in any way that s/he desires and thereby ignore state sponsored pressures to act in certain ways. Rather, the concept of competitive individualism being promoted here is that of a person whose "self-discipline" lines up with the state's rules for living the life of the good citizen, as these rules are promulgated by such state agents as school teachers. We can confirm this interpretation by looking at the material in table 8.1 that reflects teachers' ideas about what makes a bad student. While two teachers specifically noted that a bad student is not independent, six teachers acknowledged that a bad student could often be very bright, nine suggested that s/he never listens to the teacher, thirteen said that a bad pupil plays up in the classroom, and nineteen stated that a bad student is a bighead who shows an excessive self-pride and a disrespect for others. Read differently, many of the traits that are said to exist in a bad student could be taken as an indication of a bright, self-reliant individual who makes his or her own judgments in the face of opposition while maintaining an almost complete personal autonomy. What is "missing" in this interpretation and what makes these traits "lacking" as *the* traits of a modern competitive individual is the idea of the person who makes rational choices about his or her own behavior. School teachers and other agents of the state (such as social workers, the judiciary, and the police) do not accept the type of behavior noted above as belonging to "bad pupils" as a true indication of the properly modernist form of autonomous individualism because it does not conform to their notion of a person who makes *rational choices* in the face of the structurally arrayed forces of state power.

In working through concepts that can be seen in different levels of information (such as classroom observations versus semi-structured interviews), we are able to change and enlarge our ideas regarding the patterns of behavior associated with the idea of competitive individualism in a specific study. This new interpretation tells us that competitive individualism does not mean selfish action but rather is thought to refer to disciplined individual actions that take place under the watchful eye of state sponsored authority. Put another way, children are only given permission to compete for those things that they are *allowed* to compete for under the rules that have been created by adults within their relatively new nation-state political economies.

If we take the basic idea of competitive individualism and also relate it to some of the material that was presented in chapter 7 on self-reported information, we can also add a more subjective dimension to our understanding of students' own ideas about what a modern Papua New Guinean individual might wish to act like in his or her own adulthood. Looking over the tables presented in chapter 7 about "my future work" in relation to the concepts that we have explored so far in our analysis here, I am immediately struck by how many grade five and grade six boys and girls tie their hopes for their individual adult futures on obtaining work that is directly tied to the state. Jobs such as being a school teacher, medical doctor or nurse, police officer, member of the armed forces, Department of Primary Industry worker or Department of Fisheries worker, government typist or clerk, member of parliament, radio announcer, or a building inspector all depend directly on government operations for employment opportunities. Other wage economy jobs mentioned by the students, such as that of engineer, mechanic, pilot, air hostess, rugby player, architect, taxi driver, and so forth depend very heavily upon government subsidies, state laws and regulations, and state sponsored educational opportunities to become a reality. These students understand very well that they will have to compete for these opportunities as individuals, while simultaneously "deciding" to display the forms of behavior acceptable to the state that will allow them to escape the notice of gatekeepers who might otherwise deny them entrance to higher educational opportunities or wage work opportunities directly or indirectly tied to the state (note that all of this occurs in education processes despite the tremendous amount of rhetoric about the "free market system" and the "open competition of capitalism" that exists in Papua New Guinea and in other similar nation-states).

It is interesting to me that many of the children seem to view their potential futures as ones that will largely be independent of the customary family and kinship obligations that exist in every village community in Papua New Guinea, while at the same time realizing that these ties may remain useful as a safety net in case of individual failure. Remember the boy discussed in chapter 7 who openly stated that if he was individually successful he would become a government clerk and try to get a posting overseas but if he was not successful in education he would return to the village and take advantage of his father's business ventures; or the girl who wanted to be a school teacher and live in the urban center of Bialla so that she could teach the children to respect her as the teacher; or the boy who wanted to be a ship engineer so that he could travel, obtain a high salary, and live the good life (while at the same time paying his parents back for his education); or the boy who wanted to be a geologist for Shell Oil so he could spend his time roaming around the bush alone looking for minerals. All of these children view "success" largely in individual terms and can be said to have learned the lessons of competitive individualism well. The emotional longing expressed in these and other self-reported essays on the topic "my future work" tell us how deeply embedded these conceptual themes have become in the new modernist notions of individual self-identity among many of the pupils of West New Britain. This adds a personal aspect to the more social analysis reported above in regard to the connection between the concept of competitive individualism and the expectations on the part of social agents such as school teachers that such individualism is "naturally" limited by the strictures of the state-sponsored social regulation of behavior.

All of these micro level sets of information can further be compared to evidence that emerges out of macro venues of research, such as newspaper accounts, government documents, literature regarding the political economy of contemporary Papua New Guinea, or historical material (whether from archival or secondary sources). These can add greatly to the social analysis that has already been accomplished through comparing concepts from the different methods of ethnographic research concerning micro research locations such as classrooms, schools, or educational meetings. Again, I remain within our theme of competitive individualism and its relationship to similar concepts in illustrating the usefulness of analytical comparison across methodological levels of information gathering. And again, what is offered here is only a small sample of what can be accomplished by using this form of conceptual comparison within your own research project.

In chapter 4, which included an explanation of how to use newspaper sources for research, I noted that there were letters to the editor complaining about a lack of opportunity for school leavers. One writer, for example, suggested that employment in government or in other good wage labor jobs should be limited to ten years, at which time the employed person should give the job up and allow another person to take their place. I also noted that in response to these types of letters to the editor in the newspapers, elected government officials often wrote replies that, in the light of the analysis that we have done above, would seem to largely be a defense of the idea of competitive individualism. As noted in chapter 4, the Deputy Prime Minister wrote that "Only hard work solve[s] problems—there is no one to blame for failure but ourselves," while the Prime Minister wrote a month later in the same newspaper that "It is now time to bury dependent thinking for good. . . . Why should the tax money of a few hard working people build schools and hospitals for people who do not lift a finger to make any contribution at all?" In other words, if some have more than others in the new Papua New Guinea it is because they have "earned it" through competitive individualism—while a lack of this kind of success can only "be blamed on oneself." Again, a new dimension of understanding becomes available through the comparison of one set of analytical material with another. In this case, this new dimension dovetails nicely with the expectation that students (or others) need to learn "self-discipline" and how to "take responsibility" for "their own" success or failure; whether in the classroom or, as the newspaper accounts seem to suggest, in the world of the wage economy long after schooling is finished.

One note here before I continue in my analysis of newspapers as a source of information. Television has also become important in many developing nations and can be gleaned for interviews, documentaries, and other material that might provide alternative "voices" to the ones that you have been able to collect through newspaper sources. At the time that I actually carried out my fieldwork in Papua New Guinea, television broadcasts did not exist in the country. This has since changed and there is no doubt in my mind that local television programs, like radio or newspapers, can be a good source of specific kinds of information if carefully used and analyzed.

Comparing concepts gleaned from micro research in classrooms and schools with macro research using such sources as newspapers confirms that what at first glance may seem to be a specific educational issue of teaching students how to compete in the classroom in the form of examinations, the adoption of "self-discipline," and so forth can actually be tied to larger social and political issues, such as the political rhetoric used by politicians to "explain" to their constituents why only a very few Papua New Guineans receive the good life promised to the masses during the period leading up to independence in the middle of the 1970s.

At the same time, this conceptual theme can be tied to related issues that emerge out of the analysis of both historical trends and the contemporary political economy of Papua New Guinea. Compare, for example, the words of the Prime Minister of Papua New Guinea in 1986 as published in the newspaper source quoted above and the words of a resident magistrate in 1908 as they were noted in chapter 2 of this book on the use of historical sources: "Nowhere in Papua, I venture to say, will you find a more lazy, indolent set of male natives than in these villages. With them laziness is carried to a fine art and their chief and only occupation is dancing" (quoted in Lacey 1983: 36). Although seventy-eight years apart and set respectively in social worlds that were colonial versus independent, both pieces of rhetoric quite clearly "blame" individuals for not living up to the speakers' notions of a modern form of competitive individualism—one that includes an energetic self-discipline and the kind of rational decision-making that leads to working hard within the labor arenas created with the full support of the contemporary nation-state. In that same earlier chapter I noted the words of missionaries such as John Holmes, who bragged about how he made every individual at Urika station in 1918 account every morning for the work they had completed the day before, and that "if there has been any slackness it has to be accounted for before all hands." Some of the many examples of the quasi-military style of "drill" used at mission stations as a part of education were also described in the same chapter. I noted then how similar this was to many contemporary practices in the community schools of West New Britain. Here we can also note how these historical trends coincide with the beginnings of attempting to create a "modern" form of individual—one who understands his or her place in the world to be defined through personal competition and tied to the lessons of autonomous actions tempered by the self-discipline of rational choice (see Fife 2001). This of course gives a dimension of depth to our analysis and allows us to consider where some of these educational patterns began and how they developed into the contemporary forms of schooling that we can view in today's Papua New Guinea.

As such, we would expect the micro lessons of competitive individualism and related concepts such as self-discipline to be strongly related to other widespread social patterns in contemporary Papua New Guinea. Instead of proving that this is so, I would like to use this set of comparisons to show the reader how the process of moving up the ladder of analytical comparison from micro analysis to macro analysis can also be turned back downward again and lead to new insights about the same basic social process that is being illuminated through these initial comparisons. As usual, clarity will be better achieved with a specific example than with abstract statements about analytical methods.

Having reached the point in our analytical comparison where we understand that the concept of competitive individualism is closely aligned with other concepts such as discipline, and that this whole bundle of concepts are themselves better understood when we further realize that competitive individualism does not refer to actions that are truly "independent" but rather to actions that are said to be independent but are in fact strongly influenced by the possibilities created for acceptable action by social agents such as teachers (who themselves interpret what kinds of personal characteristics might best serve a modern nation-state), we can then move on to new insights. The researcher who arrives at this point of the analysis will often realize, because of his or her new level of knowledge regarding the patterns of behavior associated with the concept of competitive individualism, that there are other concepts that can be taken from micro level research material and "recognized" now as also being relevant for the analysis of this particular constellation of related behaviors. By turning the analysis back upon itself, the researcher gains an understanding that the interpretation of larger patterns is something that not only builds through an expansion "upward" through the many levels of the methodologically driven collection of information, but also "downwards" and "sideways" through a continual reappraisal and re-comparison of older material that sits "beside" the material from which the original concept came. I illustrate this point by taking two related concepts from classroom observations, explain how they are related to what we have considered so far, and link them to concepts taken from the macro level of research involving the contemporary political economy of Papua New Guinea.

I noted in chapter 5 on the use of the participant observation method of research that two of the concepts that I coded for in my notes on classroom observations were "authority" and "hierarchy." By now, it should become apparent to a researcher that both of these concepts are also closely related to the idea of "competitive individualism." Authority, for example, involves the hidden curriculum of classroom instruction that emphasizes that each individual has a very specific social place to occupy in a modern nation state and that each of these roles contains a specific amount of social authority. This lesson is taught, for example, by drilling students with charts that show how educational, political, and other forms of social organization all move along a pyramid style system. In this sense, the educational system, as one example, can be thought of as a giant pyramid with the federal minister of education at the top of it and the community school students forming the base of the structure, with teachers, head teachers, inspectors and so forth arrayed along various middle levels of the pyramid. The "higher" the level, the more social authority the occupier of that position holds. As I've mentioned, students memorize these conceptual schemes and are often amazingly capable of describing, for example, which individual occupies which political position in a complex alignment leading from themselves through to local politicians and all the way up to the prime minister of the country.

In the strongly related concept of hierarchy, teachers reinforce the idea that an order-giving / order-taking hierarchy is part of the "natural order of things." Both this notion of hierarchy and the concept of authority that are taught in the class-rooms of West New Britain justify (I suggest in my analysis), and are in turn justi-fied, by the concept of competitive individualism. For example, let us turn back to one of the fieldnotes that I used to illustrate the idea of hierarchy in chapter 5.

> She [the teacher] is teaching the class how to pronounce certain words: fun, run, sun, etc. She will say a word out loud, such as "run," and then asks "What sounds the same?" Individual children often call out a correct answer, but she persists in waiting for the person she herself chooses to answer "correctly." (English, Grade Two, Bialla C.S.)

The hidden curriculum of this lesson teaches several things at once: that only the teacher (properly constituted authority) gets to decide when something is correct; that students have to compete with each other not only for knowing the correct form of knowledge but also for getting the attention of authority in an acceptable manner in order for their knowledge to "count," and that the world is divided up into universally acknowledged correct (non-contextualized) information versus incorrect (particular) information. Here, we can see the very strong tie created in these classrooms between learning to exercise competitive individualism and the notion that such actions are only allowable under the strict authority of a state-sponsored arbiter of (modern and therefore universal) human knowledge.

How do these concepts relate to other concepts that emerge out of the political economy of contemporary Papua New Guinea? There are many examples that I could give here, but the most salient one concerns the work situation that students will face if they hope to be one of the lucky few that find a job in the wage-based economy. Whether working directly in a cash economy situation (e.g., as a miner, or a store clerk, or a bank clerk) or for the government (e.g., as a bureaucrat in the Department of Education or as an employee of the Department of Primary Industries) a worker in Papua New Guinea will be faced with the standard struc-ture of employer/employee relationships that characterize modern bureaucratic capitalist economies. The basic structure of this form of political economy is of course that of the boss/worker. The boss, by definition, is the person who decides what constitutes correct work behavior in a specific situation. It is his or her authority, often expressed as an appeal to that person's special relationship to a supposed universal standards of action or knowledge ("I'm a qualified engineer, so I know how to build this road") that is held to be more important than the assumed inferiority of the worker's knowledge. "Your twenty years of actual road building does not matter (that is, context does not matter), because you did not go to Australia and get your engineer's degree along with training in standard road building techniques" (that is, I am the authority because I have been taught the assumed-to-be-universal techniques of road building, or banking, or business accounting). In other words, the worker is only allowed to express his or her (assumed to be natural rather than socially taught) competitive individualism through gaining sufficient credentials to qualify for a specific job, beating out other competitors for the same employment, and working hard to continually prove that s/he deserves to keep the job as opposed to being replaced by another worker. Self-autonomy ends when and if it conflicts with the "right" of the bosses to assume their properly constituted authority (whether that authority is bestowed by the state, a corporation, or a small business owner). Again, a modern individual is expected to make a "rational" choice in the face of structural author-ity and exercise his or her own individualism in a manner consistent with the rules laid down by this authority. Competitive individualism may only be expressed at the service of the state, corporation, or business for which one works. Anything else is likely to lead to dismissal or other form of disciplinary action. The parallel between the hidden curriculum of classroom instructions and the world of work in a bureaucratic capitalist economy is striking. The teacher is the boss, the stu-dents are the workers, and correct knowledge or actions are defined in relation to both authority and authority's presumed understanding of universal (rather than contextual) forms of knowledge.

Comparison, then, can be worked sideways within methodological categories, up or down between different levels of methodological analysis, and in various combinations (sideways, upward from micro to macro, downward back to micro, sideways again and then back upward, and so forth). As in the gathering of infor-mation, analysis is partly a science and partly an art form, or partly a matter of rea-son and logic well grounded in evidence and partly a matter of inspiration or intuition about what concepts to compare and what might point to an interesting relationship if a bridging piece of evidence could be found to bring two or more concepts together to form a larger unified analytical whole. As a rule of thumb, your goal as an ethnographic scholar is to build larger patterns out of well-grounded smaller conceptual elements, while maintaining plausible connections between small pieces of evidence and the overall (holistic) picture within which they seem to fit. The whole picture is what we mean when we say that we are writ-ing "an ethnography" (but more on this in chapter 10).

Differences Within Patterns (Or, Why Patterns are Never Exact)

If only things could remain that simple. If only ethnography were a straightfor-ward matter of adding up the evidential elements, making larger patterns out of smaller patterns, and then forming the larger patterns into an overall whole. Unfortunately, there is often dirt on the ethnographic floor. This "dirt" comes in the form of inconsistent or contradictory evidence. Any good ethnography should take such evidence into account and not simply sweep it under the analytical rug (where the reader can't see it). In fact, such inconsistencies often make the ethnog-raphy stronger in the long run, adding idiosyncratic dimensions and enlarging our understanding of the complexities of social and cultural patterns. More impor-tantly, such "dirt" is a normal part of social and cultural life and is only seen to be "unusual" by both insiders and the researcher because of our expectations regarding the orderliness of life. In this sense, it is researchers grasp of these normal inconsistencies that help make their ethnographies unique. Any good study of education in developing countries (or any other specific topic) should produce common themes that can be compared to similar studies conducted in other countries around the world. Each project, however, should also produce unique or original material that can then be used by other researchers to enlarge their notion of what they might themselves study in their next piece of research. If this were not so, there would be no reason for all of the work on context that I have consistently pushed for in this book. It is context that helps make sense of "breaks" or inconsistencies in the information and, as we explore in chapter 9, that often lead to insights that can be turned into new theory.

During my initial periods of coding my raw information from the classrooms of West New Britain, I quickly saw that "competitive individualism" formed one of the most important lessons of hidden curriculum. At the same time, I noted that other contradictory messages were also present in my observations about classroom behavior. Although almost all teachers stressed the idea of competitive individualism on a consistent basis when it came to tests, spelling bees, or other directly competitive situations, there were considerable variations in the extent to which individual or group responses, working alone or in ability groups or as a whole class together, occurred in the day-to-day functioning of various classrooms. Several teachers that I observed, for example, seemed to prefer working at the level of the class as a whole and/or in ability groups much of the time rather than in the individual modes of interaction patterns that were favored by a strong majority of teachers. For example:

> Math. She is teaching them to count, each group uses sticks that they arrange on the floor in front of them. She tries to get them to add two groups of sticks together. "What's the answer?" A few children call out "seven," even though she means it as a rhetorical question. "Hey, no shouting," she says, "I don't like children who shout—then the others know the answer too." She walks over to each group and asks them what the answer is. They certainly find out fast if they are "slow" in comparison to some of the other groups. It is interesting the emphasis she puts here on group work, group answers, etc. But it means that being typed as "dumb" leaves the child little room to change the teacher's mind about them, because they are grouped with other "dumb" partners. (Math, Grade One, Kimbe C.S.)

This particular teacher generally favors, as do a few others, organizing her work through the agency of ability groups rather than through forms of teaching/learning that emphasize individual progression. Notice, however, that although she emphasizes the importance of group work she does not negate the message of hierarchical inequality. In this case, groups rather than individuals are set up to compete with each other as to how quickly they can solve particular problems. This may teach individuals that they are not more important than the group to which they belong, but it does not teach them that all members of the class are in some essential sense equal to each other. And of course, during examination periods she is just as vigilant as any other teacher in enforcing the notion that tests are a measure of individual "ability" alone and will not allow her students to "cheat" by working cooperatively together in their ability groups—even though almost all of the learning in her classroom occurred within that kind of a context.

Other examples could be given here to show that a few individual teachers actually seem to prefer to work with the class together as a whole (e.g., encouraging collective responses from students, often chanted in unison, to questions). Of course no teacher uses only one method of instruction exclusively, but these examples do show that the researcher should expect to find considerable individual differences within the overall patterns of educational instruction inside of classrooms and must be prepared to account for these differences (more in that regard later).

Every so often in my notes I came across a stronger lesson that was given by the teacher about the importance of collective relations over individual performance. In this form, these particular lessons most directly reflected customary Papua New Guinean concerns with limiting the actions of an individual and reminding each person that individual performances depended heavily upon the ability to enlist the active support of their fellow human beings (on customary limitations, see Fife 1995a). I give an example of this below.

"Alright, count to a hundred." The class responds "One, two, three, . . . one hundred!" "Alright, counting in twos?" he asks. "Two, four, six, . . . one hundred!" "Counting in fives?" A few seconds after they begin he stops them. "Domi, you are rushing. Begin again." "Five, ten, fifteen, . . . one hundred!" "Tens?" he commands. Again he stops them just after they begin. "Domi, who said you could go first?" The class laughs, then continues the exercise. (Math, Grade One, Kimbe C.S.)

Examples from my notes indicate that teachers who are working in this fashion will often chastise a student who tries to charge ahead of the class or shame individuals who lag behind. The ideal, when performing as a collective body, is for everyone to move at the same pace. There are no star pupils, nor should anyone be left behind. Notice that while this seems to contradict the message of competitive individualism, it also reinforces the hierarchical authority of the teacher—who alone determines who is over-performing or who is not keeping up in a satisfactory manner. Despite this lesson in hierarchy, these teaching methods also resonate with the customary concerns of Papua New Guineans—who generally embrace cultural forms that suggest that individuals need to be, or at least should appear to be, roughly in step with the other members of their social group.

What do these inconsistencies mean? As I read and reread my classroom notes, I became convinced that many individual teachers had an intuitive understanding of the "need" to balance the dominant message of competitive individualism with lessons about the desirability of cooperative individualism (or individual performance versus fitting into the group). When I arrived at this understanding, I began to note occasions when the same teacher "mixed" his or her messages within a single set of lessons. For example:

She has a very ritualized pattern of teaching. Spelling today. "Sundays, always, holidays, etc." The teacher asks Rachel to spell "always." The girl stands up, but spells it wrong. "Is she right?" the teacher asks the class. "No!" they respond. She then asks the girls to [collectively] spell always, then the boys. Then she continues to call on individuals to spell specific words. "Everybody, spell the word holidays." Class: "Holidays, H-O-L-I-D-A-Y-S." They follow with this cadence, three times: "Holidays, holidays, holidays!" (Spelling, Grade Two, Ewasse C.S.)

The teacher groups the class into a semi-circle, facing the front chalkboard. "Alright, close your eyes, I want you all to say your times." In unison: "Sixty seconds equals one hour, twenty-four hours equals one day . . ." All the way up to reciting the number of days each month has. "Alright, keep your eyes closed. I want you to think about how many shapes we learned about." Hands go up. "How many?" she asks one boy. "Five shapes," he answers. They then go on to name each shape: "Triangle, square, oblong, . . ." Individual answers, then all together. "Okay, the three colours in our shapes?" (Math, Grade Three, Kimbe C.S.)

The teacher indicated in the last example repeats the individual/group question and answer pattern in very regular intervals, not only in Math lessons but also in her teaching as a whole. The teacher from Ewasse school whom I mentioned above, however, showed a general preference for asking individual students questions, only occasionally asking for group responses in most of her lessons. These two teachers can be further contrasted to a teacher from Bialla (not noted above) who demonstrated a general preference for group answers, alternating with individual answers only at irregular and unpredictable intervals. Collectively, these teachers show how complex patterns of hidden curriculum can be. Taken alone, the Ewasse teacher noted above displays her own individual complexity. Within this one small example, she not only shows that she is willing to soften her general preference for individual answers on occasion, but also gives a hint of a preference for gender differentiation. These are very useful reminders that hidden curriculum is a matter of emphasis and degree rather than a clear-cut case of either/or, this or that. My qualitative analysis, based on over two hundred and fifty hours of direct classroom observation time, convinces me that the vast majority of teachers in the three schools that I studied emphasized the importance of individual performance first and only then went on to include the secondary message about the importance of group performance. Why this should be so is an important question and one that I attempt to answer in chapter 9 in relation to the creation of theory in ethnographic research. I should also note here, though, that because this analysis largely arose inductively after the study had been completed I was not able to construct a counting schedule to verify my observational findings. Such verification could of course occur in my own future research, or in the research of others who might wish to test out the idea of whether most teachers in West New Britain truly do favor individual over group performances in their classrooms.

Differences and contradictions will always exist in ethnographic research because individuals are not automatons and are themselves exposed to disparate influences at various times of their lives. Even when we "function" (in a social sense) as an agent of the state, or as a representative of our social class, or age grade, or gender group, we are always more than this as individual human beings. Actual behavior spills over from our social conditioning and individuals variously rebel against structures, embrace them with both hands, and/or become confused about what "I am supposed to do in this situation." At times, a person may experience and express all three feelings within a single set of interactions, or even draw upon yet another social influence that—at this particular moment—becomes the most important guiding principle for immediate behavior. This is what makes analysis so endlessly challenging—relating the words and actions of real people to the larger social and cultural patterns that give such behavior meaning.

Perhaps this is another way of saying that analysis requires imagination. Not the kind that involves flights of fancy or the invention of information, but rather an imagination firmly grounded in the ethnography of everyday life in relation to its larger context. What are commonly called "facts" cannot speak for themselves—as they do not exist in this sense. They exist only as part of the over-all research goals of a project and in relation to the theory that guides it. It requires human intuition to link facts to concepts and finally to larger patterns of analysis. This of course leads us to theory, which is the topic of chapter 9.

9

Creating and Testing Theory

E thnography can be thought of as a simultaneous conversation between the ethnographer and at the very least two other groups of people. One group is made up of the people with whom we conduct our research. The other group includes the relevant scholars (such as researchers in anthropology, education, sociology, history, folklore, and so forth) and policy makers (such as government bureaucrats, community leaders, etc.) to whom we communicate our results. Theory might be thought of as the language that makes this second conversation possible. Any dialogue needs a common language in order to proceed. It is theory, or more accurately shared theoretical concepts, that allow us to talk to one another about the results of our research. Pragmatically, theory is the matrix that creates "facts" and that gives us the framework from which we can have a meaningful discussion with others about the evidence or information gathered through our ethnographic methods.

Theory is both "made" and "tested" in ethnographic research. It is created, for example, every time the researcher suggests a linkage between one analytical concept and another, such as that which might be suggested to exist between student dropout rates and employment opportunities in a developing country. It is tested whenever a researcher takes an analytical suggestion from a previous writer (or even from their own earlier work) and questions it as an explanation in his or her own research project in order to see how well it "fits" or explains the situation. Testing, in this sense, does not refer to the kind of positivistic assumptions that underlie most forms of quantitative research (though of course this research tradition can yield a tremendous amount of useful information itself). Rather, it simply refers to the idea that the analytical framework of one ethnographic researcher can be critically evaluated by a second researcher through trying to apply it to what seems to be a similar social situation and considering whether or not the theory increases or decreases our understanding of that situation. In other words, does a specific theoretical element increase or decrease our ability to make rational sense out of the various pieces of information that we are trying to fit together and understand as a larger pattern of human behavior in a particular time and place? If the answer is yes, then that bit of theory is worth holding onto and even expanding so that it might be used again in future research projects. If it works to some extent but not fully (a common finding), then it may be worth modifying (through reference to the explanation of information in the current research) and then passing it along in this changed though not fully "new" format. If it does little to help us understand our own ethnographic work, then we have to decide that either it does not fit my particular research situation or perhaps that it is simply a bad theory and should be abandoned. If we take either of the latter two positions then we need to either create new theory ourselves or search for alternative existing theories that make better sense out of our information.

All of this can be restated in an alternative manner. Information is potentially infinite. Therefore, the only way to render information useful to us as researchers (or indeed as a human beings) is to organize it. Theory is the tool that we use for the organization of information. Part of the creativity of ethnographic research involves the invention of new theories in order to better explain what we are finding "in the field"; part of the discipline of ethnography is using our findings to critique what others have suggested can be used as theory in order to organize the understanding of similar social situations (such as, for example, the relationship between hidden curriculum and social inequality in a country similar to Papua New Guinea). How this actually works can best be illustrated with specific examples from my own work. I continue to use my own project, then, to show how a researcher can both test old theory and create new theory in the course of an ethnographic study. This is not an arid academic exercise—it is what allows us to have conversations with others about the social worlds we are trying to understand. It is also, as we see in chapter 10, what determines how writing or other forms of ethnographic presentation will proceed. Without theory, there is no true ethnographic writing (but more on this later).

Testing Theory

I wish to begin our exploration of theory by considering the idea that qualitative theory can be "tested" in some very real sense. Let me begin with an example that involves witchcraft accusations. At one time it was a truism among those who worked on witchcraft issues in the social sciences that witchcraft accusations rose and fell in relation to times of high or low social stress. High social stress might refer to an economic crisis, an environmental crisis, or another major event or situation that was sure to have a substantial impact on the society being considered. The suggestion that witchcraft accusations will become much more prevalent during such periods of intense social stress can be thought of as a theory of witchcraft accusations. Such a theory can of course be "tested," in my sense of the word, through new ethnographic research by scholars who concern themselves with witchcraft accusations. It might subsequently be found, for example, that accusations in a specific society actually seem to be spread relatively evenly across time and do not change appreciably during periods of great social change. Or, another researcher might find that witchcraft accusations seem to be largely a gender issue in a specific society, as most accusations in that group are directed toward women.

Alternatively, a scholar might discover that accusations are primarily made by older men against younger men, and speculate that they are related to a political form of gerontocracy in which older men try to control access to young brides through various social means (including witchcraft accusations). After some time, each pattern of witchcraft accusation might be found to exist by different researchers in separate ethnographic projects. Clearly, with such findings, the simple theoretical formula that "witchcraft accusations increase in times of high social stress" becomes an inadequate theoretical idea and must either be rejected altogether, severely modified, or replaced by a newer theoretical explanation. For example, as an alternative theory, a scholar might suggest that all members of hunting and gathering societies are dominated by X type of witchcraft accusations, while horticulturalists are dominated by Y type of accusations. Someone else might offer the idea that all witchcraft accusations are really about gender relationships, and that whenever we find a rapid increase in gender tensions (e.g., high rates of divorce), we will also find escalating witchcraft accusations. A third person might put forth the notion that accusations are best thought of as a form of political control and create a theory that places them in a specific relationship to societies that rely on a particular type of political organization. It is common for many alternative theories to be presented in a relatively short period of time after the initial theory—one that inspired a great deal of ethnographic research—begins to be strongly questioned. This is basically how theoretical testing proceeds in ethnographic settings. The more circumstances involving witchcraft accusations that ethnographers working in different part of the world find are not well explained by the simple formula of "high social tension equals high witchcraft accusations" the more the original theory will be considered to have been "tested" and found wanting as a good explanation for that particular social process.

Let's turn now to some of my own research in Papua New Guinea and consider the issue of testing theory in relation to educational issues. I actually considered a large number of theoretical issues in my original study, but we concentrate here upon only one specific issue in order to retain as much clarity as possible.

As I mentioned earlier in this book, in the late 1970s Frederick Gearing made a laudable attempt at creating a "cultural theory of education and schooling." In this theory, Gearing assumed that hidden curriculum was the key to understanding cultural transmission and to explaining why some students became successful in specific classroom environments and others did not. As Gearing (1979a: 170) put it:

> . . . the theory is intended to *explain* how it comes about that some members of certain definable categories of persons predictably will, and all members of other categories of persons predictably will not, come competently to perform some task . . . [T]he explanation of how such competencies predictably get distributed would entail the identification of those kinds of restraints that are interactional, and that are not mental and not motor in nature.

My own research taught me that I was very much in agreement with Gearing in respect to the importance of hidden curriculum and hence about the need to study human interaction on a very close level, but that I did not agree with him about where we could find the "constraints" that informed these interactions. For example, I agreed with his statement "one cannot adequately comprehend any one part of a system of education or schooling in a community unless one comprehends as well something of the variety of the other parts that coexist and may compete" (Gearing 1979b: 174). In other words, his theory contained the idea that the researcher must take the larger social context of education into account. Where we differed, however, was in where we would locate that larger social context. He suggested (177), for example, that it could be related in a good old-fashioned "structural-functional description." In this description, the researcher would have to learn about the basic social organization of a community, the kinds of jobs or work that community members engaged in, and the kinds of smaller groups into which they gathered. Gearing defined these groups "behaviorally" and suggested that a researcher following his theoretical position could gain an understanding of the social context that informs the micro process of education simply by focusing upon the interactional behaviors of members of the community (170).

My research led me to believe that Gearing's theory fell into the error of relying on a much too narrow definition of what constituted the "context" or "structure" of a situation and that societies could not be defined by the easily observable limit of their communities but rather were embedded within much larger social and economic systems. I also felt that these systems had to be taken into account—at least to the extent that they might reasonably be thought to impinge upon the everyday behavior that researchers such as Gearing and myself like to observe and analyze. To take an example outside of education, a researcher can watch laborers planting coffee on a plantation and interview them in order to get their views regarding what they think they are doing, but without some notion of where they stand as workers in relation to the larger market conditions for coffee in their region and the ways that these conditions are affected by outside forces such as the global coffee market, we would only be able to reach half an understanding of the meaning of their "interactions" within their community. In other words, it is not enough to observe members of the community at work, it is also necessary to have some idea about why they continue to do that particular work. Much the same can be said of education, which is a global process as much as it is a national or a local one—a process that may be as much about "the economy" or "religion" as it is about "education." That is why, for example, I insisted in this book that the researcher begin his or her project by investigating the broader context of any ethnographic topic in a specific country. This context, as I explained earlier, may well involve historical trends over the last few centuries and larger patterns involving the political economy of a country and a region (such as a province or a state). One of the major problems with Gearing's theory as it was formulated in the late 1970s was that it largely ignored history. If we think of social "structure" as a snapshot in time, then it seems obvious to me that it is necessary to have some knowledge of what goes into making the picture the way it is at this particular moment in time. We also need to know about the kinds of larger social forces that might alter this picture in the very near future. In short, we must consider the context that only a historically informed political economy can give us if we are going to connect micro and macro levels of influence together to create a more holistic ethnographic understanding of education in a particular developing country. The same of course is just as true if our ethnographic topic were tourism in a marginalized region Canada, temporary emigrants who found a niche for themselves as construction workers in Germany, unionized versus non-unionized hospital employees in the Caribbean, and so forth.

As I stated earlier in this chapter, testing theories through ethnography seldom leads to either a complete acceptance or rejection of them. As was true in the case of my own ethnographic research in relation to Frederick Gearing's cultural theory of education and schooling, we most often find that some aspects of a theory will help explain parts of our own information well and that other aspects will seem to be lacking or otherwise inadequate in our own use for organizing our information into coherent patterns that "make sense" of the situation we are investigating. When this happens, the researcher normally suggests ways that the original theory might be modified to better explain similar research situations to our own and presents it in written formats so that others might try these new analytical suggestions out for themselves. In my own West New Britain study, for example, I suggested (Fife 1992a: 377):

> It is at this level of analysis [i.e., hidden curriculum] that Gearing's emphasis on language and micro-interactions are most valuable, for it is in these interactions and not in macro assumptions about such interactions that actual differences in hidden curricula will be found. Gearing gives researchers the room to find differences in both teacher and student performances. But we must go beyond his model to include historical and larger social relations in order to give researchers the room to understand how these differences relate to widespread changes in developing societies. This will expand Gearing's model to one that can be used more effectively for research in both developed and developing societies.

Creating Theory

When we suggest changes to an already established theory, we are in a way of course also making theory. The creation of theory that I am most interested in here, however, involves a more active inductive process—one that proceeds largely from the gathering of information to the invention of new theoretical ideas based upon that information. I say "largely" because this process is never a pure one, in the sense that it is probably impossible to invent a totally new theoretical idea based strictly upon ethnographic research that has not been influenced in some fashion by the ideas of others. In reality, ideas come from all kinds of places at once and it is very difficult to separate what strikes you as a new analytical approach to understanding information from something that you may have read about years ago but consciously forgotten, or something that you discussed one late night with a colleague and no longer remember who said what about which concept, or something that you picked up in a classroom a decade ago and have modified to suit an entirely new situation. That is why, when we do remember some of these influences, we cite them to the best of our abilities within our writing. However, it is useful for the purposes of this discussion to consider what kinds of theories we can invent that are based primarily upon our encounters with field research situations rather than based primarily upon the written work of other researchers. I use what I think is an excellent example from my own work to illustrate how such theoretical creation can proceed in ethnography. The example is, I think, particularly appropriate as it began as an investigation into an already existing theory and, through my own encounter with field research, evolved into an original theoretical formulation.

I have already indicated in chapter 3 of this book that prior to my field research I had read the work of numerous scholars concerning the idea of hidden curriculum and its usefulness for understanding some of the ways that human interactions in classrooms help to create social inequalities in a specific place. None of these writings, however, prepared me to expect the kind of systematic contradictions in my evidence (see chapter 8) that I observed. These contradictions led me to conclude, after many hours of classroom research that teachers not only created a classroom atmosphere that gave off such primary messages as competitive individualism but also contradicted themselves to a greater or lesser extent (depending upon the individual) and in so doing created secondary messages such as ones about cooperative individualism as well. Over time, although I had no reason to expect that such a process existed from any of the readings I had done regarding other scholars' research, I theorized that at least in developing countries such as Papua New Guinea, two kinds of hidden curriculum existed simultaneously in the same classrooms—I called these primary forms of hidden curriculum and secondary forms of hidden curriculum (e.g., Fife 1992a, 1992b, 1994).

Primary forms of hidden curriculum, I theorized, resonated with the responsibilities that teachers felt they had to use to bring students into the "modern" world of the new Papua New Guinea. This was a country undergoing rapid social changes that were primarily aimed at creating social formations that would correspond to political and business leaders' notions of a "developed" country. Among many other trends, these included the notion that teachers should help create autonomous competitive individuals who would see themselves as separate social units who made rational choices in pursuit of personal goals. In other words, a "modern citizen" for a "modern nation-state."

I further postulated that many teachers, who had grown up within an uneven mixture of village style social life alongside of urban-informed social changes, were often personally uncomfortable with completely negating customary Papua New Guinean ideals. These ideas included the importance of pursuing an individualism that was acknowledged in village areas to depend upon group cooperation and that were ultimately required to feed back into the well being of such collective social units as lineages and clans. Because of this, according to my theory, the secondary message of cooperative individualism, even though it seemed to directly contradict the primary message of competitive individualism, sometimes appeared in my classroom observations. My theory suggested that primary forms of hidden curriculum satisfied what teachers felt to be their responsibilities as agents of the state (or, as they would put it, "leaders in a modern Papua New Guinea"); while secondary messages satisfied the emotional hunger that many teachers felt for remaining connected to more customary conceptions of the social world and the place of individuals within it. Stated in another fashion, using both primary and secondary forms of hidden curriculum in the classroom might be said to allow teachers to act as agents of the state without *feeling* as though they were acting as agents of the state.

Creating this theory helped me make sense of the ethnographic information that constantly produced widespread contradictions that seemed to counter or at least call into question the easy formulation of there being a single "hidden curriculum" in the classrooms of West New Britain. In addition, this theoretical formulation was not limited to the issue of competitive versus cooperative individualism but rather expanded to help explain a whole range of "primary versus secondary" forms of hidden curriculum that I found to exist in my study (such as hierarchy versus egalitarianism, or the importance of abstract versus practical knowledge). Simultaneously, it allowed me to explain individual differences that existed in specific classrooms—some teachers personally "needed" to retain stronger emotional ties to customary ideals and would therefore contradict their own primary messages more often, while other teachers were almost fanatically committed to what they saw as modernizing social change and hence contradicted themselves relatively seldom.

Like any good theory, my idea probably created more questions than it answered. Since I worked it out through long periods of analysis well after my fieldwork was completed, I was not able to test it further in the field. One way to know if something is a theory is to consider whether it can be tested (either by yourself or by other researchers) and also to what extent it generates a large number of specific theoretical ideas. For example, the notion that primary versus secondary forms of hidden curriculum exist in the classrooms of developing countries (and quite possibly the classrooms of industrialized countries as well), and that each form is tied to either messages of social change or messages of cultural continuity, suggests all kinds of specific theoretical questions that can be answered through either qualitative or quantitative research. Is there anything different in the social backgrounds of teachers who make a greater use of secondary messages in their classrooms than teachers who make very little use of such messages? Does the use of primary versus secondary messages show patterned differences in some subjects rather than others (e.g., Math versus English)? Do male versus female teachers systematically differ in their reliance on primary versus secondary forms of hidden curriculum in their classrooms? Do differences occur in higher versus lower grades? If so, why? And so on. A useful theory should be divisible into many smaller parts, with each part able to be subjected to investigation on its own.

Notice that in my theoretical formulation the term "customary" is expandable to any developing (or for that matter industrialized) country as it does not depend on a specific notion of "traditional" culture, but rather simply assumes that local people have customary ideals that can themselves be investigated and related to secondary forms of hidden curriculum in the region's classrooms. In fact, in West New Britain alone there are over a dozen different language groups (including recently arrived immigrants from other regions of Papua New Guinea) and many different specific customs. At the same time, there are some overarching themes of concern despite these differences, such as a reliance on kinship for organizing social formations and the idea that individuals should remain firmly connected to their kinship groups through complex webs of reciprocity, obligations, and rights. Because the concept of secondary hidden curriculum remains attached to "customary ideals" in general rather than to specific local formulations of "tradition," the concept remains potentially useful for any educational situation in developing countries (and, quite possibly, any situation in which education in a particular place involves more than one cultural group).

Theory does not need to be this "big" or expandable in order to be useful. A great deal of ethnography produces quite specific theoretical ideas that are closely tied to the evidence gathered in one particular location, yet still retains the potential to inform other similar situations. I take a few further examples from my own work to illustrate this point. In one of my earliest articles written from my West New Britain research (Fife 1992b), I suggested that the "shared fiction" of education might be much more fragile in developing countries than in industrialized ones and hence that schools might disappear or cease to function as social entities at a much greater rate in developing countries. I tied these "cracks" in the institutional armor to specific problems or tensions that I found to exist in education through my own work in West New Britain and suggested that other researchers begin looking for similar situations in their own studies. In turn, I also tied the issue of "disappearing schools" to the emergence of secondary forms of hidden curriculum in the classrooms of West New Britain. All of these ideas came from rereading my research notes and noticing a number of instances in which schools became threatened with institutional entropy, whether the danger existed for a single afternoon or threatened the continued existence of the school as a social entity altogether. I analyzed these situations, much as I instructed the reader to do in chapter 8, and started formulating connections between these and other patterns such as classroom interactions (e.g., secondary messages of hidden curriculum) or the relative shallowness of the historical concept of "school" in at least some developing countries. This illustrates the idea that theory is often "made" as we attempt to connect one set of patterns with another (or even several other) set(s) of patterns that emerge from our ethnographic evidence.

Another example of creating theory largely out of information gathering rather than primarily from the research of others came at a later period in my project, after I had conducted more primary archival research and began to tie that work into some of the things that I had seen first-hand in the contemporary country of Papua New Guinea. I was struck, for example, by the changes over time in what I eventually came to call "models for masculinity." I suggested in an article "that one of the legacies of colonialism and missionization in Papua New Guinea is a hierarchy of masculinity, in which some male personas become considerably more profitable than others, and some become considerably more problematic" (Fife 1995a: 277–278). In this article, I linked the emergence of specific forms of masculinity to particular moments in history and to the simultaneous emergence of specific kinds of social institutions in Papua New Guinea as a "developing country." Such statements are not descriptions of fact, but rather theories that try to explain why specific patterns form in particular times and places. As such, my theories about the emergence of various styles of masculinity become available to be tested by other ethnographers (through both ethnography and the use of historical material). To be a "theory," an idea must be subject to correction, modification, rejection, or confirmation in the light of new information. In other words, it has to be able to be tested as an organizing principle for handling increasing amounts of information.

By definition, all theory is useful. Some theories, however, may be more useful than others. Analytical concepts that remain closely tied to small bits of information are unlikely to be as useful as concepts that cut across and tie together information that comes from both macro and micro levels of evidence gathering. For example, a theory that explains why a teacher named John systematically shows a pattern of bias in his interactions with male versus female students is less useful than a theory that shows the existence of a more complex yet consistent pattern of gender bias among all of the teachers in an entire school. And the latter theory is likely to be less useful than one that links this gender bias in the school to other noneducational social processes in a society as a whole. Useful, in this sense, quite simply refers to the amount of "use" that other researchers are likely to gain from reading about a specific theoretical formulation and attempting to apply it to their own projects. In general, the more (micro and macro) levels of information a given theory takes into account the more important it will prove to be to other researchers interested in the kind of social situation that theory attempts to illuminate. Keep that in mind when you are formulating your writing—the subject of the concluding chapter of this book.

10

Academic and Practical Writing

Writing ethnography can be thought of as a problem in communication. How can we best communicate the results of our study through the use of a written format? As usual, there is no single answer for this question. In fact, writing is the most "artistic," and therefore the most variable, part of the ethnographic enterprise. There are, however, procedures that are worth following and issues worth considering before undertaking any writing project. The first thing that has to be considered is the intended audience. For a researcher, a potential audience can normally be divided into two major branches: an audience that primarily has an academic orientation versus an audience that tends to share a practical concern about a specific issue. In reality, the two audiences overlap, as a piece of writing primarily intended for academics (e.g., a Ph.D. thesis) may contain much that is of interest to practitioners (such as school teachers), and vice versa. However, each primary audience orientation calls for its own writing style or styles and each therefore should be considered in some detail by itself.

All ethnographic writing contains implicit assumptions about how we think the human social world is constructed. There is no such thing as neutral writing. Even the idea of objectivity and objective writing styles, for example, is really a theoretical position (related to philosophies such as logical positivism and to the Enlightenment project of the natural sciences) and *not* a neutral, nonpolitical or nontheoretical position. With this in mind, the first question that you want to ask yourself is: what kind of a social world do I want to construct for my reader and how much reflexivity do I want in that world? Reflexivity, in this sense, refers to both the personal and professional position of the researcher him or herself and the effects that this positioning may have had on the scholarly research and resulting writing product. In most contemporary forms of ethnographic writing, the researcher appears in at least some guise or form within the writing, so that readers might judge for themselves to some extent how the researcher's biases may have affected or influenced the overall work. There are many ways to accomplish reflexivity within writing. Sentences such as "I have been strongly influenced by Marxist forms of political economy," or "The reader will no doubt note my huge intellectual debt to the theories of Michel Foucault in this work" alert audiences to the author's analytical biases without interrupting the main narrative flow of the paper or book. Reflexivity need not play a huge role in the writing in order to be effective. I believe that most professional ethnographers think, and I am among them, that while a little bit of reflexivity is a good thing, a great deal of it can be very distracting at best and at its worst can turn into an exercise in self-indulgence. In other words, don't forget that while the reader should be alerted to some of your biases there is no need to give him or her a bulletin every three lines about what you were "really feeling" as you gathered each piece of evidence. Nor do you have to regale the reader with "my fifteen major influences and how they have affected my life" every time you make an analytic statement. Much of this is accomplished far more effectively by carefully citing influential scholarly sources (which should make it obvious to anyone where your theoretical sympathies lay) and a short word or two about anything else you specifically think the reader needs to know (e.g., such as the point that where you sat in the classroom might have affected the behavior of students in your presence). Reflexivity most commonly comes in small batches throughout the whole written product, but it is also possible to write it into a separate chapter or an appendix (e.g., "Appendix A: A Natural History of the Project"), into footnotes or endnotes (e.g., "My thinking here was . . ."") or in some other form of a relatively self-contained text that does not intrude directly into the main narrative. These kinds of extra notes may be the only way to inject reflexivity into your writing if your field of research requires that you compose primarily in an "objective" or objectifying style of prose (e.g., as a thesis on the topic of scientific education might be required to be written for a scientific faculty).

Academic Writing

Most researchers will do at least some (and many will do all) of their writing for an academic audience. This audience may be the members of your thesis committee, the readers of scholarly peer-reviewed journals, or the primary group of potential readers for that book you hope to write about "A Century of Education in South Africa" or "A New Approach to Tourism Studies in the Caribbean Islands." Because of this, it seems sensible to begin with a more detailed consideration of academic writing.

Who are you writing for? An audience that consists largely of a six-member thesis committee, for example, is quite different from the audience you hope to address for your major treatise on "The Problem of Drop-Outs in Pacific Island Education." Most theses for graduate degrees, for example, require very extensive literature reviews (often in the form of one huge chapter); while most book writers "review" the scholarly literature in a more limited fashion and scatter their comments about the work of other writers throughout the book as a whole. Why? Thesis committee members need to be convinced that you have mastered a large body of theoretical and informational literature and that you know precisely where your own work fits into this body of thought. Most book readers would find such a detailed rendering of the scholarly field boring—they want to learn, as directly as possible, about "the problem with small-business practices in West African countries," or about "successful experiments with industrial education in the Solomon Islands." Context is just as important for writing as it is for research. What and how you want to write depends largely upon scholarly and aesthetic choices (i.e., the narrative style you choose to pursue), the goal of the writing, and the intended audience.

I cannot possibly consider the many variations on writing style or forms of narrative here (but see Clifford and Marcus 1986; Fetterman 1989; Sanjek 1990; Emerson, Fretz, and Shaw 1995; and Kutsche 1998), and will instead limit myself to a consideration of how to construct a written product that coincides with the information that you have been able to gather and analyze through the kinds of research methods discussed earlier in this book. Again, we will make use of my own experiences in relation to education in Papua New Guinea. The most important piece of advice that I have for any would-be ethnographic writer is to make a writing outline. In its briefest form, for example, the writing outline for the Ph.D. thesis that I wrote from my field research experience in Papua New Guinea looked something like this:

Chapter One: Introduction
    A Note about Method
    Constructing a Thesis
    On Reflexivity
Chapter Two: Theory and the Search for a Balanced Method
    Micro Approaches
    Macro Approaches
    Development and the Issue of Education
    Hidden Curriculum and a Balanced Method
Chapter Three: Patterns in the History of Papua New Guinea
    Prehistory and Change
    Historical Forces and Changed Realities
    The Coming of Administration: 1884–1945
    Toward Independence: 1945–1975
    Trends in the History of Papua New Guinea
Chapter Four: Education as Social Change
    The Social Organization of Education
    Social Change as Hidden Curriculum
Chapter Five: Culture and Continuity
    Cultural Continuity: Expressing the Past in the Present
    The Hidden Curriculum of Traditional Culture
Chapter Six: Toward a Theory of Cultural Transmission
    Education in Papua New Guinea
    Theoretical Questions: Lessons from Papua New Guinea
References Cited

This is the basic outline of a Ph.D. thesis of some four hundred pages in length (Fife 1992a). Notice how the organization of my writing follows the research methods that I have taught about in this book. Chapter one simply states the main goal of the thesis and deals with the issue of reflexivity. Chapter two, the main "review of the literature chapter" in most theses, includes what I found about how other researchers have approached similar educational topics. Rather than simply "reviewing" the literature, I organized the chapter so that the review had a specific purpose—finding a guiding theoretical stance that could inform the work in the rest of the thesis. In effect, this chapter involved finding the "reason" for writing the thesis. I did this by splitting the approaches to educational research into those that primarily centered on the use of macro-level information versus those that primarily dealt with micro-level situations. In that way, I was able to "resolve" this contradiction in the literature through the use of a theoretical orientation that focused on the issue of hidden curriculum—an issue that, as I would show in the thesis, required the use of both macro and micro perspectives in a balanced format if it was to be used effectively to study education in a country such as Papua New Guinea. Chapter three dealt with the historical context that I had been able to piece together through the use of largely secondary sources on the history and political economy of the region that eventually became Papua New Guinea. In other words, chapter three begins to create the context for the research itself versus the context that was created for the study as a whole in chapter two. Chapters four and five form the bedrock of the thesis—they report on the main findings of the field research and upon my analysis/interpretation of those findings. Specifically, chapter four concentrates upon primary forms of hidden curriculum and how they are linked to wider issues of "development" and social change; while chapter five follows this by considering secondary forms of hidden curriculum and what they might mean in relation to the concerns of customary culture and teachers' roles as arbiters of both change and continuity in a developing country. Finally, chapter six brings the thesis back to where it began and tries to answer the question of what a good theory of cultural transmission might involve and how we could go about constructing it. Using the findings of the study, this chapter offers an analysis of both the shortcomings of previous theories of education and their relationship to the process of education in developing countries and then offers my own theoretical suggestions for a better, more holistic theory of education in this context.

A book outline might look similar, but not identical, to what I have presented above. Chapter two, for example, would either be eliminated altogether or reduced to a fraction of its roughly seventy-five pages. Elimination would probably occur by incorporating only the most directly relevant "review" material into the introductory chapter of the book. Chapter six would also likely be cut in half (versus its length in the thesis) and focus much more directly upon my own theory of cultural transmission rather than paying so much attention to "showing" the weaknesses of earlier theorists.

In each case, book or thesis, the outline above is only the beginning. It tells the writer what s/he wants to write about, but it does not show him or her how to do the writing. In order to be able to actually do the writing, the outline must be elaborated. Take chapter four from the outline above, for example. An elaborated or expanded outline might look something like the following.

Chapter Four: Education as Social Change
  The Social Organization of Education
  Education and Employment
  Themes in the Organization of Social Change

Social Change as Hidden Curriculum
  Abstract Knowledge and Modern Life
  Actions: The Importance of Being Correct
  Persons: Good versus Bad Students
  The Desire to be Modern
  Competitive Individualism: A World of Winners and Losers
Authority and Discipline: The Hidden Curriculum of Hierarchy
  Hierarchy in the Modern World
  Authority Relations in the Classroom
  The Power of Discipline
Summary: Hidden Curriculum and Social Change

The reader will recognize a number of research themes in this outline that have been discussed in earlier chapters of this book—such as the theme of competitive individualism. This kind of a detailed outline is created after the analysis of the research material has been completed. Major analytical themes and the sub-themes that are most closely related to them are used to formulate this kind of a more detailed outline. In this fashion, the writer can be confident that s/he has the necessary research material at hand to illustrate both how each analytical category exists in the classroom or other educational venue *and* how each can be considered in relation to other similar or contrasting analytical categories. The outline itself, and hence the manner by which the narrative will unfold within a chapter, suggests the relationship between various analytical categories. Thus, "authority relations in the classroom" is more closely related to "the power of discipline" than it is to "the importance of being correct"; while all of these categories are more similar to each other than they are to the category "reciprocity and the group," which is one of the analytical themes that occurs in chapter five which follows it.

The outlining process need not stop here. It can become even more fine-grained and act as a step-by-step instruction manual for writing your paper, book, or thesis. For example, take the heading from chapter four that says "actions: the importance of being correct." This heading can itself be divided in the following manner:

Actions: The Importance of Being Correct
  What it means (brief explanation)
  Example: Math, Grade 2, Kimbe C.S. (Clapping for being correct)
  Analysis: draws attention to "rightness" versus "wrongness" as defined by teacher's own method/answer
  Example: English, Grade 4, Ewasse C.S. (group participation in correctness)
  Analysis: rote teaching encourages "correct" answers in group formats, but not true understanding of language; constant reinforcement: being "correct" more important than real understanding
  Example: English, Grade 3, Bialla C.S. (variation: a clap for "trying" versus being correct—encouraged by teacher)
  Analysis: an unusual teacher; show other examples of this teacher being almost excessively "even-handed"

And so it goes. The outline above covers only three written pages of an eight-page section in the thesis about "the importance of being correct." By breaking my writing down into smaller and smaller pieces through the use of outlines, I have found that when it comes to the writing itself I simply have to follow my own outline to create a narrative that seems to flow "naturally" from one set of information and analysis to another one. A detailed outline also destroys the excuse "I can't write, because I don't know what I'm going to do next." By creating a writing outline around your research and analysis *before* you begin writing you ensure that the paper, book, or thesis will remain a rationally ordered guide to your research results—no matter what specific forms of language or which kind of narrative style you add to the mix.

A cautionary word is in order here. I have taught the above writing method to everyone from first year students to Ph.D. students. Often, a student, especially an undergraduate one, will complain "but, that is a lot of work—I don't have time for that, why can't I just write the paper?" It has been my experience that whether one is writing a journal article, a field report, a thesis, or a book (e.g., this one) a well constructed outline saves a great deal of time in the long run. Often, it can also end up being the difference between whether something ever actually gets written or not. Whenever I am stuck in a writing project, I take the next section of writing that I want to do and begin to break it down into smaller and smaller pieces— elaborating as much as I wish (sometimes to the point where I can lift whole sentences from my outline and put them in my text). In virtually every case, this shakes me loose from the conceptual problem that I was experiencing and allows me to get on with the task of writing. I *know* that this works for other writers as well. Just recently, for example, I had a good Master's student who was having great difficulty getting down to the business of writing his final project for the completion of his degree. We met on a weekly basis and each week he would come to me and say "I really don't have anything written yet." Then, he would suggest that maybe he should do some more reading, or that perhaps he needed to learn about more theories in relation to his topic, or that maybe he should even consider another topic altogether. During this period, he steadfastly refused my suggestion that he create an outline for the work. He quite openly told me that he had done so in the past, but felt that he was experienced now and that he was therefore really "beyond" such tricks of the trade. Finally, in exasperation and knowing that if he did not begin writing almost immediately he was going to miss his final deadline for getting this work done and therefore be unable to complete his degree and graduate (as a foreign student, he had to leave Canada by a very specific date), I virtually forced him to create a first, tentative outline for the paper. Each week, a small section of that outline became elaborated during our meeting and he would then leave and write that section of the project. Relatively soon, he could see how the rest of the project would have to be written. That is, he understood that the writing now "had to" proceed in a certain direction because of the logic of the outline and the ongoing narrative weight of what he had already completed. The end result was that he graduated with his M.A. degree and in fact finished his requirements slightly ahead of several other students who were on the same degree track.

This student was right in one sense. It is possible for very experienced researchers/writers to do some of the outlining process in their heads rather than on pieces of paper. This is of course much more the case for smaller works such as articles than for books or theses. However, it is also true that most people seem to do better with the guidance of a physical outline, and that virtually everyone can benefit from this method of writing when trouble strikes the writing process.

In a similar manner, I strongly suggest that that you write introductory paragraphs for a paper or an introductory chapter for a book or a thesis *before* going on to write the larger work. This flies in the face of much standard writing advice. Students and colleagues whom I suggest this process to normally come back with "but, I've always been told that you should write the introduction last, as the paper (book, etc.) is most likely to change direction as I write it and therefore I will just have to write it over again anyway." Sometimes, this is true. But, I would much rather rewrite part of my introduction than sit for months wondering how I can possibly begin writing a book or, worse yet, find myself in the middle of a book (thesis, etc.), with several chapters written, and then discover that they really do not fit together into a single coherent piece of work. In addition, I find that if you write a good outline, one that is well grounded in the research that you are trying to explain in the first place, then the basic direction of the work does not change that much as you write it. Perhaps many introductions have to be rewritten because the writer did not yet know what he or she really wanted to say. Why not find out what you want to write about by constructing an outline that can easily be modified, and invest a relatively small amount of time writing an opening section or chapter of the work, rather than struggling for six months (or even three days, in the case of a conference paper)—only to find out that you do not really know what you want to say in this particular piece of writing anyway? In short, the old advice about writing the introduction last is wrong—follow it at your peril.

Practical Writing

In the course of your career as an ethnographic researcher there is a very good chance that you will be asked at some point to "write up a report about your work" for a nonacademic audience. That is, a government department, a development committee, a school board, a nongovernmental organization, or a similar social agency will request that you write anything from a few pages to a few hundred pages for them so that they might make use of your research findings. In fact, there is every chance that the provision of at least one such report will be a requirement for you to gain permission to do research in a developing country in the first place. In industrialized countries, Indigenous Band Councils, Business Development Boards, Municipal Councils, Administrations of Homes for the Aged, and so forth will often also make it a prerequisite for their cooperation with your project. This is fine, as it dovetails nicely with the standard ethical requirement of research that we make every reasonable attempt to distribute our findings to the people who might wish to hear about them. In my case, I was asked by education officials in the capital city of Port Moresby to give them both a short oral summary of my findings in the form of a seminar just before leaving the country and to promise to provide them with a longer, more substantive report regarding the most "practically" useful part of my research after I had finished analyzing the material. Some months after I left Papua New Guinea, I mailed them back a sixty-page report. In it, I concentrated on the issue of hidden curriculum, the main results of my study relating to that issue, and suggestions about actions that teachers could themselves take to monitor their own performances in the classrooms. I took great care to provide "positive" as well as "negative" findings (i.e., outlining things that my research showed they were "doing well" and not simply things that seemed to be "going wrong" in the classrooms of West New Britain). Often, these reports are locally published or otherwise circulated among educational bureaucrats, school inspectors, other researchers, Head or other teachers, and possibly even among interested parents. Because of the specialized nature of the audience, practical writing tends to use a different format and style than the more variable kinds of academic writing.

To begin with, government bureaucrats the world over do not like to read material that offers them five different "possible" interpretations of an event, or three separate ways to theoretically consider gender inequality in the classroom, or eight factors that "might" influence better results in math testing. Generally speaking, you will have to abandon experimental narratives, first person viewpoints, and elaborate or flashy vocabularies if you want to write a report that adequately communicates your findings and your concerns to a bureaucrat or practitioner involved with a specific topic (and this is true in both "developed and industrialized" countries). This audience generally expects to read material that uses positivistic styles of writing (e.g., "male teachers are discriminating against female students in math classes" rather than nondeterministic writing such as "it is difficult for me to decide to what extent discrimination is occurring against female students in math classes and who is doing such discrimination. On the one hand . . ."). Of course, you cannot write in this style if you are truly unsure of your results. This is why reports normally focus upon the most distinct findings of a study, leaving ambiguous information and less clear-cut interpretations for other, more academic, venues (though you will want to mention in the report that such material exists, and that it can be found in such and such a venue).

It is standard to use third person, objective styles of writing in reports rather than the first person (or even a mixed style of first, second, and third person) format that is found in most ethnographic forms of writing. Many scholars will object to these positivistic forms of report writing (I do so myself), but the truth is that if we wish to have any influence over practical policies concerning social processes such as education in developing countries then we have to be willing to use the language that best communicates itself to audiences like educational bureaucrats, practitioners, and parents. Similarly, if we want to influence government policies in relation to the environmental pollution of a specific place due to its over usage by tourists, we likely have to couch our prose in the 'measurement' style of narrative (e.g., "lead in the soil has increased by 30% in the last ten years since Main Harbour has become a major tourist destination. This can be traced directly to the increased use of X because of the demand by tour operators that . . ."). We need to do this because it is that form of narrative that tends to have an impact on politicians and government bureaucrats in these situations. Think of it as an exercise in "the native's point of view."

Consider why most members of a topically involved but nonacademic audience want your writing in the first place. Government workers may want it so that they can use it to help convince those higher up than themselves in the decision-making hierarchy that more money must be spent on math education for girls, or that there is a great need for alternative forms of economic development in the West Coast region, or that quick action will have to be taken to avoid a major crisis in the health care system because of an aging population. Specialists such as educational practitioners may want to use it to show government bureaucrats that their new alternative program for high school dropouts is having real results or to argue that they have not received their fair share of funding for after-school sports and that the results can clearly be seen in levels of school vandalism. Nonspecialists such as parents or citizen's groups may want to use the report to question the local school board about why their son "can't really speak English properly," or why they have not receive their "fair share" of tourism funding in relation to region X and Y. This is why I refer to this form of narrative as "practical writing"—the primary concern of a research report audience of any type is to be able to use sections of the report to achieve practical results through a process of argumentation that can be "backed up" by your report.

As such, these readers are generally happier to see results reported in the no-frills language of counting schedules, summary results, and clear conclusions. You need to include enough information to convince the reader that you grounded your analysis in evidence and not in flights of fancy, but generally speaking, most "practical" readers will skip right to the summary statements of the report. Because of this, these statements (whether they summarize findings, analyze trends, or suggest future actions) have to be made in very clear, concise language. A one paragraph to two-page "executive summary" is normally included at the front of any report longer than a few pages. This includes the most important findings of the study and any key suggestions the author has about changing the direction of negative trends or affirming and strengthening positive patterns. In addition, key findings and recommendations are often summarized in the form of "bullets" (short, punchy phrases in objective sounding language) that can be listed at the back of the report as part of the conclusion or at the front of the report right underneath the executive summary. For example: "it was found that nearly half of male school teachers discriminated against female students in math classes." Including a short appendix that refers to the research methods used to gather information during the study is often a good idea as well. It makes a difference, for example, if you can say that classroom observations in regard to the effects of hidden curriculum were based upon over three hundred hours of observation in six different schools rather than on a dozen hours in only two classrooms of a single school. In a positivistic narrative, research methods are what give the report its authority. Therefore, do not hesitate to take the time to describe how you arrived at major conclusion X and to explain that you checked the accuracy of this conclusion using three separate methods of information gathering (you might also want to cite a number of "authorities" that state how reliable research method Y is in for educational, medical, tourism, or other studies). Emphasize how careful you have been, for example, in your use of counting schedules in order to "verify" important ethnographic results from classroom observations.

Outlines work just as well for practical reports as they do for more academic forms of writing. Staying close to your evidence is a good idea in any form of writing, but especially so in reports. Leave your more elaborate theories for other audiences who want to read about them.

Research and writing, in this sense, are part of the same single process and in each case it is the context that will determine how you should proceed. Therefore, always consider the context when deciding what to do next, but never to the extent that you let it freeze your actions or your thoughts. Developing an in-depth understanding of a specific ethnographic topic in relation to its social, cultural, and historical context can occur only as a result of a great deal of time and effort spent both inside and outside of the fieldwork situation. It is our careful use of ethnographic research methods that allows us to achieve a greater insight into a particular issue than we had before we undertook our work. Hopefully, this book will help you to do your part as a researcher interested in furthering our collective understanding of human beings who live in disadvantaged situations.

Appendix

A Methodological Check List

Review of the History of the Region
Review of the Basic Political Economy of the Region
Review of Theoretical Literature Relevant to the Topic of Research
Creation of a Theoretical Orientation
Collection of Relevant Newspaper Sources
Collection of Government Documents and Statistics
Preliminary Interviews: Government Bureaucrats, Educators, Academics
Unfocused Observations of Classroom Interactions
Unfocused Observations of the School
Unfocused Observations of Other Educational Settings
Initial Analysis of Unfocused Classroom, School, and Other Observations
Focused Observations of Classroom Interactions
Creation and Implementation of Counting Schedules in the Classroom
Collection of Self-Reporting Exercises (Essays, Diaries, Art, etc.)
Semi-Structured Interviewing of Pupils, Parents, Teachers, and/or Officials
Unstructured Interviewing of Pupils, Parents, Teachers, and/or Officials
Completion of Preliminary Analysis of All Evidence
Completion of Secondary Analysis of All Concepts
Consideration of Differences Within Patterns and Why They Exist
Preliminary (Gross) Outline of the Book, Thesis, Paper, or Report
Elaborated (Fine) Outline of the Book, Thesis, Paper, or Report
Completion of the Book, Thesis, Paper, or Report

Notes

1 Introduction to Ethnographic Research Methods

1. For an overview of this basic argument see Fife 1992a. For some of the publications that I have written using this and closely related material, see Fife 1992b; 1994; 1995a; 1995b; 1995c; 1996; 1997; 1998; 2001; 2002.
2. For good examples of studies that insist upon this more contextual approach, see Singleton 1967; Roberts and Akinsanya 1976; Gearing and Sangree 1979; Haig-Brown 1988; McLaren 1989; Weis 1990; Lofty 1992; Thapan 1989; Pomponio 1992; Stromquist 1992; King 1999; Spindler and Spindler 2000.

2 Using Historical Sources for Ethnographic Research

1. For a small sample of secondary sources on the history of education in Papua New Guinea available around the time of my research, see Bray and Smith 1985; Griffin 1976; Meek 1982; Dept. of Education 1985; Pomponio and Lancy 1986; Smith 1985, 1987.
2. For examples of secondary sources regarding the more general history of the political economy of the country available during the late 1980s, see, Amarshi, Good, and Mortimer 1979; Delbos 1985; Good 1986; Griffin, Nelson, and Firth 1979; Lacey 1983; Levine and Levine 1979; Nelson 1976; Willis 1974.
3. Papua New Guinea is made up of half of the large island of New Guinea (the other half belonging to Irian Jaya, a colony of Indonesia) and a number of smaller islands (such as New Britain, which contains the provinces of East New Britain and West New Britain). Historically, the large island was most commonly referred to as New Guinea, and I follow this convention here when referring to the whole island, including of course that portion of the island that later became the largest part of the country known as Papua New Guinea.
4. I have written extensively about the "Polynesian teachers" elsewhere (e.g., Fife 1991, 1992). The term "Polynesian teacher" was normally used for the first few waves of indigenous Pacific Island evangelists who came from London Missionary Society mission stations established on islands to the east of New Guinea. Not all of them were actually from "Polynesian" societies, although LMS missionaries at that time believed them to be so. In contrast, the term "native teacher" was normally reserved in the Papua New Guinea mission for indigenous evangelists who were native to the New Guinea mainland or to the immediately surrounding islands. However, the L.M.S. directors back in London, England often used the two terms interchangeably. I follow the New Guinea in-mission usage of these two separate terms in this book.

4   Newspapers and Government Documents: Popular and Official Sources of Information

1. Any scholar who has ever been interviewed by a newspaper reporter and has had his or her words "quoted" in a newspaper article will tell you that reporters clearly do not operate under the same canons of accuracy that guide the work of professional researchers.

2. Readers who are not anthropologists may not be familiar with these kinship terms. A lineage is a descent group that traces its members though *either* the mother's line or the father's line backward to a known ancestor. A clan, on the other hand, is a descent group that traces its membership back through *either* the mother's or the father's line to a real or mythical ancestor. The main difference is that the case of a clan the actual genealogical linkages are not known.

3. *Tok Pisin* is the name for the pidgin language that is spoken by roughly half of the people in Papua New Guinea and it is one of the official languages of the state. It began as a trade language and remains important in a country in which the usual estimate is that there are over 800 separate languages (not dialects, languages). *Tok Pisin* combines mainly modified English words with a Melanesian-style grammatical system. So, for example, the English sentence "That's all; there is no more" comes out as "No gat moa; em tasol" (e.g., Mihalic 1971). A small literature has developed in *Tok Pisin*, including the national newspaper *Wantok*. All translations from that newspaper in this text are my own.

4. Schools that encompass grades one to six are referred to as community schools in Papua New Guinea. I use the term interchangeably with the more universal term of primary school. Some community schools, especially those in more remote rural areas, may offer less than the full six grades.

5. I should note as well that the British sociologist who was already in West New Britain studying the high schools and whose work necessitated a change in my research plans also turned out to be both a friend and an invaluable colleague. Graham Vulliamy whole-heartedly welcomed me to the field upon my arrival on his "turf" in West New Britain and offered both excellent advice about specific local situations and played a key role in my securing a very hard to find habitation in Kimbe town itself. Later, he and Michael Crossley invited me to contribute a chapter about the use of ethnographic research methods for their extremely useful book *Qualitative Educational Research in Developing Countries: Current Perspectives* (1997), which initiated my interest in methodological issues. I am indebted to both of them for trusting what was then a largely unproven scholar to participate in their important book project.

5   Participant-Observation as a Research Method

1. I have purposefully written about "participant-observation" here in such a way as to make it useful for a wide variety of projects. I trust that the readers of this work will have their own opinions about what we might call the politics of participant-observation. Many contemporary scholars (e.g., Paine 1985; Fetterman 1993), including but not limited to feminist (e.g., Shenk 1995; Gailey 1998) and Marxist (e.g., Wolf 1999, 2001; Sider 2003) researchers, would suggest a more "committed," "partisan," or "advocacy," style of participant-observation than most of the people I cite in the main body of this text. I am certainly in sympathy with the idea of a more partisan ethnography, as this book as a whole should make very apparent, but wish to present the basic method of participant-observation and

leave it up to potential researchers to decide for themselves the extent to which they will become committed to a particular point of view in their research projects.

2. I use the masculine pronoun here because at the time of my field research all such officer holders were males. This was not always true, though it was a rare occasion when a woman was able to win an election for public office at either the provincial or federal levels of government.

Bibliography

Allen, Bryant. 1983. "Paradise Lost? Rural Development in an Export-Led Economy: The Case of Papua New Guinea," in *Rural Development and the State*. Eds. D. A. M. Lea and D. P. Chandhri. 215–240. New York: Metheun.

Amarshi, Azeem, Kenneth Good, and Rex Mortimer. 1979. *Development and Dependency: The Political Economy of Papua New Guinea*. Melbourne: Oxford University Press.

Apple, Michael. 1979. *Ideology and Curriculum*. London: Routledge and Kegan Paul.

Axline, W. Andrew. 1986. *Decentralization and Development Policy: Prinvincial Government and Planning Process in Papua New Guinea*. Port Moresby: Institute of Applied Social and Economic Research.

Beharall, C. 1917. L.M.S. Reports. Box 3. London: SOAS, University of London.

Bernard, H. Russel. 1994. *Research Methods in Anthropology: Qualitative and Quantitative Approaches*. London: Sage Publications.

Blackledge, David and Barry Hunt. 1985. *Sociological Interpretations of Education*. London: Croom Helm.

Blythe, Jennifer. 1978. *Following Both Sides: Processes of Group Formation in Vitu*. Ph.D. Dissertation, Department of Anthropology, McMaster University, Hamilton, Canada.

Bourdieu, Pierre and J. C. Passeron. 1977. *Reproduction in Education, Society and Culture*. Trans. R. Nice. Beverley Hills: Sage Publications.

Bowles, S. and H. Gintis. 1976. *Schooling in Capitalist America*. London: Routledge and Kegan Paul.

Bray, Mark and Peter Smith. 1985. *Education and Social Stratification in Papua New Guinea*. Melbourne: Longman Cheshire.

Bruner, Jerome. 1982. "The Language of Education." *Social Research*. Winter: 835–853.

Burnett, J. H. 1978. *Anthropology and Education*. Washington National Academy of Education.

Chessum, Rosemary. 1980. "Teacher Ideologies and Pupil Disaffection," in *Schooling, Ideology and the Curriculum*. Eds. L. Barton, R. Meighan, and S. Walker. 113–129. Sussex: The Falmer Press.

Chowning, Ann. 1985. "Kove Women and Violence: The Context of Wife-Beating in a West New Britain Society," in *Domestic Violence in Papua New Guinea*. Ed. S. Toft. 72–91. Port Moresby: Law Commission of Papua New Guinea.

Clement, Dorothy. 1976. "Cognitive Anthropology and Applied Problems in Education," in *Do Applied Antrhropologists Apply Anthropology*. Ed. M. V. Angrasino. 53–71. Athens: University of Georgia Press.

Clifford, James and George Marcus. 1986. *Writing Culture: The Poetics and Politics of Ethnography*. Berkeley: University of California Press.

Comitas, Lambros. 1978. "Report of the Chairman," in *Report and Working Papers: The Committee on Anthropology and Education*. U.S.A.: National Academy of Education.

Conroy, J. D. 1977. "A Longitudinal Study of School Leaver Migration," in *Change and Movement: Readings on Internal Migration in Papua New Guinea*. Ed. R. J. May. 76–116. Canberra: Australian National University Press.

Crossley, Michael. 1981. "Strategies for Curriculum Change and SSCEP in Papua New Guinea," in *The Politics of Educational Change*. Ed. A. R. Welch. Armidale: University of New England.

Crossley, Michael and Graham Vulliamy. 1986. *The Policy of SSCEP: Context and Development*. Waigani: University of Papua New Guinea.

Crossley, Michael and Graham Vulliamy. 1997. *Qualitative Educational Research in Developing Countries: Current Perspectives*. New York and London: Garland Publishing.

Davies, Lynn. 1997. "Interviews and the Study of School Management: An International Perspective," in *Qualitative Educational Research in Developing Countries*. Eds. M. Crossley and G. Vulliamy. 133–159. New York: Garland Publishing.

Delbos, Georges. 1985. *The Mustard Seed: From a French Mission to a Papuan Church: 1885–1985*. Port Moresby: Institute of Papua New Guinea Studies.

Department of Education. 1985. *Growth of Education Since Indpendence: 1975–1985*. Papua New Guinea: Department of Education.

Downs, Ian. 1980. *The Australian Trusteeship*. Canberra: Australian Government Publishing Service.

Durkheim, Emile. 1961. *Moral Education*. London: Collier MacMillan Publishers.

———. 1977. *The Evolution of Educational Thought*. Trans. Peter Collins. London: Routledge and Kegan Paul.

Easton, Mark. 1985. "Papua New Guinea," in *Oceania: A Regional Study*. Eds. F. M. Bunge and M. W. Cooke. 137–206. Washington: United States Government.

Emerson, Robert, Rachel Fretz, and Linda Shaw. 1995. *Writing Ethnographic Fieldnotes*. Chicago: University of Chicago Press.

Errington, Federick and Deborah Gewertz. 1995. *Articulating Change in the "Last Unknown."* Boulder: Westview Press.

Escobar, Arturo. 1995. *Encountering Development: The Making and Unmaking of the Third World*. Princeton: Princeton University Press.

Feinberg, Walter and Jonas Soltis. 1985. *School and Society*. New York: Teacher's College, Columbia University.

Fetterman, David. 1989. *Ethnography: Step by Step*. London: Sage Publications.

———. 1993. *Speaking the Language of Power: Communication, Collaboration, and Advocacy*. London: Falmer Press.

Fife, Wayne. 1992a. *"A Certain Kind of Education": Education, Culture and Society in West New Britain*. Ph.D. Thesis, Department of Anthropology, McMaster University, Hamilton, Canada.

———. 1992b. "Crossing Boundaries: Dissolution as a Secondary Message of Education in Papua New Guinea." *International Journal of Educational Development*. 12(3): 213–221.

———. 1994. "Education in Papua New Guinea: The Hidden Curriculum of a New Moral Order." *City and Society Annual Review*. 1: 139–162.

———. 1995a. "Models for Masculinity in Colonial and Postcolonial Papua New Guinea." *The Contemporary Pacific*. 7(2): 277–302.

———. 1995b. "Education and Society in Papua New Guinea: Toward Social Inequality 1870–1945." *Man and Culture in Oceania*. 11: 61–79.

———. 1995c. "The Look of Rationality and the Bureaucratization of Consciousness in Papua New Guinea." *Ethnology*. 34(2): 129–141.

———. 1996. "Education and Society in Papua New Guinea: Toward Independence 1945–1975." *Man and Culture in Oceania*. 12: 1–18.

———. 1997. "The Importance of Fieldwork: Anthropology and Education in Papua New Guinea," in *Qualitative Educational Research in Developing Countries: Current Perspectives.* Eds. M. Crossley and G. Vulliamy. 87–111. New York: Garland Publishing.

———. 1998. "The Bampton Island Murders: Exploring the Human Face of Colonization in Early Papua." *The Journal of the Polynesian Society.* 107(3): 263–286.

———. 2001. "Creating the Moral Body: Missionaries and the Technology of Power in Early Papua New Guinea." *Ethnology.* 40(3): 251–269.

———. 2002. "Heroes and Helpers, Missionaries and Teachers: Between Mimesis and Appropriation in Pre-Colonial New Guinea." *People and Culture in Oceania.* 18: 1–22.

———. 2004a. "Semantic Slippage as a New Aspect of Authenticity: Viking Tourism on the Northern Peninsula of Newfoundland." *Journal of Folklore Research.* 41(1): 61–84.

———. 2004b. "Penetrating Types: Conflating Modernist and Postmodernist Tourism on the Great Northern Peninsula of Newfoundland." *Journal of Amerkican Folklore.* 117(464): 147–167.

———. n.d. "National Parks and Disappearing People: Romantic Landscapes and the Urbanization of Rural Spaces in Newfoundland," will appear in the *Proceedings of the Second International Linkages Workshop on Newfoundland and Galician Studies.* Eds. Xaquin Rodriguez and Xose Santos, Santiago de Compostela: Universidade de Santiago de Compostela.

Freire, Paulo. 1983. *Pedagogy of the Oppressed.* New York: The Continuum Publishing Corporation.

Gailey, Christine Ward. 1998. "Feminist Methods," in *Handbook of Methods of Cultural Anthropology.* Ed. H. R. Bernard. 203–223. Walnut Creek: AltaMira Press.

Gearing, Frederick. 1979a. "Introduction," in *Toward a Cultural Theory of Education and Schooling.* Eds. F. Gearing and L. Sangree. 1–5. The Hague: Mouton Publishers.

———. 1979b. "A Reference Model for a Cultural Theory of Education and Schooling," in *Toward a Cultural Theory of Education and Schooling.* Eds. F. Gearing and L. Sangree. 169–230. The Hague: Mouton Publishers.

———. 1984. "Toward a General Theory of Cultural Transmission." *Anthropology and Education Quarterly.* 15(1): 29–37.

Gearing, Frederick and B. Allan Tindall. 1973. "Anthropological Studies of the Educational Process." *Annual Review of Anthropology.* 2: 95–105.

Gearing, Frederick and Lucinda Sangree (eds.). 1979. *Toward a Cultural Theory of Education and Schooling.* The Hague: Mouton Publishers.

Gearing, Frederick and Paul Epstein. 1982. "Learning to Wait: An Ethnographic Probe into the Operations of an Item of Hidden Curriculum," in *Doing the Ethnography of Schooling.* Ed. G. Spindler. 241–267. New York: Holt, Rinehart and Winston.

Geertz, Clifford. 1976. "From the Natives' Point of View: On the Nature of Anthropological Understanding," in *Meaning in Anthropology.* Eds. K. Basso and H. Selby. 221–238. Albuquerque: University of New Mexico Press.

Gewertz, Deborah and Frederick Errington. 1991. *Twisted Histories, Altered Contexts: Representing the Chambri in a World System.* Cambridge: Cambridge University Press.

Giddens, Anthony. 1986. *The Constitution of Society: Outline of a Theory of Structuration.* Berkeley: University of California Press.

Good, Kenneth. 1986. *Papua New Guinea: A False Economy.* London: Anti-Slavery Society Report No. 3.

Gramsci, Antonio. 1971. *Selections From the Prison Notebooks.* Eds. and Trans. Q. Hoare and G. N. Smith. London: Lawrence and Wishart.

Griffin, James. 1976. "The Instant University," in *Papua New Guinea Education.* Ed. E. B. Thomas. 99–123. Melbourne: Oxford University Press.

Griffin, James, Hank Nelson, and Stewart Firth. 1979. *Papua New Guinea: A Polictical History*. Australia: Heinemann Educational Australia.

Haig-Brown, Celia. 1988. *Resistance and Renewal: Surviving the Indian Residential School*. Vancouver: Tillacum Library.

Harber, Clive. 1997. "Using Documents for Qualitative Educational Research in Africa," in *Qualitative Educational Research in Developing Countries: Current Perspectives*. Eds. M. Crossley and G. Vulliamy. 113–131. New York: Garland Publishing.

Harding, T. G. 1967. *Voyagers of the Vitiaz Strait: A Study of a New Guinea Trade System*. Seattle: University of Washington Press.

Hargreaves, David, Stephan Hester, and Frank Mellor. 1975. *Deviance in Classrooms*. London: Routledge and Kegan Paul.

Harrington, Charles. 1970. *Anthropology and Education*. United States of America: National Academy of Education.

Hecht, Susan. 1981 *Muruk and the Cross*. Port Moresby: Educational Research Unit, University of Papua New Guinea.

Holmes, J. H. 1918. "Daily Routine at Urika." Papuan Reports, Box 3, Folder 1. London Missionary Society Archives. London: SOAS, University of London.

Howe, K. R. 1984. *Where the Waves Fall: A New South Seas Islands History From the First Settlement to Colonial Rule*. Honolulu: University of Hawaii Press.

Hunt, Archibald. 1888. "A New Guinea Examination," in *The Chronicle*. September 1888. London: SOAS, University of London.

Jackson, Michael. 1989. *Paths Toward a Clearing: Radical Empiricism and Ethnographic Inquiry*. Bloomington: Indiana University Press.

Kerber, A. and W. Smith. 1972. *A Cultural Approach to Education*. Des Moines: Kendall/Hunt.

King, Linda (ed.). 1999. *Learning, Knowledge and Cultural Context*. Hamburg: UNESCO Institute for Education. Dordrecht: Kluwer Academic Publishers.

Kiste, Robert. 1984. "Overview," in *Oceania: A Region of Study*. Eds. F. M. Bunge and M. W. Cooke. 12–29. United States of America: Department of the Army.

Kneller, George. 1965. *Educational Anthropology*. New York: John Wiley and Sons.

Kutsche, Paul. 1998. *Field Ethnography: A Manual for Doing Anthropology*. New Jersey: Prentice Hall.

Lacey, R. 1983. *Our Young Men Snatched Away: Labourers in Papua New Guinea's Colonial Economy 1884–1942*. Occasional Paper in Economic History, No. 3. Port Moresby: History Department, University of Papua New Guinea.

Langmore, Diane. 1989. *Missionary Lives: Papua, 1874–1914*. Honolulu: University of Hawaii Press.

Levine, Hal and Marlene Levine. 1979. *Urbanization in Papua New Guinea: A Study of Ambivalent Townsmen*. Cambridge: Cambridge University Press.

Levy, Robert and Douglas Hollan. 1998. "Person-Centered Interviewing and Observation," in *Handbook of Methods in Cultural Anthropology*. Ed. H. Russell Bernard. 333–364. London: Altimira Press.

Lofty, John. 1992. *Time to Write: The Influence of Time and Culture on Learning to Write*. Albany: State University of New York Press.

McLaren, Peter. 1986. *Schooling as a Ritual Performance*. London: Routledge and Kegan Paul.

———. 1989. Life in Schools. New York and London: Longman.

Mead, Margaret. 1975. *Growing up in New Guinea: A Comparative Study of Primitive Education*. New York: William Morrow and Co. Inc.

Meek, V. L. 1982. *The University of Papua New Guinea: A Case Study in the Sociology of Higher Education*. Brisbane: University of Queensland Press.

Mihalic, F. 1971. *The Jacaranda Dictionary and Grammar of Melanesian Pidgin*. Port Moresby: The Jacaranda Press.

Moresby, John. 1873. *March 19 Letter*. Correspondence, Box 1, Folder 1, Jacket B. London: SOAS, University of London.

Munroe, Robert and Ruth Munroe. 1975. *Cross-Cultural Human Development*. Belmont: Wadsworth Publishing.

Murray, A. W. 1873. *March 19 Letter*. Correspondence, Box 1, Folder 1, Jacket B. London: SOAS, University of London.

———. 1873. *Report*. Journals, Box 1. London: SOAS, University of London.

Nelson, Hank. 1976. *Black, White and Gold: Goldmining in Papua New Guinea 1878–1930*. Canberra: Australian National University.

Omokhodion, J. O. 1989. "Classroom Observed: The Hidden Curriculum in Lagos, Nigeria." *International Journal of Educational Development*. 9(2): 99–110.

Paine, Robert (ed.). 1985. *Advocacy and Anthropology: First Encounters*. St. John's: Institute of Social and Economic Research, Memorial University of Newfoundland.

Parkin, Frank. 1982. *Max Weber*. London: Tavistock Publications.

Parsons, Talcott. 1951. *The Social System*. London: The Free Press of Glencoe.

Pomponio, Alice. 1992. *Seagulls Don't Fly Into the Bush: Cultural Identity and Development in Melanesia*. Belmont: Wadsworth Publishing Company.

Pomponio, Alice and David Lancy. 1986. "A Pen or a Bushknife? School, Work, and 'Personal Investment' in Papua New Guinea." *Anthropology and Education Quarterly*. 17(1): 41–61.

Postman, Neil and Charles Weingartner. 1969. *Teaching as a Subversive Activity*. New York: Dell Publishing.

Roberts, Joan I. and Sherrie K. Akinsanya. 1976. *Schooling in the Cultural Context: Anthropological Studies of Education*. New York: David McKay Company, Inc.

Sanjek, Roger. 1990. *Fieldnotes: The Makings of Anthropology*. Ithaca: Cornell University Press.

Shenk, Dena (ed.). 1995. *Gender and Race Through Education and Political Activitsm*. Arlington: American Anthropological Association.

Sider, Gerald. 2003. *Between History and Tomorrow: Making and Breaking Everyday Life in Rural Newfoundland* (second edn.). Peterborough: Broadview Press.

Singleton, John. 1967. *Nichu: A Japanese School*. New York: Holt, Rinehart and Wintson.

Sim, Stuart. 1999. *The Routledge Critical Dictionary of PostModern Thought*. New York: Routledge.

Smith, Peter. 1985. "Colonial Policy, Education and Social Stratification, 1945–1975," in *Education and Social Stratification in Papua New Guinea*. Eds. M. Bray and P. Smith. 49–66. Melbourne: Longman Cheshire.

Smith, Peter. 1987. *Education and Colonial Control in Papua New Guinea: A Documentary History*. Melbourne: Longman Cheshire.

Spindler, George. 1974. "Why have Minority Groups in North America been Disadvantaged by their Schools?" in *Education and Cultural Process*. Ed. G. Spindler. 69–81. New York: Holt, Rinehart, and Winston.

Spindler, George and Louise Spindler. 2000. *Fifty Years of Anthropology and Education: 1950–2000 (A Spindler Anthology)*. London: Lawrence Erlbaum Associates, Publishers.

Spradley, James. 1979. *The Ethnographic Interview*. New York: Holt, Rinehart and Winston.

———. 1980. *Participant Observation*. New York: Holt, Rinehart and Winston.

Springhall, John, Brian Fraser, and Michael Hoare. 1983. *Sure and Steadfast: A History of the Boy's Brigade 1883–1983*. London and Glasgow.

Stoller, Paul. 1989. *Fusion of the Worlds: An Ethnography of Possession Among the Songhay of Niger*. Chicago: University of Chicago Press.

Stoller, Paul and Cheryl Olkes. 1989. *In Sorcery's Shadow: A Memoir of Apprenticeship Among the Songhay of Niger*. Chicago: University of Chicago Press.

Stromquist, Nelly P. 1992. *Women and Education in Latin America: Knowledge, Power, and Change*. Boulder and London: Lynne Rienner Publishers.

Thapan, Menakshi. 1989. *Life at School: An Ethnographic Study*. Delhi: Oxford University Press.

Thomas, E. Barrington. 1976. "Problems of Educational Provision in Papua New Guinea: An Area of Scattered Population," in *Papua New Guinea Education*. Ed. E. B. Thomas. 3–17. Melbourne: Oxford University Press.

Thompson, Kenneth. 1982. *Emile Durkheim*. Emile London: Tavistock Publications.

Toft, Susan (ed.). 1985. *Domestic Violence in Papua New Guinea*. Port Moresby: Law Reform Commission.

Toft, Susan and Susanne Bonnell. 1985. *Marriage and Domestic Violence in Rural Papua New Guinea*. Port Moresby: Law Reform Commission.

Trent, William, J. H. Braddock, and R. D. Henderson. 1985. "Sociology of Education: A Focus on Education as an Institution," in *Review of Research in Education* (second edn.). Ed. E. W. Gordon. 295–336. Washington: American Educational Research Association.

Vulliamy, Graham. 1985. *A Comparative Analysis of SSCEP Outstations*. Educational Research Unit Report 50. Waigani: University of Papua New Guinea.

Weber, Max. 1948. "The Rationalization of Education and Training," in *From Max Weber: Essays in Sociology*. Eds. H. H. Gearth and C. Wright Mills. 240–244. London: Routledge.

Weeks, Sheldon and Gerard Guthrie. 1984. "Papua New Guinea," in *Schooling in the Pacific Islands*. Eds. R. M. Thomas and T. N. Postlethuaite. 295–329. New York: Pergamon Press.

Weis, Lois. 1990. *Working Class Without Work: High School Students in a De-industrializing Economy*. New York: Routledge.

Weller, Susan. 1998. "Structured Interviewing and Questionnaire Construction," in *Handbook of Methods in Cultural Anthropology*. Handbook of Methods in Cultural Anthropology. Ed. H. Russell Bernard. 365–409. London: Altamira Press.

Williams, Raymond. 1983. *Keywords: A Vocabulary of Culture and Society*. Cambridge: Fontana Press.

Willis, Ian. 1974. *Lae: Village and City*. Melbourne: Melbourne University Press.

Willis, Paul. 1981. *Learning to Labour*. New York: Columbia University Press.

Wolf, Eric. 1999. *Envisioning Power: Ideologies of Dominance and Crisis*. Berkeley: University of California Press.

———. 2001. *Pathways of Power: Building an Anthropology of the Modern World*. Berkeley: University of California Press.

Young, Michael. 1971. *Knowledge and Control*. London: Collier-MacMillan Publishers.

Index

Page number in italics denote notes.